The Pubs of
Hay-on-Wye
and the
Golden Valley

The Pubs of Hay-on-Wye and the Golden Valley

by

John Eisel & Frank Bennett

Logaston Press

LOGASTON PRESS
Little Logaston Woonton Almeley
Herefordshire HR3 6QH

First published by Logaston Press 2005
Copyright © John Eisel & Frank Bennett 2005

ISBN 1 904396 46 1

Set in Times New Roman by Logaston Press
and printed in Great Britain by
Bell & Bain Ltd, Glasgow

Contents

page

Sources of Illustrations		vi
Acknowledgments		vii
Introduction		viii

Chapter One	Alehouses, Taverns & Inns	1
Chapter Two	Cider & Beer, Brewing and Breweries	19
Chapter Three	Hereford to Pontrilas, with a diversion to Kingstone	37
Chapter Four	Pontrilas to Llanfihangel Crucorney, Llanthony & through to Hay	51
Chapter Five	The Ewyas Harold area	73
Chapter Six	Clodock & the Monnow Valley	87
Chapter Seven	The Valley of the Escley Brook	107
Chapter Eight	Up the Golden Valley: Abbey Dore to Peterchurch	123
Chapter Nine	Up the Golden Valley: Peterchurch to Dorstone & Hardwick	141
Chapter Ten	Hereford to Bredwardine	155
Chapter Eleven	Bredwardine to Hay	169
Chapter Twelve	Hay-on-Wye: Broad St.	185
Chapter Thirteen	Hay-on-Wye: Lion St., Bell Bank & Bear St.	213
Chapter Fourteen	Hay-on-Wye: High Town, Castle St. & Church St.	231

Sources & References	255
Index of Pub Names	257
Index by Place	261
Paterson's 1828 Road Maps	230 & 254

Sources of Illustrations

t-top; b-bottom; m-middle; r-right; l-left

Eric Pugh
33, 181, 188, 194 t, 201, 202, 208 b, 220, 222, 223, 234, 236 t, 238, 244, 247,

Hereford Record Office
17, 32, 35, 209

Hereford Reference Library,
12, 13, 14, 15, 16, 20, 22, 26, 27 t, 31 t, 34, 40 r, 46 t, 69 t&b, 75, 80, 90 t, 100 b, 111, 116, 129, 130, 137, 142 b, 148, 148 t, 152, 164 t, 174, 196, 210

Derek Foxton
27 b, 112 t, 113, 138 t, 142 t, 145, 146 b, 155, 157, 163, 170, 171, 173

Tim Ward
74, 77, 120

Frank Bennett
80, 123, 146 t, 149 b, 182, 185, 189, 190, 191, 193, 195, 197, 199, 200, 206 b, 207 b, 208 t, 211, 212, 213, 215, 216, 217, 219, 221, 224, 225, 226, 228, 229, 231, 232, 236 b, 237, 239, 241, 242, 245, 246, 248, 253, 254, 255

John Eisel
40 l&b, 41, 47 b, 48, 49, 53, 56, 57 t&b, 61, 63 t&b, 71b, 76, 81 b, 83, 88 t&b, 92 t&b, 94, 95l, 96 l&r, 98, 99, 100 t, 101 t&b, 102, 104, 107, 108, 109, 110, 112 b, 114 t&b, 117 t&b, 120 t&b, 122, 126, 128 t&b, 131 l&r, 132 t&b, 136, 139, 141, 143, 144, 150, 151, 153, 154, 156 t&b, 160, 162 b, 164 b, 165, 167 l&r, 168, 169, 175, 177, 179

Ron Shoesmith
viii, 8, 27 m, 31 b, 44, 46 b, 47 t, 67, 70 t&b, 71 t, 79 t, 81 t&r, 85, 90 b, 125, 134, 138 b, 158, 162 t, 176, 186, 187, 194 b, 204 b, 206 t, 207, 227, 249, 252

Bryan Burrell
79 b

Gabbs (Hay)
178, 180, 204 t

Maureen Beauchamp
28 l&r

RCHM
95 r

City of Hereford Archaeology Unit
115 t&b

Acknowledgments

Whilst two names appear as co-authors, this book would not have been possible without the help of many others who freely provided information and helped with interesting stories, or just a piece of information that completed a jigsaw. Eric Pugh has been most helpful about pubs in Hay, and information gained through the good offices of Gabbs in Hay, in particular Liz Charles, has added an extra dimension, as have the reminiscences of Lucy Powell and her brother Albert Powell. The extensive local knowledge of Brian Cleaton of Craswall has been most helpful with the licensed premises in that remote but beautiful area; Mrs. C.J.F. Comyn has supplied much information on the Red Cross Inn in Turnastone, and Brian Smith on the New Inn and shop in Vowchurch; John Sprackling provided the stories of the Prince of Wales in Ewyas Harold and Bob Bowyer of pubs in Peterchurch; George Charnock has provided documentary information on Newton. To all these, and anyone else whose name is accidentally omitted, we extend out grateful thanks.

We are also grateful to those who provided historic photographs and other material to illustrate this book. The extensive collections of Dr. Derek Foxton and Tim Ward have again supplied a variety of material and this is much appreciated. Jennifer Shoesmith read the text and corrected typographical and spelling errors and Katy Shoesmith provided the map. A number of photographs have been taken to illustrate the book where no old photographs are known to exist, and our reception when calling and asking for permission has always been most cordial. In a number of cases it was not known that the building had formerly been licensed, and we were happy to provide information.

Inevitably, much time was spent in searching out documentary evidence, either in the Reference Library in Hereford, or the Record Offices in Hereford and Llandrindod Wells, and all of these allowed us to copy original material and to use it if required. Thanks are extended for the courtesy of the staff in each of these places during many visits over a period of several years.

Andy Johnson and Ron Shoesmith of Logaston Press have been most helpful, as ever. The sources of most of the illustrations are given on the opposite page. Others are from the authors' private collections and a few are from unidentified sources.

Introduction

This book is the fifth and final one in the series on the pubs of the county of Herefordshire. It covers the area to the south-west of Hereford, bounded on the south-east by the A465 Hereford to Abergavenny road, on the north by the River Wye and on the south-west by the county boundary. Hay-on-Wye is the centre for the north-west corner of the area and the pubs of that town are also included.

A wide variety of sources have been used, including licensing records, newspaper advertisements, directories, deeds, sales particulars and published works, as well as local memories. However, even with the limited number of pubs in the area, it is not possible to put in all the information available and a selection has been made to give a flavour of the area. A number of amusing stories have come to light, and these have been used to give human interest to the story. While pubs that are open are easy to locate, some of the smaller, short-lived, establishments, usually beer houses, have proved more difficult, and this is where local knowledge has played an important part. Inevitably one or two will have escaped the net and we would be delighted to hear from anyone who has any further information.

The text is organised in a structured way. After two introductory chapters, based on those that appeared originally in Ron Shoesmith's *The Pubs of Hereford City* but much altered and expanded, each chapter has a geographical basis. Chapter three starts at Hereford and follows the main road to Pontrilas with a detour to Kingstone, while chapter four continues the journey to Llanfihangel Crucorney, and then up the Vale of Ewyas and so to Hay. Ewyas Harold merits a chapter on its own (five), whilst the Ewyas Lacy area, west and north of Ewyas Harold, merits two chapters (six and seven). Chapters eight and nine follow the Golden Valley from Ewyas Harold through Dorstone to Hay, whilst ten and eleven take the back road from Hereford to Hay via Bredwardine. All roads lead to Hay, and so the concluding three chapters (chapters twelve to fourteen) deal with pubs within the parish of Hay.

Chapters three to eleven were written by John Eisel and chapters twelve to fourteen by Frank Bennett.

John Eisel and Frank Bennett,
September 2005.

CHAPTER ONE

Alehouses, Taverns and Inns

It was during the 350-year period when Britain was just within the boundaries of the Roman Empire that roads were first laid out on a formal basis throughout the country. In the first instance the roads were built for military purposes — to enable Roman troops to travel quickly and safely from one part of the country to another. Forts were built along the roads, sometimes only for short term use, known ones within the area of this book include Blackbush at Abbey Dore, Clifford and Clyro. Roads and forts were particularly important in the Welsh border area where there was a main road joining the legionary fortresses of Chester in the north with Caerleon in the south. In the first instance this road probably crossed the river Wye at one of the Hereford fords but, following the foundation of *Magnis* five miles to the west of Hereford and just below the Iron Age hillfort of Credenhill, it appears that a bridge was built across the Wye to the south of that town. The line of the road is apparent leading down to the Wye and shows particularly well on the south side of the river as Stone Street, just to the east of Madley. Throughout most of the Roman period there is likely to have been a roadside house close to the bridge which would have provided refreshment and accommodation for travellers should the river be in flood. Alcoholic refreshments would doubtless have been available to those who required them — the Romans imported wine from other parts of the Empire and made every effort to grow vines in the southern part of England. They would also have made mead from honey and possibly cider from the locally-grown apples that they had originally imported and, as wheat and barley were both available, some form of ale.

It may have been a little later in the Roman period that a road was built from Worcester, passing to the north of Hereford and continuing westwards towards the Roman fort at Brecon. It would have passed close to the Roman fort at Clyro, possibly the earliest settlement in the Hay area. Another Roman road was exposed in the old goods yard at Abbey Dore railway station. It comprised a roughly-cobbled layer, some 13 feet wide with distinct ruts 4½ feet apart. It is possible that this road followed the western side of the Golden Valley past Vowchurch, Peterchurch and Dorstone and over the head of the valley towards the Roman fort at Clifford. It would seem very likely that there was some form of crossing of the Wye in the Clifford/Hay area during a major part of the Roman period.

Magnis, with its broad main street and large public buildings would, without any doubt, have had guest houses providing overnight accommodation and places where soldiers, returning from a stint of duty in Wales, could drink and enjoy themselves. The area to the west of *Magnis*, throughout most of the Roman period, would have been in the military zone and not subject to the civilising influence of Rome. There were no towns, and any settlements that the Roman army allowed would have been relatively primitive. There is no evidence for any permanent settlements within the area covered by this book during the Roman period.

The break-up of the Roman Empire in England took place following the withdrawal of all the Roman troops, shortly after A.D. 410, after which the country was plunged into the Dark Ages. It was not long before raids on farms meant that crops were not produced and animals were no longer available for slaughter. This meant that food was not delivered to the local towns — trade had come to an end and starvation, in a land that should have been able to provide plenty, was a real possibility. Virtually all Roman towns, forts, villas and even small farmsteads, were abandoned within a relatively short period.

The slow climb out of the Dark Ages is not well defined in the border of Wales, but a major part of the area covered in this book was within Archenfield — the English name for the area bounded by the rivers Wye, Monnow and Worm. The post-Roman kingdom of Ergyng, from which the first part of the English name is derived, covered Archenfield and also lands east of the Wye. This appears to have been a predominantly Christian area with the kings of Ergyng providing lands for the church at such places as Bredwardine, Moccas and Preston-on-Wye. This semi-independent Anglo-Welsh tribe continued to exist up to the time of the Norman Conquest. However, the nearest town of any significance would have been Hereford which, apart from the early religous establishment dedicated to St. Guthlac, was unlikely to have been of any size until after the 7th century when the Hereford diocese was first created.

As Hereford grew it would gradually have become the focal point for the rural areas to the west and south-west — the Wye and Golden valleys. This was also a time of growth for drinking houses throughout the country. Indeed, as early as A.D. 750 the then Archbishop of York issued a Canon 'That no priest go to eat or drink in taverns', and there were so many inns by the time of King Edgar (959-75) that he issued a decree limiting their number to one per village.

At the beginning of the 9th century Hereford was a well-established small town complete with a strong earthwork and timber defence against possible incursions by the Welsh and the Vikings. By the time of the Norman conquest Hereford had become one of the most important towns in the country — mainly because of its ford and its strategic position on the Welsh border. Its importance continued after the conquest when the Normans built a new town for their French settlers. This was to the north of the old Saxon defences in the area that now includes High Town and stretches along Commercial Street and Union Street to the Kerry Arms. Such a development would inevitably have resulted in a sizeable increase in the number of inns and taverns.

There is no indication of any settlement at Hay before the Norman Conquest. The earliest feature would seem to be the motte to the south-west of the walled town, which was probably the *castello de haia* mentioned in 1121. The nearby church of St. Mary is also recorded in the early 12th century, having been granted to the Benedictine priory at Brecon. There is no record of any borough charter for Hay, it being a borough by prescription only. The first certain references to the town are rather unfortunate — that of 1216, when the castle and town were burnt by King John, and the one of 1231 when the town was again burnt, this time by Llywelyn ab Iorwerth. Following this double tragedy, it is not surprising to find that the citizens obtained grants of murage to build their town walls in 1232 and 1237, and a new castle soon followed. However, the large central market place is indicative of the trading potential of this small town which would also have led to a growth in the numbers of inns, taverns and ale-houses.

There was a general growth in the population of Britain following the Norman conquest, and with this growth came various measures, both to limit the numbers of drinking houses and to protect the customer. Thus, one of the provisions of Magna Carta in 1215 was that there were to be standard measures for wine, ale and corn.

A later, but important, measure was the 'Assize of Bread and Ale' of 1266. This act accepted the principle that both bread and ale were necessities for all people in the country and, for a period of some 300 years, it ensured that the retail price of ale was

A 14th-century inn with its pole and bush

3

fixed according to the price of grain. At that time ale was usually made from malted barley, or occasionally wheat which was steeped in water and then fermented with yeast.

During the 13th century there was a gradual increase in the sale of wine, and a separation came into being between 'taverns', which sold both ale and wine, and 'alehouses' which sold only ale. In addition to these there were the 'inns' or 'hostels' that provided accommodation for travellers as well as food and drink.

The Hereford city regulations of 1554, 1556 and 1576 all open with the command that the peace

A 14th-century tavern with a cellar in which to keep the ale

should be kept and that any visitors to the city should leave their weapons at their inns and not carry them about the city. Every knight and esquire, however, could have a sword borne after him. The innholders were enjoined to acquaint their guests with this regulation, upon a pain or penalty of 6s. 8d. for each omission. One wonders how many of these visitors came from the villages in the Golden Valley and the wilds of Hay and the Black Mountains.

Outside the towns and villages the principal hospitality for travellers during the medieval period was provided by monasteries — it was only along the more important pilgrim routes that guest houses and wayside inns were established, and these would have been well beyond the purse of all except the richest of travellers.

During the 14th and 15th centuries, a gradual change occurred as merchants began to travel and the influence of the church started to wane. Wayside inns became features of the countryside and hotels providing accommodation and food began to appear in the market towns.

For perhaps 1,000 years ale had been the basic drink for practically everyone, but a fundamental change occurred during the early 15th century.

This was due to the introduction of hops, described by the authorities in Shrewsbury at that time as that 'wicked and pernicious weed', and the resultant manufacture of 'beer'. The hop not only gave the new drink a more bitter flavour, it was also of considerable importance for its preservative properties enabling the beverage to be kept much longer than ale before 'going-off'.

Of course, there were the adherents of ale:

> Though I go bare, take ye no care,
> I nothing am a-cold:
> I stuff my skin so full within
> Of jolly good ale and old.
>
> Back and side go bare, go bare;
> Both foot and hand go cold:
> But, belly, God send thee good ale enough,
> Whether it be new or old.

(part of a 16th-century drinking song by William Stevenson
'Jolly Good Ale and Old')

A 16th-century brewer

In the 16th century there was a Hereford city regulation that 'no bruer shall sett Any hopes or asshes in theire Ale upon peyne of xxs. For ev[er]y defalte'. This pain or penalty of 20s. was quite severe. This regulation is more concerned with preserving the quality of the ale than prohibiting the brewing of beer, as the regulations also refer to beer. In 1554 regulations fixed the cost of a sester (four gallons) of 'good & able Ale & bere' at 20d., but by 1557 this had gone up to 2s. (24d.). In 1576 inflation had taken this to 2s. 6d., and it was stated that this price was to remain 'untill further mynde of mr Mayor and the Com[m]en Counsaile' was known, upon pain of forfeiture of the value of the drink sold and a 'paine' of 10s. The price in the country areas around Hereford would doubtless have been similar.

Hops have been grown in Herefordshire for many years and the round and square oast houses, with a swinging cowl above, used for drying the hops, are a common sight in the countryside. Charcoal was used for heating and during the drying process sulphur was added to destroy insect life and fungal and bacteriological infections. Dried hops are still pressed tightly into jute sacks called pockets. These pockets had to be marked with the name and address of the grower to identify the tax liability. Hops have other benefits — a bine of hops that is hung next to the ceiling in the kitchen or in the public bars of many an inn in Herefordshire keeps the smoke and smells down, and if you can't sleep at nights try a pillow stuffed with hops. However, the former use may begin to disappear as more 'no smoking areas' are provided in local inns, and conscientious officials decide that hops hung in a bar could be a fire hazard!

For well over 100 years brewers produced both ale and beer, but the popularity of the former gradually declined and beer eventually became the national drink — apart from in Herefordshire where cider reigned triumphant for many years. It was early in the reign of Henry VIII that cider orchards became a branch of the rural economy, but it was the Redstreak, the famous cider apple developed by the first Viscount Scudamore on his Holme Lacy estate near Hereford before and after the Civil War, that revolutionised the trade. It was recommended that the Redstreak 'was to be preferred for your Plantation to any other apple whatsoever, especially remote from your House. First, because it yields the best of British Drinks. Secondly, because the fruit is harsh and unpleasant, not tempting the Palates of lewd Persons'. The poet John Philips, who died in 1709 aged 32 and is buried in the entrance to the north transept of Hereford Cathedral, wrote of the Redstreak in his poem *Cyder*:

John Philips' brass in Hereford Cathedral includes a branch from an apple tree

Of no regard till Scudamore's skilful hand
Improv'd her, and by courtly discipline
Taught her the savage nature to forget,—
Hence styl'd the Scudamore plant.

So important was cider to Herefordshire that, in the 14th century, when Nicholas de Hereford was helping Wycliffe to translate the Bible into English, he changed the warning given to the mother of the still unborn Samson which read 'Now therefore beware, I pray thee, and drink not wine nor strong drink' to read 'drink no cider' (Judges, Ch. 13 v. 4). Surely the translation, in the well-known 'Cider Bible', was no more the worse for it.

Change was gradual — it was not until the end of the 17th century that there was any serious competition to ale, beer and cider in the retail market. Even then, the cost of the new beverages, coffee and tea, was prohibitively expensive, at least for the next half-century or so.

Although there had been previous attempts at curtailing the number of drinking houses, the first formal licensing law came at the end of the 15th century. It empowered Justices of the Peace to obtain sureties for good behaviour from the landlords and, if necessary, to close alehouses. Some 50 years later the Justices obtained the power to both licence and suppress alehouses — hence 'licensed premises'. Legislation continued and 1553 saw an Act of Parliament that curtailed the number of 'taverns', and thus the sale of wine. The limits on taverns provide an indication of the size and importance of the towns at that time — London was allowed 40; York, nine; and Bristol, six. Hereford was limited to three, the same as Lincoln, Worcester, Southampton and Oxford.

This did not mean that the population of the country was being deprived of places in which to drink — there were approximately 44 alehouses for every tavern in the latter part of the 16th century! This was equivalent to more than one drinking establishment for every 200 persons, a far higher ratio than exists today. These early alehouses were probably little different from the timber-framed and thatched houses that surrounded them. The larger ones would have had sheds at the rear where brewing was carried out and possibly cellars in which to store their brew at a constant temperature.

The taverns, being of a higher status, were probably of a superior construction, which may well be the reason that the more important towns and cities in the country tend to be well-endowed with substantial stone cellars of a late medieval date. They were obviously designed for public use and usually had well-constructed vaulted roofs and entries leading directly from the streets. In Hereford, the cellars underneath what was the Greyhound Hotel, next to All Saints church and, a little further to the north-east, those under the now closed Pippin, may well be cases in point. No such cellars have been noted in Hay.

Throughout most of recorded history it was a legal requirement that a sign should identify all drinking establishments. Poles, which gradually became longer, heavier, and more noticeable, had the sign suspended from them. In the case of a tavern, there would also be an evergreen bush, which represented the vine and indicated that wine was for sale, giving rise to the saying that 'Good wine needs no bush'. Alfred Watkins, in an

16   99

Whereas by the Laws and Statutes of This Realm

NOTICE

IS HEREBY GIVEN TO ALL

INN KEEPERS, ALEHOUSE KEEPERS, SUTLERS, VICTUALLERS

and other Retailers of

ALE and BEER,

AND EVERY OTHER PERSON or PERSONS KEEPING A PUBLIC HOUSE
IN ANY
CITY, TOWN CORPORATE, BOROUGH, MARKET TOWN, VILLAGE, HAMLET, PARISH,
PART or PLACE IN THE *Kingdom of England*

That, as from the **24**th *day of* **JUNE, 1700**

THEY SHALL BE REQUIRED TO RETAIL and SELL THEIR ALE & BEER

by the **FULL ALE QUART** or **PINT**

According to the Laid Standard

IN VESSELS DULY MARKED *with* W.R *and* CROWN

be they made of

WOOD, GLASS, HORN, LEATHER or PEWTER *etc.*

Any Person Retailing Ale or Beer to a **TRAVELLER** *or* **WAYFARER** *in Vessels not
signed and marked as aforesaid will be liable to a* **PENALTY** *not exceeding*

FORTY SHILLINGS

FOR EVERY SUCH OFFENCE

By Act of Parliament ~ at WESTMINSTER
In the Reign of Our Sovereign ~ WILLIAM III by the Grace of God, King,
Defender of the Faith &c

*In 1700 it became a legal requirement that vessels in which ale and beer
were served should be accurate and marked*

An evergreen bush, indicating an inn, from a 14th-century manuscript

article published in the *Transactions* of the Woolhope Naturalists' Field Club, also mentions a 'chequers' sign, which was apparently common in Hereford and elsewhere. This consisted of alternate diamonds or lozenges of green and red painted on the door-frame on each side of the entrance to the inn. Watkins suggested that the sign originated in the counting board (like a chess board, but used for counting money) and that it was an indication that the innkeeper kept one of these boards for the benefit of his customers.

Various attempts were made during the Civil War to levy duty on both the manufacture and the sale of beer and ale — attempts which were consolidated after the war and are still in force. At this time beer was brewed in three different qualities: strong, table, and small, and each variety attracted a different rate of duty. It was not until the late 19th century that the duty levied became based on the original gravity of the beer.

Although there was a duty on beer, spirits were exempt and towards the end of the 17th century and well into the 18th there was what Monckton in his

A mid-18th-century brewhouse

History of the English Public House described as 'one of the biggest orgies of over-indulgence our island history has ever seen'. Every small alehouse in the country was in a position to sell cheap brandy and in particular, gin. The result was that consumption of spirits increased from half-a-million gallons in 1684 to over eight million gallons in 1743 — an increase of well over one gallon per person per year! The horrific effects of this vast consumption of gin were pictorially illustrated by William Hogarth, and even a provincial paper such as the *Worcester Journal* of 14 February 1751 carried the following epitaph to a gin drinker, no doubt designed to highlight the problem:

> Half burnt alive, beneath this *Dunghill* lies
> A Wretch, whose memory the Sage despise,
> *Her* brain all Tumult; ragged her Attire
> The Sport of Boys, when Wallowing in the Mire.
> Life did to her, as a wild Tempest seems;
> And Death, as sinking to a horrid Dream:
> Hence learn, ye *Brutes*, who reel in Human Shape;
> To you, superior is the grinning Ape:
> For Nature's wise Impulses he'll pursue,
> Whilst each dread *Start of Frenzy* governs you.

The various 'Gin Acts' that followed, together with increased duties and a strengthening of the powers of the justices, rapidly changed this trend and by 1758 excise duty was paid on less than two million gallons per year. The 'gin era' was over.

However, means of regulating the public house continued to attract government interest and from 1729 licence renewal had to be made at annual Brewster Sessions, originally in September then, at a later date, in February. While no 18th-century records survive for the county, in the records of the Clerk of the Peace there are lists of alehouse keepers and their securities for the period 1818-1828. No names of pubs are given, as the recognizance for good behaviour was personal to the licensee, and he or she had to provide two sureties. However, the names of the alehouses can mostly be deduced from other sources.

Following the closure of the monasteries in the late 1530s, inns began to provide food and accommodation for travellers, the latter often in rooms on several levels around galleried courtyards. By the 18th century most of these establishments had lost their earlier reputation for being rat-infested hovels and were becoming orderly and well-equipped. However, there was still room for improvement as Viscount Torrington's experiences around 1790 show:

> I look upon an inn, as the seat of all roguery, profaness, and debauchery; and sicken of them every day, by hearing nothing but oaths, and abuse of each other, and brutality to horses ... all town inns are so noisy by low company and intemperance.

However, James Boswell in his *Life of Samuel Johnson* gives a totally different picture:

'There is no private house,' said Johnson, 'in which people can enjoy themselves so well as at a capital tavern ... The master of the house is anxious to entertain his guests; the guests are anxious to be agreeable to him; and no man but a very impudent dog indeed can as freely command what is in another man's house as if it were his own. Whereas, at a tavern, there is a general freedom from anxiety. You are sure you are welcome; and the more noise you make, the more trouble you give, the more good things you call for, the welcomer you are. No servants will attend you with the alacrity which waiters do, who are incited by the prospect of an immediate reward in proportion as they please. No, sir, there is nothing which has yet been contrived by man, by which so much happiness is produced, as by a good tavern or inn.'

The early 19th century was the culmination of coach travel and inns were at the height of their prosperity. They had an enviable reputation which is well expressed by Washington Irving in *Travelling at Christmas*:

As we drove into the great gateway of the inn, I saw on one side the light of a rousing kitchen fire beaming through a window. I entered, and admired for the hundredth time, that picture of convenience, neatness, and broad honest enjoyment, the kitchen of an English inn. It was of spacious dimensions; hung round by copper and tin vessels, highly polished, and decorated here and there with a Christmas green. Hams, tongues, and flitches of bacon were suspended from the ceiling; a smoke-jack made its ceaseless clanking beside the fireplace, and a clock ticked in one corner. A well scoured deal table extended along one side of the kitchen, with a cold round of beef, and other hearty viands upon it, over which two foaming tankards of ale seemed mounting guard. Travellers of inferior orders were preparing to attack this stout repast, while others sat smoking or gossiping over their ale, on two high-backed oaken settles beside the fire. Trim housemaids were hurrying backwards and forwards under the directions of a fresh, bustling landlady; but still seizing an occasional moment to exchange a flippant word, and have a rallying laugh with the group round the fire.

It was during the 19th century that most of the legislation that affects the present-day consumption and sale of alcoholic drink was enacted. The Alehouse Act of 1828 meant that the licensee no longer had to find sureties for his behaviour. However, he was bound to use the legal, stamped measures, not to adulterate his drinks, and not to permit drunkenness on his premises. The Beerhouse Acts of 1830, 1834 and 1840 followed — the first allowed premises to open for the sale of beer, but not spirits, on payment of a simple excise licence; the second differentiated between 'on' and 'off' licences and made 'on' licences more difficult to obtain; whilst the third ensured that licences were issued only to the occupier of the premises.

The first Act, pushed through by the Duke of Wellington against a number of vested interests, abolished all duty on beer and enabled any householder to sell beer on the purchase of a two-guinea licence from the Excise. As a consequence, a number of illegal drinking places became legal, and many craftsmen also sold beer as part of their business,

January 12, 1775.

Coach-Office, Gloucefter, Nov. 2, 1774.

Gloucefter Flying Machines,

In ONE DAY, Six Times a Week,

CONTINUE Flying from the Coach-Office in Gloucefter, and the Bolt-and-Tun in Fleet-ftreet, London, every Evening, (Saturdays excepted) at Eight o'clock. Fare 14s.—Outfides Half-Price.

HEREFORD MACHINE,

In a Day and a Half, Twice a Week,

CONTINUES Flying from the Swan-and-Falcon in Hereford, Monday and Thurfday mornings, and from the Bolt-and Tun, Monday and Thurfday evenings. Fare 19s. Outfides Half.

There would have been a connection from Hay to join the 'Flying Machine' from Hereford to London

naming the beer-house after their craft. Such small beershops were known as 'tiddlywinks', a word also used for unlicensed public houses or pawnshops. The Duke of Wellington later declared that the passing of the 1830 Act was a greater victory than any of his military triumphs! Within a year of the passing of the Act more than 24,000 licences had been issued, and Sidney Smith, a supporter of the Bill who seems to have changed his mind, later wrote:

> The new Beer Bill has begun its operations. Everybody is drunk. Those who are not singing are sprawling. The sovereign people are in a beastly state.

The effects of this Act were also commented on in the pages of the *Hereford Journal*. On 2 March 1831 a letter from J. Benbow appeared in its pages on 2 March 1831 — a glove manufacturer in a large way of business at the Friars in Hereford, he was concerned at the increase in over-indulgence in beer among his workforce. His letter was taken up in the editorial, which commented on it as 'one instance amongst many others that have been communicated to us, of the evils the Beer Act is inflicting on the working classes of this community'.

At about the time of the Beerhouse Acts the temperance movement was also getting under way. Organised temperance societies had originated in America in 1808, crossing to Ireland by 1818 and then to Liverpool where American ships' captains distributed temperance tracts. By 1830 there were temperance societies in Ulster, Lancashire and Yorkshire having 23,000

DRUNKARD'S CATECHISM

1. Q. What is your name?
   A. Drunken sot.
2. Q. Who gave you that name?
   A. As drink is my idol, Landlords and their wives get all my money; they gave me that name in one of my drunken sprees, wherein I was made a member of strife, a child of want, and an inheritor of a bundle of rage.
3. Q. What did your Landlords and Landladies promise for you?
   A. They did promise and vow three things in my name; first, that I should renounce the comforts of my own fireside; second, starve my wife and hunger my children; third, walk in rags and tatters, with my shoe soles going flip flap, all the days of my life.
4. Q. Rehearse the articles of the belief.
   A. I believe in the existence of one Mr. Alcohol, the great head and chief of all manner of vice, the source of nine-tenths of all diseases; lastly, I not only believe, but am sure when my money is all gone and spent, the Landlord will stop the tap and turn me out.
5. Q. How many commandments have ye sots to keep?
   A. Ten.
6. Q. Which be they?
   A. The same which the Landlord and Landlady spoke in the bar, saying, We are thy master and mistress, who brought thee out of the paths of virtue, placed thee in the ways of vice, and set thy feet in the road which leadeth to New South Wales.
   I. Thou shalt use no other house but mine.
   II. Thou shalt not make for thyself any substitute for intoxicating drinks, such as tea, coffee, ginger pop, or lemonade; for I am a jealous man, wearing a coat that should be on thy back, eating thy children's bread, and pocketing the money which should make thee and the wife comfortable all the days of thy life.
   III. Thou shalt not use my house in vain.
   IV. Remember that thou eat but one meal on the Sabbath day, for six days hast thou been drinking, and nought else wouldst thou do; but the seventh is the sabbath day, and thou canst have no trust; therefore thou skulketh on the seventh day and abominates it.
   V. Thou shalt honour the Landlords and Landladies and Gin-shops with thy presence, that thy days may be few and miserable in the land wherein thou dwellest.
   VI. Thou shalt commit murder, by starving, and hungering, and beating thy wife and family.
   VII. Thou shalt commit self-destruction.
   VIII. Thou shalt sell thy wife and children's bread and rob thyself of all thy comforts.
   IX. Thou shalt bear false witness when thou speakest of the horrors, saying thou art in good health when thou art labouring under the barrel fever.
   X. Thou shalt covet all thy neighbour is possessed of, thou shalt covet his house, his land, his purse, his health, his wealth, and all that he has got, that thou mayest indulge in drinking, help the brewer to buy a new coach, a pair of fine horses, a new dray and a fine building, that he may live in idleness all his days: likewise to enable the Landlord to purchase a new sign to put over his door, with 'Licensed to be drunk on the premises', written thereon.

An 1850s Temperance Society Tract based on the Ten Commandments paying members, and 60,000 registered abstainers. The main impetus came in 1833 with the founding of the Preston Temperance Society by Joseph Livesey, who instituted the idea of 'the pledge'. The word 'teetotal' was coined by Dicky Turner, a drunkard reformed by Livesey, as a consequence of his stammer! The Preston Temperance Society met with strong opposition, and one early meeting was disrupted by a bear which was unchained and let loose on the audience, which dispersed more quickly than it had assembled! The tracts distributed by such societies were often dressed up in religious form; the one on the previous page probably dating from about 1850.

The Apprentice's Monitor.
O R,
INDENTURES
IN VERSE
Shewing what they are bound to do.

Proper to be hung up in all Shops.

EACH young Apprentice, when he's bound to Trade,
This folemn vow to God and Man has made,
To do with joy his Mafter's juft commands,
Nor truft his fecrets into other hands.
He muft no damage to his fubftance do,
And fee that others do not wrong him too.
His Mafter's goods he fhall not wafte nor lend,
But all his property with care defend.
He fhall not buy nor fell without his leave,
Nor lie, nor injure, nor at all deceive,
Taverns and Ale-Houfes he fhall not haunt,
Thofe fnares to Youth, thofe fcenes of vice and want,
At Cards and Dice he fhall not dare to play,
But fly from fuch temptations far away.
    O Youth ! remember thou to this art bound.
    See that no breach of this in thee be found.

Apprentices were not allowed to visit taverns and ale-houses

In Hay the temperance movement found much work to be done, at least in the view of its supporters. The Rev. W.L. Beavan, vicar of Hay from 1845 until 1901, was a strong supporter of the temperance movement and of him it was said:

> His work for the cause of temperance was noteworthy and necessary in a town which had an unbelievably high proportion of inns per head of population.

One aspect of the movement was the founding of temperance hotels, the first of which was opened in 1836, and by 1865 there were some 200. Generally these were not a success, being of poor standard and often run by failed landlords or reformed drunkards with no business sense or experience.

At the time of the Beerhouse Acts there were few restrictions on licensing hours. As a whole, the only non-permitted hours were during Divine Services on Sundays, Christmas Day and Good Friday, but there were more restrictions on beer houses which could only open between 4 a.m. and 10 p.m., with local variations. The regulations had to be kept in

Published for Bettering the Condition and Increasing the Comforts of the POOR.

CAUTION

To Alehouse Keepers, & their Guests.

It is better that Offences against the Laws should be Prevented, than that Offenders should be Punished.

THE PROPER USE OF INNS, &c.

THE proper use of Inns and Alehouses, is to furnish Refreshment and Lodging to Travellers, upon a reasonable profit; to accommodate persons meeting on *necessary* business; Soldiers in his Majesty's service; and some whose occupations require a frequent change of residence, or who cannot provide themselves with meat and drink in a more convenient manner.

The neighbouring Justices of the Peace have the Power of granting a License for keeping a Publick House, and they have the like Power of refusing to grant a License, without giving any reason whatever for such refusal, which is entirely at their discretion; it is therefore the Interest as well as the Duty of an Alehouse keeper to take care, that he conduct himself and his House in a becoming manner, lest he forfeit the good opinion of the Justices and be deprived of his License.

A principal duty of an Alehouse keeper is to prevent Artificers and Labourers from drinking more than for their necessary Refreshment; and not to allow them to lose their time and spend their money to the injury of themselves and their families: therefore, almost all debts (commonly called Ale Scores) are incurred in an improper manner; and are such, as the lawful means (if any) of recovering such debts would often discover bad conduct in the Alehouse keeper, and hazard the loss of his License.

The Law protects the Alehouse keeper from losses, by giving him the power of detaining the Person of any Guest who refuses to pay the reasonable charges for the meat and drink which have been furnished him: Debts are seldom incurred by Travellers, who are generally Strangers, and when they are incurred by Artificers and Labourers, great blame will attach to the Alehouse keeper from the manner in which such Ale Scores must have been contracted.

An Alehouse keeper is liable to heavy penalties for allowing Tippling, Drunkenness, or disorderly behaviour in his House, extending to the Forfeiture of his Recognizance, and that of his Surety or Bondsman, and the loss of his License.

The Guests who are guilty of Tippling, Drunkenness, and disorderly Behaviour are also liable to heavy penalties; and Artificers and Labourers who waste their time and their money at Publick Houses, ought to consider that although they may avoid punishment from the forbearance with which the Laws are executed, yet their Wives and their Families cannot escape from the miseries of Poverty, the certain consequence of their Husband's misconduct; and that the wholesome restraint which the Law lays upon a man in this respect, gives the best assurance of protection to his Family and to Himself, when it forbids him to waste his time and his money in a Publick House, and disturb the peace of others by his intemperance and bad example.

To   *Alehouse keeper.*

You are desired to have this Paper pasted up in your Kitchen, or some other usual place where your Guests take their Refreshment.

SIGNED

T. DAVIES, BRITANNIA PRINTING-OFFICE, HEREFORD.

Should this notice still be posted in landlords' kitchens?

15

the inn and notice was given in the *Hereford Journal* of 18 September 1839 that:

> Constables and police-officers are authorised to enter these houses [in Hereford] whenever they think proper, and any landlord refusing them admittance, is liable to a penalty of five pounds for the first offence and suspension of the license for the second.

The 1872 Licensing Act, amended in 1874, tidied up and tightened the complex legislation, but at the beginning of the 20th century public houses were, in general, still allowed to open for some 20 hours each day. The notable exception was Wales, where Sunday drinking was banned from 1881 onwards. However, liquid refreshment could be supplied at any time to *bona fide* travellers (defined as travelling over three miles), or to residents of the licensed premises. Those who only had six-day licences were not allowed to serve travellers on a Sunday, only residents.

In the early 20th century there was pressure to reduce the number of licensed premises. This was aided by an Act of 1904, which established the principle of compensation for the owners and landlords whose licences were suppressed or surrendered. The powers of the magistrates were considerably increased by the Licensing (Consolidation) Act, 1910, which, among other things, gave them the power to either insist on or veto proposed structural alterations. On this basis a number of licences were refused, and in Hereford, by 1919, the Compensation Authority had approved the closure of no less than 35 public houses at a cost of some £16,000. Similar closures happened at the same time in Hay, but only a few records of closure and compensation survive for the 1920s and '30s and these will be considered in the appropriate place.

An Act to prohibit the Sale of Intoxicating Liquors on Sunday in Wales.
[27th August 1881.]

WHEREAS the provisions in force against the sale of fermented and distilled liquors during certain hours of Sunday have been found to be attended with great public benefits, and it is expedient and the people of Wales are desirous that in the principality of Wales those provisions be extended to the other hours of Sunday :

Be it therefore enacted by the Queen's most Excellent Majesty, by and with the advice and consent of the Lords Spiritual and Temporal, and Commons, in this present Parliament assembled, and by the authority of the same, as follows :

1. In the principality of Wales all premises in which intoxicating liquors are sold or exposed for sale by retail shall be closed during the whole of Sunday. — *Premises where intoxicating liquors sold to be closed on Sundays in Wales.*

2. The Licensing Acts, 1872–1874, shall apply in the case of any premises closed under this Act as if they had been closed under those Acts. — *Application of Licensing Acts. 35 & 36 Vict. c. 94. 37 & 38 Vict. c. 49.*

3. This Act shall commence and come into operation with respect to each division or place in Wales on the day next appointed for the holding of the general annual licensing meeting for that division or place. — *Commencement of Act.*

4. Nothing in this Act contained shall preclude the sale at any time at a railway station of intoxicating liquors to persons arriving at or departing from such station by railway. — *Sale of intoxicating liquors at railway stations.*

5. This Act may be cited as the Sunday Closing (Wales) Act, 1881. — *Short title.*

The 1881 Welsh Sunday Closing Act

A rather hesitant letter concerning children being served with 'liquors' in 1898

It is not often realised that the regulations concerning licensed houses, alcohol and children are mainly of 20th century origin. Although the 1872 Act made it an offence to sell spirits to those using licensed premises under the age of 16, it was not until the Children's Act of 1908 that children under the age of 14 were prohibited from being in licensed premises. It was only in 1923 that it became, in general, an offence to serve alcoholic drinks to those under 18.

Regulations brought in at a time of war often have a habit of staying. It was during the First World War that limited opening hours were instigated — in Hereford this meant that closing time was 9 p.m! Also in 1915, Monmouthshire was included in the Welsh ban on Sunday drinking.

Warnings of transgressions were common and in the *Hereford Times* for 12 February 1916 Mr. Wallis (the magistrate) warned landlords that:

> great as were these difficulties, they should set their faces against any drinking by soldiers. To see soldiers about the streets under the influence of liquour was a very sorry sight. The bench also regarded with much displeasure any encouragement of women to spend the money they received from the Army in the public houses of the city. They knew that in the great majority of public houses this would not be allowed.

The Licensing Act of 1921 regularised this situation by defining 'permitted hours' as being eight hours between 11 a.m. and 10 p.m. except for Sunday, which was limited to five hours. In 1934, there was a slight improvement — an extension could be granted to 10.30 p.m. during the summer months, especially in rural areas where it was appreciated that evening work was necessary.

The 1920s were again a time when the Temperance Movement came to the fore and their activities occupied many pages in the *Hereford Times*. Typical of their attitude is a letter from Charles Smith of Sheffield, included in the edition of 17 July 1920:

> Herefordshire devoted over 30,000 acres to the growth of barley, hops, and cider apples wherewith to produce a poison which intoxicates; which lands carters in the street drunk, wounded, and helpless, and leaves the horses straying; and men reeling on horseback, drunk, clamouring for more beer, creating a disturbance, and ending in custody. All this is evil for the community, however profitable to the brewers. I observe that your Herefordshire Fruit Company are using £50,000 value in early fruits, only two-fifths of which are obtained in the county and three-fifths from outside. Why are not the 30,000 acres mentioned above given to the production of fruit wherewith to feed the people, instead of to the production of a drug wherewith to poison them?

After the Second World War there were several minor Acts. One, of considerable importance to the Hay area, was included in the 1953 Licensing Act which directed that Sunday closing in Wales and Monmouthshire would only apply in administrative districts where the electors so decided. Following this, Wales gradually became 'wet' on a Sunday, starting with the districts closest to England. Sunday closing could return and the Licensing Act of 1964 made provision for a poll on this issue to take place on request every seven years. In 1989 the district of Dwyfor, Gwynedd, voted, on a very low turnout, to become dry on a Sunday and as a result remained so for the next seven years. This meant that anyone in Porthmadog who wanted a Sunday pint went over the border to Penryndeudraeth in neighbouring Meirionydd!

Restrictions continued to be simplified and the 1961 Act provided for 'restaurant' and 'residential' licences and also gave the customers' grace — the ten minutes of 'drinking-up time'.

A late 20th-century Act restored the situation as regards opening hours to more or less what it had been at the beginning of the century by allowing inns to stay open throughout the day if they so wished, most commonly any times between 11 a.m. and 11 p.m., with a somewhat shorter 'window of opportunity' on Sundays. A new millennium has brought new thought and the 2003 Licensing Act has led to the possibility of 24-hour opening once again. However, there seems to be no local need or take-up of this opportunity. The same act also removed the provision for polls on Sunday opening — Wales will now remain permanently 'wet' on Sundays!

CHAPTER TWO

Cider & Beer – Brewing and Breweries

From a surprisingly early date cider, one of the main products of Herefordshire, was sent long distances, even as far as London. First it was sent in barrels, but the boastful Andrew Yarranton, writing in 1677, claimed credit for himself and his business partner for bottling 'sider' and that they 'caused vast quantities to be Bottled up and sent to *Glocester*, from thence to *Lechload* [Lechlade] and so to *London* by Water'. Others copied his example 'and now there is a great Trade, and a great number of persons are now driving great Trades with Bottle-Sider; and it hath been the occasion of erecting Five or Six Glass Houses in them parts'.

When Daniel Defoe passed through Herefordshire at the beginning of the 18th century he noted that the populace were 'diligent and laborious people, chiefly addicted to husbandry, and they boast, perhaps, not without reason, that they have the finest wool, the best hops, and the richest cyder in all Britain'. As far as cider was concerned, he went on to say:

> here it was, that several times for 20 miles together, we could get no beer or ale in their publick houses, only cyder; and that so very good, so fine, and so cheap, that we never found fault with the exchange; great quantities of this cyder are sent to London, even by land carriage tho' so very remote, which is an evidence for the goodness of it, beyond contradiction.

The importance was that both cider and ale were safe to drink at a time when most water supplies were at the best suspect and often could cause serious illnesses. Cider was also considered invigorating as *Berrow's Worcester Journal* of 31 July 1755 reported:

> Last Tuesday a very fat Man, who weighs 20 Stone, undertook to go on Foot from Bromyard to Worcester (being ten computed Miles) in three Hours, for a Wager of a Guinea, which (with Difficulty) he perform'd in 4 Minutes less than the Time allow'd. 'Tis thought he would have lost, had he not eat a large Quantity of Bread and Cheese, and drank two Quarts of Cyder, on the Road.

The production of cider was an important part of the local economy. It was also a source of revenue, and taxed from time to time. An additional duty on cider was proposed in the budget made by Sir Francis Dashwood, the then Chancellor of the Exchequer, on 7 March 1763. (Dashwood is, of course, better known as the founder of the Hell Fire Club). The initial proposal, to add an additional duty of 10s. per hogshead, to be paid by the retailer, met with fierce opposition from the cider-producing counties, and this was altered to one of 4s. on each hogshead of cider, to be levied on the makers. This duty was to be collected by the excise department, and officers had the right of entry into the cider-makers' houses. The poor

Old   C Y D E R   for   Ever!

A woodcut celebrating the repeal of the cider tax

were exempt, and those producing cider for their own use were permitted to pay 5s. per head composition. Despite protests, the Act received royal assent on 8 April 1763.

This did not go down well in Herefordshire and on 29 November 1763 a meeting of the gentlemen, clergy, and freeholders of the County took place at the Swan and Falcon in Hereford and passed a resolution against the Cyder Act — a resolution endorsed by a meeting of the Common Council the following day. Nothing happened, but the discontent evidently simmered on and *Berrow's Worcester Journal* of 17 October 1765 reported:

> We hear; that at a very numerous Meeting of the Gentlemen, Clergy, and Freeholders, of the County of Hereford, held at the Swan and Falcon in the City of Hereford on Wednesday last Week, it was unanimously resolved to present a Petition to Parliament for at total Repeal of the late Act for laying a Duty on Cyder and Perry.

A petition complaining of the effects of the Act and the increased powers of the Excise was agreed at a meeting of the Common Council on 6 January 1766 and sent to Parliament. This was all part of a general move to have the Act repealed and this was finally achieved some three months later. The news reached Hereford on 14 April and there were immediate celebrations which were reported in *Berrow's Worcester Journal* of 24 April 1766:

They write from Hereford, that on Monday se'nnight, upon the Arrival of the News that the Bill for the Repeal of the Cyder Act had received the Royal Assent, that City gave the Strongest Testimony of its Joy and Gratitude which could possibly be expressed. – At Noon the Populace were entertained in the Market-Place with Two Hogsheads of Cyder, and in the Evening the Town was universally illuminated. – Grand Exhibitions of Fire-works were made at the Cross and on the Castle-Hill, whilst Bonfires blazed in every Street, and on all the Eminences within Five Miles of the City.

No doubt the bells were also rung, although the payment of 5s. to the ringers of All Saints' church for ringing 'for the ceasing of the Cyder Tax' was not recorded in the church accounts until 2 July 1766. A pamphlet announcing the repeal was sent to Hereford from London and this contained the following:

A new SONG, sung by the *Herefordshire* Society

Rejoice, here's welcome News, come let us merry be,
 Since GEORGE, our gracious King in his great Clemency,
So kindly has consented his Subjects Wants to ease,
 By taking off the CYDER-TAX, which does the Kingdom please.

Then let the merry Bells all ring
 In every Village round,
 And nought but Joy and Harmony
 In every Place be found.

Come jolly *Hodge*, and *Will*, lay by your Pike and Flail,
 For *Susan*'s gone to fetch our largest Milking-pail
Brimfull of brave old Cyder, such, such as B*te never knew,
 Tis Liberty we'll drink until the Skies look blue.

Then let the merry Bells ...

It makes each Farmer smile to see the good old Dame
 So nimble with her Liquor, which from the Red-Streak came.
Handing it to her Neighbours, by which their Spirits rise,
 Rejoicing that their Mills are free from the Excise.

Then let the merry Bells ...

A Health to all our Members let's drink in merry Vein,
 To *Rockingham* and *Pratt*, let's fill it up again,
Likewise *Pitt* and *Dowdeswell*, we'll stretch our Throats still wider,
 And all the neighbouring Hills shall echo back Old CYDER.

Then let the merry Bells all ring
 And Musick sweetly play,
 Let shining Bonfires blaze around
 To close this joyful Day.

Cider was collected from small wharves along the Wye and stored in warehouses in Hereford for export down the river on barges. The warehouses were often of considerable size, and some at Pearce's Wharf in Hereford, advertised in the *Hereford Journal* in November 1788 as being to let, were capable of holding two to three hundred hogsheads of cider. The trade depended on the state of the river. If there was too little water the barges could not float and the movement of trade had to wait for rain. If there was too much water in the river from heavy rain or melting snow, the barges were at risk and had to remain tied up. There was a particularly bad flood in February 1795 caused by a rapid melt, and several bridges across the river were carried away and cider was lost from the warehouses in Hereford.

Not only cider, but grain and other commodities were exported down the Wye. On the return journey the barges were filled with a variety of goods, including coal. There was also an import trade in beer and on 26 December 1804 Jonathan Crompton of Pipe Lane, Hereford (now Gwynne Street) was advertising that he had received a large quantity of Bath Porter, Brown Stout, and Taunton Beer. However, the river trade declined by the middle of the 19th century, other better and more reliable means of communication with the outside world having been established.

Until relatively recently cider was made on almost every farm in Herefordshire. It was sometimes produced as a cash crop, but was usually made by the farm labourers for their own use, once the harvest was in. It was made from special cider apples, which are rather unpleasant to the taste as they contain a lot of tannin. In 1782 the method of making cider was described by Rev. Treadway Nash in volume 2 of his *Collections for the History of Worcestershire*. In the section on Mathon parish (then in Worcestershire but transferred to Herefordshire in 1897) he states that that area was renowned for the production of cider and perry, and goes on:

A cider press depicted on Taylor's 1786 map of Herefordshire

22

Let the fruit stay on the tree till quite ripe; those apples that do not fall naturally must be shaken off; when got together, it will be better (if it can be done conveniently) to lay them in the open air upon wattled hurdles, which will let the damp through, and keep the fruit from the damp and vermin of the ground; the heaps must not be above six inches deep, least they heat.

When the apples begin to decay, they are then fit for grinding; those that are black rotten being first thrown away. You are advised to grind the fruit till it becomes a kind of pap, that the kernels being thoroughly bruised may give a pleasant flavour to the liquor. This must or pap should then be put into a vat or large open tub, and remain there for two days; then press the *must* between hair-cloths very hard, and return the liquor into the vat, where it must remain until the lees are all settled at bottom, which may take two, three, or four days, according to circumstances. The fine part of the cider must be drawn out of the vat by a cock placed about three inches from the bottom. The liquor must then be put into a cask (the larger the better, if the quantity is sufficient), and should be filled within about four gallons. If it should fret much (which you will know by listening at the bung-hole), it must be returned into the vat for four and twenty hours, whilst the vessel is new cleaned, and then drawn off by the cock in the same manner as before, when the remaining lees will finally settle at the bottom. The bung-hole must be left open for two months; the cask then filled up with the same cider, and kept at least two years before it is drank or bottled. If for draught, that is, not for bottling, it may be drunk at the end of one year, but in any case, particularly in a vessel smaller than a hogshead, it should be tasted frequently; as the smaller the vessel, the more subject it will be to become sour; after the fermentation is over, it is best to fill up the vessel every three or four months with cider of equal, if not superior quality.

Where apples grow so do pears, which when processed in the same manner as cider apples are converted from unpalatable varieties of that fruit into that pleasant, heart-warming drink called perry. Nash goes on to describe how to make perry, and points out that it is possible to make spirit out of both. More details of the production of cider are given by the Rev. Jonathan Williams in his 1808 *Leominster Guide*:

The colours of good cider fruit are red and yellow; of an astringent taste: green colour is to be avoided. Ciders composed of the juices of mixed fruits generally succeed with greater certainty than those made with one kind. In grinding the fruits, care is taken to have as much of the juice of the rinds and kernels as can possibly be obtained. The must or pomage should be suffered to remain about twenty-four hours before it is taken to the press. The quantity of apples sufficient to fill the provincial hogshead of one hundred and ten gallons, varies from twenty four to thirty bushels.

Ciders manufactured from good fruit will retain a considerable portion of their sweetness at the end of three or four years. The best time for bottling cider is when it is from eighteen months to two years old; if perfectly secured from the air, by the tightness of the cork, it may be kept to any age. The annual produce of the fruit, in a plentiful year, is almost beyond conception. Twenty hogsheads of cider have been made from the produce of a single acre of orchard ground. This excessive fruitage, however, seldom occurs more than once in four years.

After crushing the apples and pressing to extract the juice, farm cider was produced without the addition of cultured yeast, fermentation relying upon the natural yeasts in the apples to produce a still, cloudy, acidic, invigorating and thirst-quenching drink. This was much appreciated during the heat of the following summer when the farmer would provide bread, cheese, and cider for those helping with the hay-making, a practice that continued into the 20th century. These delights of making hay, and possibly others, are described by Laurie Lee in his best-selling book *Cider with Rosie*.

Farmhouse cider was not universally acclaimed. In *Hereford in 1892*, the author comments:

Those who have seen the wretched looking farm-house cider-mills in various parts of the country, the uncleanly surroundings, and the rough-and-ready methods used in the production of this beverage, can only wonder at the good luck that so often favoured the cider maker. All sorts and conditions of apples, some green, some over-ripe, and some half-decayed windfalls, all mixed without care or selection and crushed up in a dirty, lumbering old mill, and the juice left to ferment or mature in something like superannuated water casks or wash tubs, covered with old sacks. Such was frequently the method of making home-made cider.

Rumours also abounded of the addition of dead rats and cats and the use of water from particularly noisome duck-ponds!

Between the wars a former Bishop of Hereford gave evidence to the Licensing Commission and clearly had a poor opinion of his flock, for he said that there was much secret cider drinking in Herefordshire. This statement was taken up by the satirical magazine *Punch*, and the poem by E.V. Knox shown opposite was published in its pages.

Clearly this particular bishop did not share the views on drinking of one of his predecessors. On 27 March 1899 the Rev. W. Glenn, rector of Wentnor, Shopshire, in the northern archdeaconry of the diocese, wrote to the proprietor of the Three Tuns brewery at Bishop's Castle in the following terms:

HELL IN HEREFORDSHIRE

The wild white rose is cankered
 Along the Vale of Lugg,
There's poison in the tankard,
 There's murder in the mug;
Through all the pleasant valleys
 Where stand the pale-faced kine
Men raise the Devil's chalice
 And drink his bitter wine.

Unspeakable carouses
 That shame the summer sky
Take place in little houses
 That look towards the Wye;
And near the Radnor border
 And the dark hills of Wales
Beelzebub is warder
 And sorcery prevails.

For, spite of church or chapel
 Ungodly folk there be
Who pluck the cider apple
 From the cider apple-tree,
And squeeze it in their presses
 Until the juice runs out,
At various addresses
 That no one knows about.

And, maddened by the orgies
 Of that unholy brew,
They slit each other's gorges
 From one a.m. till two,
Till Ledbury is a shambles
 And in the dirt and mud
Where Leominster sits and gambles
 The dice are stained with blood!

But still, if strength suffices
 Before my day is done,
I'll go and share the vices
 Of Clungunford and Clun,
And watch the red sun sinking
 Across the March again
And join the secret drinking
 Of outlaws at Presteign.

E.V. Knox, *Punch*

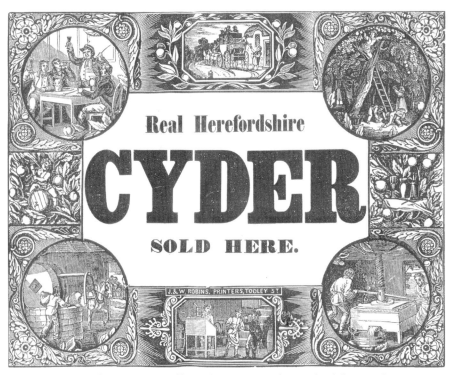

An early poster extolling the virtues of Herefordshire cider

My Dear Roberts

I hope you will not forget to send me some beer tomorrow, Tuesday, as I have not had a glass since I last saw you. Please send it good as I shall have the Bishop and some clergy here on Monday week and you know there are no people in the world better judges of drink than they are. I want them to be able to exclaim as with one voice, after they have tasted your brew, 'Roberts deserves well of his country as he is the only man who has discovered a cure for agricultural depression'.

Late in the 19th and during the first half of the 20th centuries, cider was made by several firms in Hereford including W. Evans and Co., H. Godwin & Son, and H.P. Bulmer & Co. In 1892, William Evans and Co.'s Cider Works were said to produce 'two favourite beverages, namely cider and perry, in greater perfection than any other town in England'. They continued to produce cider in Hereford until well after the end of the Second World War, but eventually closed and the buildings had all been demolished by 1975. Godwin & Son had premises at Holmer, where their factory was enlarged and remodelled in 1913, but they too have been closed for many years.

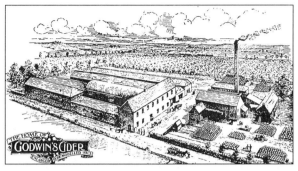

Top: Godwin's cider works after enlargement in 1913.
Bottom: Bulmers appreciated the possibilities of aerial advertising

Bulmer's firm was founded in 1887 by the sons of the rector of Credenhill who was determined that his sons would make cider in a scientific way. By 1888 this scientific adventure had prospered to such an extent that the business had moved to premises in Maylord Street. They eventually centralised their operations in Ryelands Street and, more recently, in Plough Lane. Bulmer's, the largest cider producer in the country, recently had financial troubles which led to the firm being taken over by the Scottish and Newcastle Brewery.

Manor Farm, Clehonger, a few years after Richard Henry Ridler started production of cider (Photo: Derek Foxton collection)

27

Two photographs of Ridler's Cider works at the time it closed

While most of the larger producers were in Hereford, there was a cider works at Manor Farm, Clehonger. In 1902 Richard Henry Ridler was farming there, but within a few years he started making cider on a commercial basis — an early example of diversification. The firm subsequently became Ridler and Son Ltd., which was run in conjunction with the farming business. After the Second World War the firm became Evans and Ridler Ltd., but it closed in 1950 after which the buildings were used for an engineering business.

As well as production by the larger manufacturers, cider continued to be made by a few farmers and inns using the old methods. However, nearly all cider is now made in plants resembling chemical engineering factories but, technology aside, the process has not changed much and most cider is only made when apples fall, or are shaken, off the trees. Now the natural yeasts are generally destroyed and replaced by cultured ones, but fermentation is still a batch process and is continued to complete dryness and an alcoholic content of over 8%. This results in many vats, each containing a slightly different cider, the cider-maker's art being in blending quantities from many vats to produce a consistent product. Alcoholic content, sweetness, and colour are all adjusted by the addition of water, glucose, and natural colour, the resultant blend being filtered, pasteurised, and carbonated before being marketed under an appropriate brand name and logo. Ciders produced by organic methods do not go through all these processes.

Many fermentation processes produce waste-products and by-products: the beer industry amongst other things produces spent malt that can be used as animal food and 'Marmite', that famous 'you either love it or you hate it' by-product. The residue left after pressing the juice from apples is called pommace and can also be used in animal feeds or ploughed into the land as a fertiliser and conditioner. An important by-product is pectin, a natural gelling agent used in the food industry. Bulmer's used to produce much of the world's requirement for pectin from the residues of Herefordshire apples, but in a global economy things change and pectin can now be produced more cheaply from the residual pulp from the citrus fruit juice industry, meaning pectin is now produced in South America near the sources of its raw material.

Until the middle of the 19th century most landlords made their own ale and beer in small brewhouses behind their inns. Few of these survive in a recognisable state today — they have either been demolished or converted to become part of the main buildings of the inn. However, many of the smaller inns and beer-houses that opened during the first half of the 19th century had no brewing facilities whatsoever and were totally dependent on other inns or on the growing number of breweries for their supply. This change accelerated as breweries bought public houses whenever they came onto the market, a process that resulted in a substantial decrease in the number of 'free houses' and of independent breweries. This was followed by a series of mergers and takeovers until only a few of the largest breweries survived. By the end of the war, the long tradition of inns producing their own beer had completely ceased in Herefordshire.

Brandy, Rum, &c.

TO be fold Wholefale, at the Brew-Houfe, at Fownhope, near Hereford, neat French Brandy, Jamaica Rum, and other Spirituous Liquors, by
NATHANIEL PURCHAS and Co.

MAY 11, 1771.

N. B. A Labouring-Man, and his Wife, of good Character, not too far advanced in Years, without any Children; efpecially fuch as are not gone out, or are able to go to fervice. The Man to have fome little Tafte for Gardening; and the Woman a good fpinner of Flax, may hear of a comfortable Being gratis, and conftant Employ for the Man, by applying to Mr. Whittlefey, at Fownhope, near Hereford.

Nathaniel Purchas used this 1771 advertisement for staff as a means of selling his wares

The first brewery of any size in the county was that of Nathaniel Purchas at Fownhope. In 1771 he was in partnership with Robert Whittlesey and the firm was in a good way of business as an importer of wines and spirits, using Purchas's barges to bring the stock of these up the river Wye from Bristol. The following advertisement appeared in the *Hereford Journal* on 15 June 1775:

NATHANIEL PURCHAS, BREWER AND BRANDY DEALER, takes the earliest opportunity, after the death of his late partner, Mr. Robert Whittlesey, of returning his most grateful thanks to all his friends and customers, and begs leave to acquaint them, that the business will be carried on in all its branches by him and his brother, Thomas Purchas, jointly; who hope for the continuance of their favours, which they will study to merit by serving them on the best terms. They have also just imported a quantity of Neat Genuine PORT and other WINES; which articles they intend dealing in for the future.

29

This demonstrates the increase in scope of the undertaking and shows that brewing had been added to the business. When he married Miss Mary Williams, daughter of a merchant of Chepstow, on 17 December 1772, he was even then described as being an 'eminent brewer' — whilst she was described as being 'liberally endowed with those engaging qualities which give permanence to the felicity of the nuptial state!' The union was blessed with several children, Nathaniel, the oldest, being baptised on 15 October 1775; he will be met with again in connection with the **Three Tuns Inn** at Hay.

The brewery was behind Nathaniel Purchas's house on the road between Mordiford and Fownhope, in a prominent position overlooking the river. It is not known how long the partnership between Nathaniel Purchas and his brother Thomas lasted, but the Ross firm of wine merchants of T.W. Purchas and Sons later claimed that it was founded in 1790. Thomas Purchas married Sarah Bird at Fownhope in May 1787, and Thomas Whittlesey Purchas seems to have been his son, although the baptismal entry has not yet been traced.

If Thomas Purchas set up as a wine merchant, then Nathaniel carried on the brewing business on his own account until his death, as recorded in the *Hereford Journal* of 26 November 1817:

> On Saturday last died, at an advanced age, Nathaniel Purchas, Esq. of Fownhope, in this county; a gentleman universally respected throughout a long life for the most undeviating integrity and uprightness of conduct, and whose death is seriously regretted by an extensive circle of friends.

The business was carried on by his 30-year-old son William, who announced in January 1827 that he had entered into partnership

> with two highly respectable Gentlemen; and that the BREWING, MALTING, WINE and SPIRIT TRADES, will be carried on under the Firm of 'REYNOLDS, PURCHAS, and REYNOLDS,' upon the same extensive scale and liberal terms as they were during the long period his late Father so successfully conducted the Business.

By 1830 the Fownhope Brewery was in the hands of William and John C. Reynolds, the name of Purchas having been dropped, and in 1834 John C. Reynolds moved the brewing business to Hereford, where he established himself as a brewer, maltster and wine and spirit merchant in new purpose-built premises in Bewell Street. By 1839 the firm had become Reynolds and Wase, and John C. Reynolds was also recorded as a maltster in Packers' Lane. The business was not a success and within a short while the brewery closed and was offered for sale by auction on 15 October 1842. At that time the brewery was capable of producing 5,000 barrels of ale and porter annually.

*The Watkins Imperial Brewery
in 1892*

*1892 advertisement for
Golden Sunlight pale ale*

What happened is not clear, but it seems that subsequently the buildings were left empty for a number of years and it was not until 1858 that the whole establishment was bought by Charles Watkins.

Watkins had previously brewed his own beer in a small brewhouse at the rear of the Imperial Inn in Widemarsh Street, but this new acquisition enabled him to put his creative energy to work in increasing output and in finding new sales outlets. He started his new business by adopting an eagle as his trade mark and by changing the name of the firm from the Hereford Brewery to the much more imposing Imperial Brewery, capitalising on the name of his inn. The beginnings of his fortune came when he transported vast quantities of his beer a few miles to the north of the city, where the navvies were digging a tunnel underneath Dinmore Hill for the Shrewsbury to Hereford railway.

Within a few years he was producing 'Imperial Household and Pale Ales', described as 'pure and sound, and unrivalled for excellence of quality and value combined'. Mild and bitter beers were available at 1s. a gallon and pale ale at 1s. 2d.; all being supplied in 9, 18, 36 and 54 gallon casks, delivered free. He was also responsible for the well-named Golden Sunlight Pale Ale, which won a gold medal at an International Exhibition in 1886 and became a best-seller for the firm.

A 1876 price list for the Imperial Brewery

*A delivery to the Hereford Brewery branch stores at
the King's Head Inn at Hay*   •

The brewery grew rapidly and with the profits Charles Watkins was able to buy and lease several public houses in Hereford and the surrounding areas including some in Hay. These purchases provided him with the main outlets to sell the beer he was brewing in ever increasing quantities. However, the brewery was still the centre of the Watkins family enterprises and eventually Henry, the eldest son, was taken into partnership. Unfortunately Charles and his son, Henry, both died in 1889, leaving the Imperial empire to be managed by Charles' two other sons, Charles and Alfred.

The quality of the many products from the brewery was said to be due to the water used in all the processes, which came from the famous Bewell

The first page of the catalogue for the sale of the Hereford Brewery in 1898

Spring by means of an artesian well some 40 feet deep. It had been discovered in 1724 and had always 'yielded an unfailing supply of excellent brewing liquor'.

The Hereford Brewery was the part of the family business that the two Watkins brothers decided to put on the market in 1898, as they were 'desirous of retiring'. Included in the sale was the brewery with its plant and all the other buildings on the site; 35 hotels, public houses and beer houses in the city and neighbourhood, including Hay; and branches in Birmingham, Cardiff and Swansea. It also included the various trademarks including the famous Golden Sunlight. It is not surprising, considering the size of the business, that the sale was held in London. The city reference library copy of the sale particulars is marked '£64,000 highest bid for the lot'.

The Tredegar Brewery Company acquired the business and a name change followed. The new firm was called the Hereford and Tredegar Brewery Co. and, in 1906 when they closed their Brecon and Tredegar breweries, the Hereford base became their main production centre. By 1950 changes were again in the air as a result of a merger, which established a new firm — the Hereford, Tredegar and Cheltenham Breweries Ltd.

These changes were also to affect the other main brewery in Hereford, which had been founded in the second half of the 19th century and, after several changes in ownership became the City Brewery which, in 1890, was bought by Arnold, Perrett & Co. of Wickwar in Gloucestershire. The brewery was situated on the south side of Maylord Street, on a more restricted site than the Hereford Brewery, and produced beer for consumption in the gradually growing number of inns in Herefordshire that belonged or were tied to the company. Arnold, Perrett & Co. were eventually associated with the Stroud Brewery, and in 1924 a Trust Deed transferred the ownership of the whole of the Maylord Street premises to the Cheltenham Original Brewery Co. Ltd. The City Brewery was eventually amalgamated with the Hereford & Tredegar Brewery and the joint firm eventually became the Cheltenham & Hereford Brewery Ltd., although it continued to make use of the trade names such as the Stroud Brewery and Arnold, Perrett & Co. for parts of its various enterprises. Brewing continued in Maylord Street until May

A Hereford and Tredegar Brewery order form printed on a postcard

1948 and in 1951 it was put up for sale because the firm was concentrating all their brewing operations in the city 'at their other extensive premises in Bewell Street'. The whole area is now part of the Maylord Orchards development.

Subsequent to the acquisition of the Cheltenham and Hereford Brewery by Whitbreads, brewing operations ceased in the Bewell Street works. After a few years of being used as a distribution centre, all the buildings on the site, apart from Bewell House, were demolished in the early 1960s. Eventually, the Tesco supermarket was built on the site, the extensive basement car park replacing in part the cellars belonging to the brewery.

Following the closure of the Bewell Street brewery, there was a period of some 30 years when beer for public consumption was no longer produced in Hereford. Indeed, beer brewed at individual inns throughout the country almost ceased, with only a few notable examples such as the Three Tuns at

Bishop's Castle surviving. Convenience beers, in pressurised barrels that did not depend on the skill of the landlord, flooded the market. For a time, it looked as though the old-fashioned beer-engine, used to draw the beer up from the carefully racked barrels in the cellars, would be a thing of the past.

A welcome change has occurred in recent years and locally produced beer is again available. The Wye Valley Brewery, based at the Barrels Inn in Hereford, now has its beer in many local inns. Indeed, such has been the demand that it moved its operations to the former Symond's Cider works at Stoke Lacy in April 2002, leaving behind its outgrown premises at the rear of the Barrels. The move has enabled the brewery to increase production from 100 to 300 barrels of beer each week.

Another brewery in Hereford was installed at the rear of the Victory Inn; this is called the Spinning Dog Brewery after the pub's resident dog which always chases her tail! It produces a range of 12 beers and ales, most of which is sold outside the county. One of these won the champion accolade at the 2003 Hereford Beer Festival, the culmination of over three years' work since the business was started. 'Specialist beers' — the products of the many smaller breweries that have opened throughout the country — are available in many pubs, and the beer-engine has made a welcome return on most bar counters.

> Say, for what were hop-yards meant,
> Or why was Burton built on Trent?;
> Oh many a peer of England brews
> Livelier liquor than the muse,
> And malt does more than Milton can
> To justify God's ways to man.
> Ale, man, ale's the stuff to drink
> For fellows whom it hurts to think.

> (*A Shropshire Lad*, A.E. Housman, 1896)

CHAPTER THREE

Hereford to Pontrilas, with a detour to Kingstone

The sprawling southern suburbs of Hereford now reach almost to Belmont, so that the Hereford to Abergavenny road is lined with houses for about two miles from the new Wye bridge. Eventually bursting into partial countryside at Belmont, it can hardly be called a country road, being now a main arterial route. From 1721 the roads in Herefordshire, notorious for their appalling condition, were gradually improved by a succession of Turnpike Acts. Roads radiating from Hereford were improved under an Act of 1730; this particular road as far as Pontrilas Bridge. Although none of the toll cottages survive, there were formerly three, one at Allensmore, another at what is now Lock's Garage, and a third in the parish of Kentchurch at Pontrilas Bridge.

Running roughly in the same direction as this road is the railway from Hereford to Abergavenny and South Wales, which has had a long and varied history, having started as a horse-drawn tramroad. In 1801 there was a proposal to build a tramroad to Hereford through the Forest of Dean, and a revised plan submitted on 30 September 1802 showed a tramroad starting from the opposite side of the river to Lydbrook and terminating in Hereford at the Wye Bridge, but this came to nothing.

However, the opening of the Brecon to Abergavenny canal in 1800 and the resultant benefit of cheap coal stimulated two proposals to create links with Herefordshire. The first, to build a tramroad from Brecon to Eardisley, was first mooted in 1810, and the necessary funds were raised and Acts of Parliament obtained. The first section, from Brecon to Hay, was completed in 1816 and the remainder to Eardisley was opened on 11 December 1818. The approach of the Hay tramroad stimulated a proposal in 1818 for a connecting railway to Kington and beyond, the section from Eardisley to Kington being opened on 1 May 1820. The second proposal made in 1810 was for a tramway to link the Brecon to Abergavenny canal at Llanwenarth to

Llanfihangel Crucorney and this was more successful. A Bill was passed in 1811, while the following year a Bill for an extension from Llanfihangel to Monmouth Cap was also passed. It was rumoured that meetings were held from time to time to stimulate interest in extending the tramroad to Hereford, but that these were broken up by people with vested interests in the failure of the project. However, in 1825 a series of public meetings was held and an application made to Parliament for an Act. This was passed the following year, and the construction put in hand. The tramroad was opened for traffic on 21 September 1829 and at 10 a.m. the first consignment of coal arrived at the Hereford terminus — the old coal wharf to the west of the south end of the Wye bridge. It had been estimated that about 6,000 tons of coal would be transported annually, but it is suggested that the peak tonnage transported in the mid 1830s was rather more than this. The subsequent decline was attributed to the increased price of coal from South Wales, which made Forest of Dean coal more competitive.

In 1845 a company was formed to develop a steam railway from Pontypool to Hereford, to join up with other projected lines. However, the three separate tramroad companies that made up the tramroad from Abergavenny to Hereford had to be purchased, and these transactions took some time, being eventually completed on 31 July 1851. Work on the railway, which had been suspended, then continued and the line was constructed, partly on the line of the old tramroad. The new railway line crossed the river over Hunderton bridge (now part of the Great Western Way) and terminated at Barton Station. This part of the line was open until the 1960s, although for many years passenger trains had used the line which looped round the south of the city and crossed the river at Eign to go to Barrs Court Station.

However, with the decline in goods traffic on the railways, the road to Abergavenny now takes most of the transport in this direction. In post-war years it has been much improved, so to find the wayside licensed establishments it is necessary to divert from the main road. The A465 Abergavenny road forms the south-eastern boundary for this volume, pubs to the south and east having been included in Heather Hurley's volume *The Pubs of Ross and South Herefordshire*.

After Belmont, which is in Clehonger parish (chapter 10), the next parish is Allensmore. The church is in a quiet spot to the left of the main road, and less than half a mile further on along the main road was an area known as Goose Pool. This was on the left-hand side just before the turning to the right leading to Cobhall Common. In the early 19th century there was a proposal to establish a public house here. On 4 September 1812 Thomas Bird, of Drybridge House, Hereford, wrote to Edmund B. Pateshall of Allensmore Court, telling him that he was engaged in letting a house that he owned at

Goose Pool to one William Lewis who had previously kept a public house in Abergavenny and wished to take out a public house licence for this building. Thomas Bird suggested that it would be a matter of convenience for the parish and asked if Pateshall had any objection, understanding that Pateshall's objections in a previous case had been on personal grounds. He went on to say:

> I have seen several of the Inhabitants who think it would be an accommodation there being no Licensed house at present in Allensmore or the adjoining places of Eaton Bishop, Clehonger, Haywood or Callow.

The following day Edmund Pateshall penned a strong reply:

> Mr. Pateshall presents his compliments to Mr. Bird. In reply to his letter he has only to say that his objections to Mr. Birds Tenement at the Goosepool being licensed as a Public house are still as great as ever they were and that he is extremely sorry to think that the many unpleasant circumstances which occurr'd some years ago on that subject have not discouraged Mr. Bird from pursuing such an object.

Not only that, but the local clergyman penned a letter in support:

> Mr. Pearce is pleased to find that Mr. Pateshall feels and expresses his dislike to the licensing of a Public House in the Parish of Allensmore. The objections to this measure upon a former occasion were not of a personal nature, but were founded upon the apprehension that if the application for a licence had been sanctioned, it might have produced dangerous consequences to the morals of the Parish. These objections therefore are now as strong as ever.

As a consequence of the objections Thomas Bird's house at Goose Pool was not licensed, and the lists of alehouse-keepers' recognizances taken out in the period 1818 to 1828 do not record any licensed premises in Allensmore. These lists survive in the records of the Clerk of the Peace — who was Thomas Bird!

In the event, a public house was subsequently established at Goose Pool, but not until the middle of the 19th century. This was called the **Pelican**, the first mention being in Lascelle's *Directory* of 1851 when it was run by Francis Sayce, who augmented his income by combining the licensed trade with that of shopkeeping. It seems most likely that it was established after the death of Edmund Pateshall in 1848. The unusual name of the pub can be explained by the fact that the family crest of the Burnam Pateshall family was a pelican vulning itself — in other words a pelican with outstretched wings pecking at its breast. Such a use of the crest of the Lord of the Manor no doubt had Edmund turning in his grave!

The one-time Pelican and a representation of the pelican as a crest

James Brisland, at the **Pelican** in the 1860s and '70s, was also a tailor. From the late 1870s James Perkins was the licensee and he may well have been the last one, for although the **Pelican Inn** is marked on the 1890/1 Ordnance Survey map, it is not mentioned in any directories after this date. Jakeman and Carver's *Directory* of 1902 records that Arthur Evans, a blacksmith, was resident at 'Laine's Cottage', by which name the **Pelican** was then known. Subsequently it was divided into two cottages, listed simply as Nos. 1 and 2. At present the north part is called Lane's Cottage, while the remainder, which has been extended, is named Davean after some previous owners.

The Cherry Tree is no longer an inn

A mile and a half further along the main road, on the right-hand side, was the **Cherry Tree Inn**. This first appears in the 1841 census when Francis Sayce was licensee; he was later to move to the **Pelican**. John Powell, who held it in 1851, was described simply as a victualler. In the late 1860s John Morgan was the licensee and his widow Martha took over about ten years later. She was still there in 1891 but it closed not many years later. In 1902 Catherine Harris, described as a cottage farmer, was at Cherry Tree Farm. The building is still called Cherry Tree and to its south is a small orchard containing two cherry trees, one of which is of considerable size and age, evidently the reason for the name of the holding.

Lock's Garage, a little further on at the next crossroads, is the next landmark on the A465. The 1810 Turnpike Act for repairing roads near Hereford describes this place as the Old Horse Shoes, named after the Old Horse Shoes Farm marked at this crossroads on Bryant's map of 1835, although a lease and release of 9 & 10 September 1817 refers to it as Three Horse Shoes Farm. All that is left of the farm is some old barns close to the crossroads. The first edition of the one-inch Ordnance Survey map, published in 1832, records the road running behind Lock's Garage, whereas Bryant's map shows the road layout as it is today, so clearly there had been an early exercise in road straightening.

Turning right along the B4348, the **Three Horse Shoes Inn** is just a short distance from the main road, but until the road was straightened in the 1830s the main road actually went straight past. The **Three Horse Shoes** is in the township known as Treville, which was extra-parochial for ecclesiastical purposes as it was not attached to a church. In the 19th century it was made a parish for poor-law purposes, and the paupers from Treville were sent to the workhouse in Abbey Dore until it closed in the early 20th century. The **Three Horse Shoes** is one of the few surviving pubs in the area and has a long history. There is an assignment of a lease of the inn executed on 20 March 1649/50, which recites a lease of 4 October 1610. However, it does not identify the building as the public house, and although the name is very suggestive but it could refer to the farm. Nor is it possible to confirm that it relates to the present **Three Horse Shoes**, although this would seem to be most likely.

An interesting news item about the **Three Horse Shoes Inn** appeared in the *Hereford Journal* of Thursday 27 February 1777:

The Three Horse Shoes at Treville in 2005

On Thursday last died, at the dwelling-house of Ann Evans, the sign of the Three Horse-shoes, in the township of Treville in this county, William Williams, of the parish of Cwmyoy, in the county of Monmouth, labourer, aged fifty-five, whose appearance of extreme poverty and distress of late had prevented many of his former employers from engaging him as a day-labourer. In the morning he was found dead in bed, and the extraordinary weight of some part of his clothing upon moving it, occasioned a strict examination of the whole, when, to the unspeakable surprise of all present the following pieces and sums of money were cut out of his patched and ragged apparel, no part of which was unprovided, viz. thirty-seven guineas, twenty-eight half-guineas, and six quarter-guineas,; one thirty-six-shilling piece, one twenty-seven-shilling piece, and one eighteen-shilling piece; eighteen pounds seven shillings in silver, and five shillings and ninepence halfpenny in copper.

In the same issue of the *Hereford Journal* was an advertisement by William Wilcox, who had conducted the search, asking for anyone entitled to the money to contact him, which he would pass on subject to proof of claim and payment of expenses.

In March 1815 an advertisement in the *Hereford Journal* stated that two tenements were to be sold by auction at the **Three Horse-Shoes**, while on 16 February 1820 land was advertised to be sold by auction at the inn. Surviving alehouse keeper's recognizances for the period 1818 to 1828 show that there was a licensed establishment at Treville at that time, and probably for a good time before that, no doubt the **Three Horse Shoes Inn**.

There was also a toll gate at the crossroads, a news item about which appeared in the *Hereford Journal* of 25 December 1844.

TURNPIKE TOLLS. — At a Petty Sessions held at the Shire-hall, in this city, upon Saturday the 14th instant, Mr. Thos. Wheeler was fined in the penalty of 30s., including costs, for allowing two horses to be taken from his wagons previously to their passing through a Toll Gate at the Three Horse Shoes, Treville, and afterwards, and on the return of the wagons, which were loaded with coal, whereby the toll upon the two horses was evaded.

Just over two months later the **Three Horse Shoes** was the venue for an illegal prize fight, but this did not happen, as the report sent by a correspondent to the *Hereford Journal* of 5 March 1845 reported:

PITCHED BATTLE. — On Thursday evening a fight was to have come off at the Horse-shoes public house (five miles on the Abergavenny road), between Edward Challenger, of Ewias Harold, and James Cooke, pieman, of this city; but, as luck would have it, an active justice of the peace of the immediate vicinity (who is famed for sanctioning and assisting in all kinds of rural amusements), having been informed by one of his *detectives*, of the intended *breach of the peace*, then and there made his appearance, severely reprimanding the parties and forbidding the performance; whereupon the countryman showed his discretion by his absence from the field, and the large assemblage separated 'ill pleased with the *no sports of the day*'.

For many years in the 19th century and into the 20th, the licence was held by a succession of landladies. In 1856 J. Berrow was here, but by 1858 the licence was held by Mrs. Sarah Hemming, who by 1867 had been succeeded by Mrs. Jane Mary Dean. She was here until 1893, and although her name appears in directories during this period without a break, the licensing records show that from 1879 to 1885 Harriette Louise Dean held the licence. Mrs. Alice Elizabeth Tipton took out a licence on 27 March 1893, and in 1896 it was issued to Alice Elizabeth Smith, she having remarried. Her name is given in the 1903 printed list of licensed premises issued by the county magistrates which also shows that the pub was then owned by Captain Percy Clive, of Wormbridge House, who had bought it around 1894; previously it had been owned by members of the Dean family. Alice Smith was at the **Three Horse Shoes** until at least 1909, but by 1913 the licence had been taken over by Albert Preece.

By 1917 the premises were owned by the Herefordshire Public House Trust Company, later called the People's Refreshment House Association Ltd. A prospectus was issued in 1904 for the Trust Company inviting subscriptions towards a capital of £10,000. The prospectus stated that:

> The Company is formed for the promotion of temperance by eliminating as far as possible the element of private profit from the retail sale of alcoholic liquors.

The idea was to take over existing public houses, and manage them as refreshment houses rather than just drinking places, so that tea, coffee, meals and non-alcoholic drinks would also be available. The sale of non-intoxicants was the prime object of the company, and each manager was to be paid a fixed salary together with commission on the sale of food and non-alcoholic liquors but none on the sale of alcoholic liquors. Thus the objects were quite clear:

> The Company seeks by such means to reduce the present excessive consumption of alcohol, to diminish the number of drinking clubs and generally to lessen the evils resulting from existing methods which in effect stimulate the demand for intoxicating liquors.

At the time that the prospectus was issued in 1904 there were already 34 such trusts in operation, operating over 130 public houses. The prospectus also stated that negotiations were already taking place for a lease of the **Hop Pole** in Commercial Road Hereford, which was then owned by the Hereford Society for Aiding the Industrious. In 1941 there were only three public houses run by the People's Refreshment House Association Ltd. — the **Three Horse Shoes**, the **Hop Pole**, and the **Biddulph Arms** in Ledbury. The direction in which the People's Refreshment House Association Ltd. tried to steer licensed premises has, in more recent times, perhaps been achieved more effectively both by economic forces and by laws against drinking and driving. The **Three Horseshoes** continues to thrive, but is much enlarged and the size of the car park is an indication that most of the trade arrives on four wheels!

Continuing through Thruxton — no record has been found of any licensed establishment there — the next village is Kingstone, where there is the **Bull Ring Inn**. It was named after the bull ring where, according to Mrs. Leather in *The Folk-lore of Herefordshire*, bear-baiting and bull-baiting took place, the last recorded occasion being in 1815. The **Bull Ring Inn** was described by the Royal Commission on Historical Monuments in 1931 as being

> at the N. angle of the cross-roads, 140 yards S.W. of the church, is partly of two storeys with cellars and attics. It is of T-shaped plan with the cross-wing at the S.W. end. The cross-wing has been refaced with brick, and there is a large modern addition on the N.W. side of the house.

This building has been licensed since at least the 18th century. In the church records is a note dated 1741 which states:

The Bull Ring in 1999

44

It was also agreed that ye Churchwardens and Overseers of the Poore shall pay the expenses not exceeding 2/- at any parish meeting lawfully called that should be held for ye future at any publick house in the parish for ale and syder then drank. We do allow of the above amount.

Entries relating to meetings often commenced with the words 'at a meeting lawfully held in Kingstone Church adjourned to ye Bull Ring'.

In 1764 the landlord was Isaac Roberts, and in that year he took on Elizabeth Roberts as a parish apprentice. No doubt she had to do all the menial tasks about the pub. The **Bull Ring** was where the manorial court met, and a court was held on 19 Oct 1767 'at the house of James Evans at ye Bulring'. It was also the centre for 'sporting' activities and on 8 May 1793 it was advertised that a main of cocks would be fought at the **Bull Ring**. Another was advertised on 4 May 1796.

In the early 19th century Thomas Preece was there, although the surviving list of alehouse keeper's recognizances show that Mary Preece was the licensee. When the **Bull Ring** was advertised as being to let on 19 December 1821 it was described as:

A Well-Established PUBLIC-HOUSE, situate in the Village of Kingstone, six miles from Hereford, known by the name of the *Bull Ring*, with about Sixteen Acres of Arable, Meadow, and Pasture Land. For Particulars apply to Mr. Wm. Parry, or the present Tenant, at Kingstone; or to Mr. Lane, Attorney, Hereford.

A new tenant was found in the person of one Richard Powell, and on 20 February 1822 Mr. Thomas Preece advertised that his farming stock, household furniture etc. would be sold on the premises at the **Bull Ring Inn**.

In the middle of 19th century the licensee was Frederick Seall, a member of a local family, who was also a tailor and draper and in 1851 employed two men. In the household were his wife Mary, seven-year-old son Frederick, a journeyman tailor, a tailor's apprentice, and an eleven-year-old house servant. Then and later there was a shop to the left of the present front door, no doubt where Frederick Seall ran his tailor's business.

By the time of the 1871 census Frederick Seall had been succeeded by his widow, Mary, who was there until the late 1870s. By the 1880s Thomas Davies was licensee, and his widow, Emma, followed the tradition and held the licence into the early 1890s. Jakeman and Carver's *Directory* of 1902 records that Charles Cowper was then the licensee and that he was also a shopkeeper. The shop was no doubt run by his wife, as she appears separately in the directory as a shopkeeper. The 1903 printed list of licensed premises records that the premises were then owned by John Bennett of The Parks, Ross. Charles Cowper was still there in 1905, but by 1909 Mrs. Emma West had taken over. She was there during the First World War, but directories do not mention her as running a shop.

In the early part of the 20th century the May Fair was held for three days and the swings and roundabouts were erected in the orchard behind the **Bull Ring**. Later in the 20th century the telephone came to Kingstone and Jack Meek, landlord of the **Bull Ring** by 1937, had one of the earlier ones with the number Madley 35. The **Bull Ring** continues to adapt to changing circumstances, and in 2004 it underwent a face-lift, reopening in the summer after the first phase of refurbishment.

At Coldwell, half a mile north-west of the church, was the **Mason's Arms**, which must have been the un-named beer house run by Thomas Morgan that is recorded in Lascelle's *Directory* of 1851. In 1867 Thomas Morgan was described as a cider retailer at Coldwell. By 1871 he had died and his widow Hannah, who was then aged 64, was described by the enumerator as an innkeeper. Her name appears in the surviving licensing records from 1872, by which time

MASONS ARMS

KINGSTONE

———

Marstons Burton Ales

Coach Parties by appointment

Bed and Breakfast

Parties catered for by appointment

———

SEVEN MILES FROM HEREFORD

———

Resident Proprietor : Mr T. Spencer

Telephone : Madley 223

A 1960s advertisement for the Mason's Arms

The Mason's Arms was looking rather run-down when this photograph was taken in September 1999

The Mason's 1960s sign

the inn had a full licence. In 1878 she was succeeded by John Lewis, and then in 1884 Arthur Preece took over and he was there until at least 1912. It seems that he had a spot of bother in 1894 as William Cleland, farmer, of Abbeydore, and Samuel Matthews, farmer of Bacton, appeared in court charged with assaulting Arthur Preece of the **Mason's Arms**, Kingstone.

The 1903 printed list indicates that he was a tenant as the premises were owned by Thomas Statham of Vowchurch, shown in trade directories of the time as an agricultural implement maker, an agent for other agricultural implements, an agent for the Prudential Assurance Co. and the local sub-postmaster! Another long-serving licensee at the **Mason's Arms** was Tom Morris, whose name first appears in a directory in 1913 and was there until about 1948. This inn, like the **Bull Ring**, was popular with the farm workers for their lunchtime pint, and in the summer and during the hop-picking time there was an increase in custom. During the war there was a shortage of supply, but as the **Mason's Arms** was a free house, Tom

By 2005 the old Mason's Arms had been partially re-built

Morris could shop around for different sources. Regretfully, the **Mason's Arms** has suffered the fate of so many rural pubs and closed about two years ago. It has now been renovated to such an extent that much of its character has been lost.

Returning from Kingstone to the main road, St. Devereux appears to have been permanently dry, but there was a former beer house in the next parish of Wormbridge, about a quarter of a mile before the church on the left. This was

Once the Carpenter's Arms at Wormbridge

the **Carpenter's Arms** which does not appear in directories by name, but from 1858 John Preece was recorded as a wheelwright and beer retailer. It is therefore not surprising that the licensing records from 1872 onwards show that the name was, the **Carpenter's Arms**. John Warby's name appears as a beer retailer here in a directory in 1891, but this was a little out-of-date as the licensing records show that the licence was not renewed in 1890. However, it seems that the wheelwright's business continued, for Thomas Watkins was recorded as a wheelwright in Wormbridge in 1902 and it is most likely that he carried on the business in the existing premises. The house is still there, but is now called Fair Acre, and the out-buildings have been converted into a separate cottage.

Next down the road is Kenderchurch, better known as the location of Pontrilas Saw Mills, a very small parish in both area and population. In 1861 the population was 99 living in some 14 houses. One of these, a beer house run by John Pugh, was called the **Oak Inn** in a directory of 1851 and the **British Oak Inn** in 1867. It had closed by 1872, as it does not appear in the surviving licensing records which start in that year. The 1851 census indicates that it was between Howton Grove and Little Howton and so just down the road from Wormbridge church. It seems to have been in a building on the roadside, almost immediately opposite Howton Grove, that is no longer in existence. The tramroad crossed the turnpike road just south of Howton Grove and the **British Oak** was in the corner of the junction, fronting onto the road with the tramroad running behind, evidently intended to pick up trade from both means of transport.

After Kenderchurch comes Pontrilas village, which is in the parish of Kentchurch. Although the modern road has been diverted so that is misses the centre of the village, historically it should still be included in this volume. It is at the southern end of the bypass that the road to Ewyas Harold (chapter 5) branches off to the right.

Just past the Saw Mills and the embankment of the former railway bridge for the Golden Valley Railway, is a left turn that was formerly the main road.

On the left, outside the old railway station, was the former **Pontrilas Inn**, which was built as a consequence of the arrival of the railway in 1853. There had been little development before the arrival of the railway, such as there was in the area having happened down the road at Monmouth Cap when it was the terminus of the tramroad. Indeed, there are no licensed premises recorded in Pontrilas village in the 1851 census, the only one in the parish being the **Bridge Inn** at Kentchurch. However, Cassey's *Directory* of 1858 records two persons resident at the **Pontrilas Inn**, one being Miss Sarah Ann Watkins and the other Amelia Dew. This could suggest that there were two places of the same name, but the 1861 census only records one inn here (although not by name), with two residents. One was Mary Watkins, an 80-year-old widow, who was described as a 'Housekeeper inn', while the other was 17-year-old Eliza Bradley, a barmaid who had been born in Manchester. Clearly Amelia Dew had left by this time.

Once the Pontrilas Inn

By 1867 an hotel had opened in the village, in what had been previously Pontrilas House. This had been built by the Baskerville family in the period 1630-40, and added to later in that century. After descending by inheritance through several families, it was purchased in 1821 by a Dr. Trenchard, and about the year 1840 was bought by Colonel Lucas-Scudamore and added to the Kentchurch Estate. In 1851 it was occupied by George Bentham, described as a magistrate, while in 1861 the occupier was Richard Watson. He had moved out by 1867 and it had been turned into the **Scudamore Arms Family Hotel and Boarding Establishment**. Littlebury's *Directory* of 1867 remarks:

> About 200 yards from the station is the *Scudamore Arms Hotel*, a first-class family hotel and private boarding house. It was formerly a baronial mansion, but is now fitted for the reception of gentlemen and families of position, with extensive right of fishing on the River *Monnow*, one of the best trout streams in England.

The 1871 census, recording 'The Hotel', states that George Jones, the proprietor, was then aged 59 and had been born in Carmarthen. He was clearly enterprising, for he had also taken over the **Pontrilas Inn**, no doubt at the same time as he opened the **Scudamore Arms**. In 1871 the only person staying at the **Pontrilas Inn** on the night of the census was the 22-year-old barmaid Louisa Bowen, who had also been born in Carmarthen. Nevertheless, the surviving licensing records, which begin in 1872, record that William Russell had taken over the licences of both premises, which he renewed the following year. However, the licence of the **Scudamore Arms** lapsed in 1874, leaving only the **Pontrilas Inn**, of which the licensee had changed to Amelia Sayce. The licensing records show that the ownership of the **Pontrilas Inn**, which also belonged to Colonel Lucas Scudamore, was transferred to Mrs. Donegan of Llangua about 1876, and then back to the Kentchurch estate in 1889. The **Pontrilas Inn** continued through the latter part of the 19th century, although with changes of tenant, until in November 1893 the licence was transferred from Harriet King, widow and executor of John King, to Sam Davis. He was there until well into the 20th century and it was his son, Mr. D. Davis, who changed the name to the **Scudamore Arms** in the 1920s. In the 1940s it was kept by Harry Bishop, and then by his son Harold. One night in December 1970 Harold Bishop had been out and returned to find that the **Scudamore Arms** was ablaze, and despite the efforts of five fire appliances the place was gutted, Harold losing all his personal possessions and his pet dog. It was repaired and rebuilt after the fire, but did not open again as a licensed establishment and is now a private house. Harold Bishop moved on to the **Red Lion** in Ewyas Harold (Chapter 5). Pontrilas House subsequently became known as Pontrilas Court and is at the south end of the former main street of Pontrilas.

CHAPTER FOUR

Pontrilas to Llanfihangel Crucorney, Llanthony & through to Hay

About a mile past Pontrilas the main road crosses the river Monnow, the boundary between Herefordshire and Monmouthsire. Just over the county boundary is Llangua, where there was a noted inn called the **Monmouth Cap**, named after the knitted headwear produced in Monmouth. The trade of capper dates back in Coventry to at least the 13th century, and the trade was later widespread. The surname Capper occurs in a roll of the Hundred Court of Monmouth in 1449, implying the existence of the trade there at that time, but it was not until in the 16th century that the term 'Monmouth Cap' was used, and such was the quality that later such knitted caps were referred to by this generic name even if made elsewhere.

A late 19th-century history of the church and surroundings refers to the congregation of the church at Llangua, and to this hostelry:

> A cluster of houses known as 'Monmouth Cap' supply the chief part of the Sunday congregation. These houses were built by the Herefordshire and Monmouthshire 'Old Tram Company' trading between Hereford and Abergavenny, in coal and iron. There was also at that time a comfortable Hostelry, well known to anglers as 'Monmouth Cap Inn', the half way house between Hereford and Abergavenny, for which the late Mrs. Le Blanc, daughter of Lady Bentham, and a visitor to Mrs. Scudamore of Kentchurch Court, painted a suggestive Sign Board, a Monmouth Cap, adding the quotation from Shakespeare's Henry V. (Scene vii.) 'wearing leeks in their Monmouth Caps'.

Shakespeare's mention of a Monmouth Cap at the time of Agincourt was, of course, an anachronism.

51

The **Monmouth Cap** is mentioned a few times in the *Hereford Journal* in the early 19th century. An advertisement in the issue of 12 April 1815 gave details of a sale by auction that would take place at the inn on 20 April, when there would be sold:

> All the valuable HOUSEHOLD FURNITURE, late the Property of Mr. Price, deceased, comprising Mahogany and other Tables and Chairs, Chests of Drawers, Linen Chests, good Feather Beds and Bolsters, Blankets, Bed Quilts, Bedsteads with and without Hangings, good Clock, Pewter Dishes and Plates, Lot of Glass Bottles, Tod of Hops, Copper Furnace and Irons, several Hogsheads and Barrels, Kitchen Requisites, Brewing Utensils, and various other Articles. – Sale to commence precisely at Ten in the Forenoon, and continue till the whole is disposed of.

Since it is unlikely that the furniture and brewing equipment would have been moved to the **Monmouth Cap** from elsewhere, it can be assumed that Mr. Price, deceased, was the former landlord. A 'tod' was a weight used in the wool trade in particular, usually 28 lbs. or two stone, but varying locally. It was also used to mean a load, either generally or of a particular weight.

There were also one or two sales of timber advertised to take place at the **Monmouth Cap** at this period. A sale of timber was advertised to take place there on 15 December 1819, the subject being:

> THE FALLAGE of several valuable COPPICE WOODS, in the Neighbourhood of Kentchurch, chiefly of Eighteen Years growth; namely, *The Meadow Wood*, about Twenty-Four Acres, and the *Wern Council Wood*, about Ten Acres, both in the Parish of Kentchurch, *Campson Great Wood*, near Eleven Acres, in the Parish of Grosmont, and *Leath Wood*, in the Parish of Langua, near Ten Acres.
> The Two last Woods lye near the Turnpike-road, and the Tram-road leading to Abergavenny, and the whole is worthy of the attention of Dealers.

The location of the timber near to the tramroad was seen as a definite advantage as it could be moved easily.

The position of the **Monmouth Cap** just over the county border was the reason for it to be chosen as the location for a prize fight in 1827. In the 1820s the **Booth Hall** in Hereford was kept by Thomas Winter Spring the famous pugilist. On 22 November 1826 it was reported in the *Hereford Journal*:

> Robinson, the celebrated Yorkshire pugilist, who is matched to fight the Gas Man for 200£. is now at Spring's, Booth-hall Tavern, in this city, for the purpose of being trained by the Champion; he will remain at the Boothall Tavern till the day of the combat, a period of six weeks. Crawley, who is matched to fight Ward, is expected at Spring's in the course of a few days, for the purpose of training.

The match between Robinson and the Gas Man (Bissell) took place on 23 January 1827, and a long report of the fight appeared in the *Hereford Journal* the next day, with a description of each of the 26 rounds — each round finished when one of the combatants was thrown to the ground — there were no Queensbury Rules

The Monmouth Cap Inn in 2005

at that time! Because of local opposition the fight took place near the **Monmouth Cap Inn**. It lasted a total of 35 minutes and at the beginning of the 26th round Robinson was unable to start and so the Gas Man was declared the winner.

The **Monmouth Cap** was clearly of note and was marked on Bryant's map of 1835. It was also a convenient meeting place, and on 26 April 1844 a meeting about the tithes of Longtown parish was held here, even though there were suitable hostelries in Longtown itself.

The 1851 census records that the then landlady of the **Cap Inn** was Amelia Dew, a 42-year-old widow who had been born in Devonport. Also in the household were her six children, her sister who acted as a barmaid, two maid servants and a bailiff. She had been in Llangua for at least ten years as one ten-year-old child had been born there.

The position of the **Monmouth Cap** recommended itself to the gentlemen of the fledgling Woolhope Naturalists' Field Club, who used it as a base for a field meeting on 22 August 1854. About 20 assembled at the inn, most having come by the recently opened Newport, Abergavenny and Hereford railway. After breakfast, one party departed to the area around Abbey Dore, Ewyas Harold and Kenderchurch, while the greater part rambled down past Kentchurch to Garway and Grosmont. The party reassembled for dinner at 5 p.m., no doubt hungry after many miles of walking, and partook of an excellently prepared dinner, which was in the opinion of the guests 'a feather in Mrs. Dew's (Monmouth) Cap'. Dinner was followed by various scientific papers read by those present, and eventually:

> The party rose from table about 8.30 p.m.; and the Hereford members
> departed from Pontrilas station. Through the kindness of Mr. Leyland, the

traffic manager, a carriage had been appended to the luggage train which [was] ordered to stop at Pontrilas for the purpose of taking up the party, who reached Hereford about 10 p.m., much gratified by their last field meeting for 1854.

In 1858 Amelia Dew, a rather unusual name, appeared at the **Pontrilas Inn**, perhaps having moved from the **Monmouth Cap**. But if so, she was not there for long, as in the following year she was recorded as being the landlady of the Golden Lion Inn in Frogmore Street, Abergavenny which, in 1862, was being run by 'Mrs. Amelia Dew and son'.

Somewhere about this period the landlady of the **Monmouth Cap** had a long period of bad luck, which was recorded by the Rev. Francis Kilvert, the vicar of Bredwardine and compiler of his well-known diaries on 26 March 1878 . He went to visit the toll collector for the bridge over the river Wye at Bredwardine and recorded in his diary:

> Called at the Bridge Gate House on the Merediths. Mrs. Meredith told me she had seen better days. She once had kept the Monmouth Gap [*sic*] Hotel and a coaching establishment of 18 horses, 16 of which died of influenza at one time. Then her husband died and she moved with their 5 children to the shop opposite the hotel, and brought them up. Her second husband was a small timber merchant who was ruined by the failure of a man in the same business. Now they have come down to keep a turnpike gate.

A moving story, told in Kilvert's usual style, which does not refer to Mrs. Amelia Dew (a later entry in the diary indicates that Mrs. Meredith's first name was Jane). Probably she was Amelia Dew's successor at the **Monmouth Cap**, and it is possible that her bad luck was part of the reason for the closure of the inn.

The **Monmouth Cap** did not survive for many years after the visit of the Woolhope Club — not that there is any suggestion of a connection — and Morris & Co'.s *Directory* of 1862 makes no mention of it, except to say that Edward McCormick, land surveyor and farmer, was resident at Monmouth Cap House.

In the late 19th century the inn was mentioned by H. Thornhill Timmins in his book *Nooks and Corners of Herefordshire*, published in 1892. He wrote:

> Down in the valley, just across the Welsh border, we espy that once notorious hostelry, the 'Monmouth Cap' of coaching days — a sign deriving its origin from that article of headgear referred to by Fluellen in 'Henry V' at the battle of Agincourt, where he speaks of his countrymen 'wearing leeks in their Monmouth caps'; and they are also mentioned, among other gifts presented to Lord Gilbert Talbot of Goodrich, as 'a new Yeare's Gifte of a Monmouth Cappe'.

Would that we knew why he called the inn notorious — there must be a story there!

The former inn is now known as Cap House, and in 1904 was the residence of Colonel Lucas-Scudamore. It is of some note, and part of the building is thought to date from the 16th century, so the reused timber in the roof must predate that period.

From Monmouth Cap, the road leads on to Pandy. This part of the road was turnpiked by the Grosmont Tramway Company, who built this section of the tramroad and a road running alongside, following all the twists and turns of the permanent way. Previously the main road to Llanfihangel Crucorney led past the **Monmouth Cap** and over Campston Hill. The Newport, Abergavenny and Hereford Railway was absorbed into the West Midland Railway Company in 1860, and they conveyed this section of road to J.L. Scudamore, no doubt as part of a policy of selling surplus assets.

This stretch of turnpike has since been straightened and widened, so that it bears little resemblance to its original state, helped by the fact that when the railway was built it did not utilise this section of tramway, mostly running along the other side of the valley, crossing over just before Pandy. Between Llangua and Pandy are the two places of Great Goytre and Little Goytre, the names suggesting that the **Goytre Inn** was somewhere in the vicinity. This was a beer house which was recorded in a directory of 1852, when William Thomas was landlord. He was in business until at least 1866.

At Pandy there was formerly a station, but it was closed many years ago as uneconomic. It was at this station that H. Thornhill Timmins alighted when collecting material for his book *Nooks and Corners of Herefordshire*.

> Shouldering our sketching-kit, we turn past the Pandy Inn, beloved of anglers, who find here a comfortable *pied à terre* after a day spent in beguiling the wary trout adown the charming reaches of the Monnow and her lively affluent, the Honddû.

Fortunately, unlike the station, the **Old Pandy Inn** is still open. It was built in the middle of the 19th century, probably to serve travellers on the railway, the station being about three hundred yards or so towards Hereford. It was at the **Pandy Inn** that the first dinner of the Pandy and Monnowside Ploughing and Agricultural Society was held on 28 November 1867, a society which was limited to a circle of radius seven miles from the Pandy station. Earlier in the day a ploughing match had been held nearby, and the dinner was provided by 'mine host and hostess Gough of the **Pandy Inn**, taken soon after four o'clock and followed by numerous toasts'. Over the years the society has met at the **Pandy Inn** many times, although the event has taken place at other locations in the vicinity. By 1881 Edwin Gough had moved down the road to the **Lancaster Arms**.

The Old Pandy Inn in 2005

In 1985 CAMRA recorded 'Strictly not in Herefordshire but half a mile over the river Monnow into Gwent, this stone-built roadside inn deserves a mention because of its excellence'. Indeed, the **Old Pandy Inn**, as it is now, is little altered since the 19th century, except for its windows. Its roadside location is a positive benefit, with easy access and basic accommodation, so it should continue to prosper.

The other inn at Pandy is the **Lancaster Arms**, not far down the road from the **Old Pandy Inn**. It was built in 1843, when the owner, Benjamin Teague, pulled down an existing house and built a roadside inn and turnpike cottage. It first appears in a directory in 1852, when it was held by Morris Jenkins. By 1871 the licensee was David Jenkins, who was described as an innkeeper and timber merchant. He was probably still there in 1873, when the **Lancaster Arms** figured in a report of a sad accident that happened after a ploughing match at Pandy. The hedging and ditching competition was held at Trevedw farm, and afterwards, James Seaborn, one of the competitors who came from Cwmyoy, decided to walk back along the railway to the **Pandy Inn**. Unfortunately he was run over by a luggage train from Abergavenny and killed, and his mutilated body was carried to the **Lancaster Arms** to await an inquest. Other, later, meetings of the ploughing society were held at the inn under happier circumstances.

The Lancaster Arms in 2005

The Rising Sun

The Rising Sun sign

The **Lancaster Arms**, like the **Old Pandy Inn**, makes its roadside position a positive advantage, dispensing food and refreshment to passing travellers, with a bed for the night should the journey prove too much!

After Pandy comes Llanfihangel Crucorney, where the modern road by-passes the village centre. On the left is a sign for Wern Gifford, and shortly after this a right turn takes the traveller onto the old road through the village. Immediately on the right is the **Rising Sun**. In the 1861 census this was described as the **Sun Inn**, and Caroline Gough, resident at that time, was described as a haulier's wife. Clearly it was her husband who held the licence, but he must have been away on business on the night that the census was taken. By 1871 it was being called the **Rising Sun** and the innkeeper was then one James George, a local man, who also worked as a stone 'tyler'. The basic building seems to have altered little in the intervening time, but has been extended at the rear and the windows have been modernised. Its position just off a main road has been turned to advantage, for as well as offering the usual hospitality it also has a park for touring caravans,

Continuing along this old section of road, the **Skirrid Mountain Inn** is on the right-hand side. It is claimed to be the most haunted inn in the country and modern publicity also states that it is the oldest inn in Wales, having been an inn since the 12th century. One web-site, reporting the haunting story, even goes as far as to state that it was a temporary court-house in the aftermath of the Monmouth Rebellion of 1685 and that 180 persons were hanged there by the order of Lord Chief Justice Jeffreys! Such a claim is easily dismissed since the Bloody Assizes only took place in the West Country, and of the 1,381 persons tried about 200 were executed, none north of Bristol.

As far as the building goes, John Newman, in his authoritative volume on Monmouthshire in the *Buildings of Wales* series, states that it is 'A remarkably complete mid- to late C17 building, constructed of the local shaley Old Red Sandstone'. He also points out that the pattern of

Above: The Skirrid Inn in 2005; Below: The doorway

relieving arches indicates that the fenestration of the lower storey has been altered, and that it was originally symmetrical. As for its use as a court house, it could have been used for the local manorial court, but this only dealt with matters relating to the administration of the manor, and should not be confused with a criminal court.

The first mention of the inn as a licensed house is in 1859 when John Richards was in charge and in the 1860s it was described as a beer house in the hands of one Joseph Davies, who was born in Clifford, Herefordshire. Because it was a beer house, it was licensed under the 1830 Act, and so unlikely to predate that Act. It soon gained a full licence, and in 1871 the name was given as the

'**Skyrryd' Inn**. It had lengthened its name before 1878 and in that year the local ploughing match was held nearby, with a dinner at the **Skirrid Mountain Inn**, finishing, of course, with the obligatory long list of toasts.

The property, which was part of the estate of the Marquess of Abergavenny, was sold to the then landlord, David Lewis, in 1900. The fortieth meeting of the Pandy and Monnowside Ploughing and Agricultural Society was held there in 1906, with a slap-up meal, followed by songs and a speech by Mr. Allen James, who had attended each one of those meetings. Part of his speech was reported thus:

> He wished that their M.P. [Mr. McKenna] was there, for he would like to say to him that he thought it was through him that the Pure Beer Bill was lost. He thought that there was nothing better than the pure beer, and nothing worse than McKenna's mixture. He did not notice many men of his age stronger in health than himself at the present day, and he put that down to the proper use of pure beer; that was a good healthy beverage, but with that dreadful mixture it was different. [Applause] If only Mr. McKenna had spoken in favour of the Pure Beer Bill, most likely it would have passed this year. But a gentleman who could afford fine old port didn't want pure beer. [Laughter]

The **Skirrid Inn** featured in the reminiscences of Stanley J. Bayley, who was born in 1901 and about 1980 recorded his reminiscences of the period around the First World War.

> The cobbled area outside the Skirrid Inn was a great attraction on Tuesday evenings, following the Market at Abergavenny; horses and carts were all tethered up outside whilst their owners were inside (my father used to tell me that they were in there for the same reason he occasionally went in 'to put their watches right by Mr. Powell's clock'). The inn was well patronised each evening by the local working men; half a pint of beer would sustain them all the evening with a game of quoits or cards (they probably could not afford to spend money on drink as we know it today). By the side of the great fireplace was a conical shaped copper jug, and into this men would pour their beer and heat it up by pushing it down into the fire. Sugar and ginger were free, in jars on the counter. A pint of beer, a round of bread and cheese, and a box of matches cost 6d. in those days.
> Charles Powell was a good landlord, had two sons, Hector, the oldest, being my particular chum. On Harvest Festival night, the long wooden benches were taken from the inn into the church to provide additional seating. The stables were always full of horses, as in my youth there were a number of timber hauliers working in the district; many of the great woods have now gone, and sadly, not replaced. Charles Powell incidentally, was the first man in the village to own a motor car, about 1910 I should think. It was in this very high, two-seater, that I had my first car ride.

The profile of the **Skirrid Inn** in recent years has been very high, and those working men of a hundred years ago would now feel quite out of place, with the offer of fine food, ales and wine, and period accommodation, complete with four-poster beds. However, despite the false claim to antiquity and notoriety, it is a splendid building and well worth a visit.

Before leaving Llanfihangel Crucorney, a mention must be made of the **Butcher's Arms**, recorded as being somewhere in the parish in 1852. It was run by Richard Watkins, described as a beer retailer and farmer; the surname of the publican suggesting that it was the un-named beer house run by John Watkins in 1859 and Elizabeth Watkins in 1862 after which it disappears from the directories.

The Vale of Ewyas

By the side of the **Skirrid Inn**, the B4423 leads up the Vale of Ewyas, the valley of the river Honddu, as far as Llanthony Priory, with a minor road eventually climbing the whole way up the valley and descending to Hay. Something over a mile along the road, at Lower Cwmyoy, is the **Queen's Head**, held in 1852 by James Pritchard and by 1862 by his widow, Margaret, who was described as a victualler. This is another place where the local ploughing match was regularly held. After a match in 1896 there were about 140 for dinner, and because the room was small, they had to dine in three relays. Despite this, it was a success as it was reported that 'an excellent repast was served up by my Host and Hostess Hughes'.

The Queen's Head at Cwmyoy

61

The building has changed little since that time, except that a porch has been built along the road frontage, and double-glazed windows have been installed to keep out inclement weather. There is, of course, the vitally necessary car park, needed for the visitors to the valley. The pub business, including accommodation, is supplemented by pony trekking and camping by the stream in the valley bottom.

After the **Queen's Head**, the left-hand side becomes very steep, with a long ridge following the line of the valley. On the far side of the ridge, and running along it, is an area called Fwddog, a hamlet in the parish of Cwmyoy, which was formerly in Herefordshire but transferred to Monmouthshire by order of the Local Government Board on 18 May 1893. For such a remote area, it is surprising that at least four drinking places have been recorded. The most recent of these was the **New Inn** which is reached by returning past the **Queen's Head** for a quarter of a mile and then turning right. This narrow road skirts the south end of Fwddog, and after a couple of miles arrives at a junction where five roads meet. Turning sharp right up a very steep minor road, the former **New Inn** is on the left-hand side; it is now called New Inn Farm. In 1837 the publican, Samuel Thomas, and his son James, who were both masons, built the Tabernacle Chapel. Later a cottage was built next door for James called, not too surprisingly, New Inn Cottage (now Fferm Newydd). The **New Inn** is recorded in the 1841 census when 50-year-old Samuel Thomas was the publican, but it does not appear in any directory until 1867 by which time James Powell was licensee. His name is also recorded in the licences issued by the Dore Bench of magistrates from 1872 onwards, which also show that he was the owner of the premises. After his death in 1883, the licence passed to Mary Powell, his widow, and then on 25 May 1885 it was transferred to Edward Jones. By then the premises belonged to Edward Thomas Husband of Pontrilas.

The **New Inn** closed in 1918 as a consequence of a minor transgression. The licence was held at that time by the wife, and she went out for a short time during licensing hours and locked the door. This was considered to be a breach of the terms of the licence which was consequently taken away. When the **New Inn** was licensed the front door was in the centre of the building, with a room on each side opening off a corridor with wooden walls. The barrels were kept on trams (trestles) in the back of the inn.

Despite the remote situation there were three other establishments up the road leading past New Inn Farm, which must have been open at different times. A short distance after the farm the road deteriorates into a stoned track, much eroded by water running down the steep hill. Where the track levels out, on the right-hand side there is a much ruined building which was formerly the **Cock Inn**, a metal sign for which was found many years ago

The remains of the Spiteful Inn

buried in the ground. It appears by name in the 1841 census when James Lloyd, described as a farmer, was resident, but there is no suggestion that it was still in operation as a public house and indeed it probably had closed many years previously.

Carrying along the track, there is another ruined cottage on the right-hand side, and not too far past this there is the remains of a building on the left, with a tree now growing though it. This was formerly the **Spiteful Inn**, whose name (found in deeds relating to the area) is said to have been given because when it opened another pub closed from lack of business. Finally, further on still, was the **Castle Inn**, which was said to have been a simple beer house, but only the foundations can now be traced.

Returning to the Vale of Ewyas, Upper Cwmyoy is somewhat further along the valley than the **Queen's Head**, and is best reached by turning off the main road by that inn. The church is in a prominent position on the side of the valley, and close inspection reveals that no part of the church is perpendicular. This is because the church was built on a fault line and, while the tower has sunk in one direction, other parts of the church have moved in another.

Immediately behind the church used to be the **Black Lion**, which was occupied in 1852 by Thomas Williams, described as a victualler. By 1862 William Exon had taken over; he also worked as a shoemaker. In 1881 the landlord was John Parry, a married man of 37, who also farmed 22 acres; not really surprising in such a remote spot, as it would not be possible to make

Cwmyoy church

a living out of the licensed trade alone. It was still open in 1926, but must have closed soon afterwards and has since been demolished. It is possible to imagine the local who was a regular at the **Black Lion** using the church as a reference point on leaving the inn. If the church appeared upright then he would know he had had too much to drink! Indeed, the local story is that the masons who built the church spent too much time in the **Black Lion** and so could not built anything upright — a calumny on the masons, of course, as the church was built long before a pub was likely to have been open.

Carrying on up the main valley road, the prime objective of most visitors is Llanthony Priory, of which there are substantial remains. Although it remains in private ownership, it is looked after by Cadw. The site has early connections, as St. David himself is said to have lived here for a few years and built a simple shrine — indeed the present name is a corruption of the Welsh *Llandewi nant Honddu* (the church of St. David by the brook of the black water). In 1100 a knight called William de Lacy, finding himself carried here in the course of hunting and no doubt influenced by the story of the residence of St. David, was seized with devotional fervour, and settled as a hermit in this out-of-the-way place. He was joined in 1103 by Ernisius, chaplain to Queen Matilda, and a priory of Augustinian Canons was founded in 1107.

After some 30 years, the monks, finding the Vale of Ewyas not to their liking, mostly moved to Gloucester where they founded another Llanthony,

Llanthony Abbey in 1800

called Secunda, the church being dedicated in 1136. Llanthony Prima was later revitalised and the church rebuilt towards the end of the 12th century. It eventually became subsidiary to its daughter foundation and survived until the Dissolution in the 16th century, when the site was sold for about £160. Although it has gradually decayed since then, the survival of the impressive remains is probably due to its remote situation, making it uneconomic for use as a quarry.

A late 18th-century print, made from a drawing of 1777, shows that the prior's lodging, to the south of the priory church, was roofed and no doubt inhabited. In 1799 the Llanthony estate was bought from the Harley family by Colonel Sir Mark Wood, and he extended the prior's lodging, taking in the south-west tower of the priory, to make a shooting box. Colonel Wood sold the Llanthony estate to the poet Walter Savage Landor for £20,000 in 1808. He made his residence in the shooting box, and started to build a new house a few hundred yards above the priory. He also removed part of Colonel Wood's buildings against the priory. His past record was an augury of things to come — expelled from Rugby, sent down from Oxford, inevitably he fell out with everyone in the area. Many of the hundreds of thousands of trees that he planted were uprooted, his tenants refused to pay their rents, and he lost so much money that he was nearly ruined. From 1814 to 1835 he lived mostly abroad and his estates were managed by his mother, who seems to have made a better job of it than he did! He retired to Bath from 1837 to 1858, but then spent his remaining years abroad, dying at Florence in 1864 at the age of 89.

Llanthony Priory has served as a magnet for tourists for many years. In 1770 it was visited by the Rev. William Gilpin, father of the cult of the picturesque, during his tour of the river Wye. He was rather disparaging in his comments on the situation of Llanthony, lending point to the improvements that Landor tried to carry out.

> If you have time to make a little excursion, you will find, about halfway between the Hay and Abergavenny, the ruins of Llantony-priory. Dugdale describes it, in his Monasticon, as a scene richly adorned with wood. But Dugdale lived a century ago; which is a term that will produce or destroy the finest scenery. It has had the latter effect here, for the woods about Llantony-priory are now totally destroyed; and the ruin is wholly naked and desolate.

Llanthony was visited in 1803 by J.P. Malcolm, who was staying with a clerical friend in Herefordshire, and he provides a graphic description of his walk over the mountains from Dore Abbey in wild and windy weather. He commended the then owner, Colonel Wood of Piercefield, for employing a mason to replace stones that had fallen from the great west door, and to do other similar repairs. However, this does not seem to have been effective, as the tracery of the west front collapsed in 1803 in the sight of Sir Richard Colt Hoare.

Colonel Wood's shooting box, used as a house by Walter Savage Landor, was subsequently converted into an inn, evidently for the convenience of visitors to the priory, and Lascelle's *Directory* of 1852 records that Richard Walker, victualler, farmer and steward, was then resident at Llanthony 'Abbey'. At that time and later the inn was called the **Traveller's Rest**. By 1862 Richard Beachamp had taken over, and he is mentioned in Kilvert's diary for April 1870. At that time Kilvert was curate at Clyro, and with friends had taken a carriage to Llanigon and walked from there over to Llanthony. He wrote:

> We crossed the field and the fold of a farm house, scrambled down a narrow stony lane and struck the main road again. About a mile above Llanthony we descried the Abbey ruins, the dim grey pile of building in the vale below standing by the little river side among its brilliant green meadow. What was our horror on entering the enclosure to see two tourists with staves and shoulder belts all complete postured among the ruins in an attitude of admiration, one of them of course discoursing learnedly to his gaping companion and pointing out objects of interest with his stick. If there is one thing more hateful than another it is being told what to admire and having objects pointed out to one with a stick. Of all noxious animals too the most noxious is a tourist. And of all tourists the most vulgar, illbred, offensive and loathsome is the British tourist. No wonder dogs fly at them and consider them vermin to be exterminated. The most offensive part of their conduct however was that they had arrived before us and already had ordered their dinner, so we had to wait till they had done, solacing ourselves with either the *Hereford Times* and the Visitors' Book from which to the great and just indignation of the landlord some of the British tourists had cut out and stolen half a year of entries from October 1865 to May 1866, including my last entry. Stout Beauchamp the landlord had not turned a hair since I saw him 4 years ago, but he did not remember me. Recollecting that Richard Beauchamp was a Somersetshire man I made capital of the West Country clannishness and introduced Bridge as a fellow countryman, and it paid very well for mine host was much pleased at having a guest from the old shire. His broad ruddy hard face softened and beamed more kindly, his manner became less surly and scratching his huge bullet head he turned to the dark-eyed servant girl Sarah and bade her make haste and put plenty of ham and eggs for the gentlemen for he knew how Somerset men could eat.

While they waited for their meal, Kilvert and his friends bought photographs of the priory and little books about it, and strolled round. Kilvert moaned that the tourists had delayed their meal by an hour, and that they were late in leaving the priory for their walk home. They left at 3.50 and arrived back at Clyro at 7.50 after a round trip of 25 miles.

Kilvert visited Llanthony again on Midsummer's Day 1870, and in his diary once again expressed his opinion of tourists:

> When we entered the Abbey precincts the courtyard was swarming with people. Some were walking about, some sitting down under the penthouse on either side of the Abbey Tavern door, some standing in knots and groups talking. The kitchen was buzzing and swarming like a hive. Beauchamp came forward and met us and we were shown into the upper long room. Here the servant girl Sarah told us it was Mr. Arnold Savage Landor's rent day. Mrs. Beauchamp came in and said she was afraid she could not cook anything for us as there was so much cooking going on in the kitchen for the tenants' dinners. However, she promised us some bread, butter, cheese and beer and boiled eggs. While these things were being got ready we amused ourselves by looking out of the window at the people in the green courtyard below. A tent or rather an awning had been reared against the wall of the Lady Chapel. The wind flapped the canvas sides and strained at the ropes. The cloth was spread on the table. No viands had yet appeared but a savoury reek pervaded the place and the tantalized tenants walked about lashing their tails, growling and snuffing up the scent of food hungrily like Welsh wolves.
>
> For our part we consumed 18 eggs amongst us and a proportionate amount of bread, cheese, butter and beer. ... We [then] amused ourselves

Tourists at Llanthony priory in 2003

by watching the dinner being carried out and the ways and customs of the natives in taking their food. They were an uncommonly short time about it and the dishes were changed fast. The agent took the head of the table and Beauchamp as steward sat next to him. Then tourists began to arrive, and two carriages, probably from Abergavenny, drove into the courtyard. The morning's rain had happily and successfully choked them off till now.

On 28 July 1891 the Woolhope Club visited Llanthony and, being the annual Ladies' Day, there were many ladies and other visitors present. The party travelled by train to Llanfihangel Crucorney and were then conveyed by brake up to Llanthony. Lunch was to be had at the priory but:

> The very threatening aspect of the weather shortened the examination of the buildings and rendered it most prudent to hurry on the preparation of luncheon. This cold luncheon, *al fresco*, on the Abbey green, was hurriedly despatched. Of provisions there were plenty, and the serving was better than is often obtained, but the unpleasant chilly blasts of wind suddenly arising caused it to be partaken of under difficulties, and necessitated an early removal of the cloth.

The visit to the priory and surroundings was much enjoyed, but there was dismay that the priory gate-house had been converted into a barn 'and the humble hostelry licensed within the precincts of the enclosure'.

One of the party on that occasion was H. Thornhill Timmins, and he was much taken with the place, recommending that:

> The wanderer in these hill cannot do better than take up his abode at the modest inn at Llanthony, once the prior's lodgings; where a room should be engaged beforehand, as visitors are numerous in summer time, and resting-places are few and far between. Here the fisherman, artist or sportsman will find quiet, homely quarters; and a snug corner of the kitchen, where many a Rembrandesque effect maybe seen beneath a vaulted ceiling; while the country-side will provide matter to suit each individual taste.

In view of the remote situation it is not surprising that the landlord of the **Travellers' Rest** brewed his own beer. A photograph of the brewhouse was taken in the early 20th century, and is preserved in the Pilley Collection in Hereford Reference Library, together with a labelled diagram of the equipment. It is headed with both the name **Traveller's Rest** and the new name of **Llanthony Abbey Hotel**. In 1926 Matthew James Knight of the **Llanthony Abbey Hotel** was advertising 'Accommodation for tourists & visitors, excellent trout fishing, conveyances to meet visitors at stations; motor garage'. Now called the **Abbey Hotel**, the exterior has changed little in the intervening years, but it is now possible to sleep in a four-poster bed in a room in the south-west corner of the tower, all very different to when the monks were in residence. As for the building itself, adjacent to the tower is a

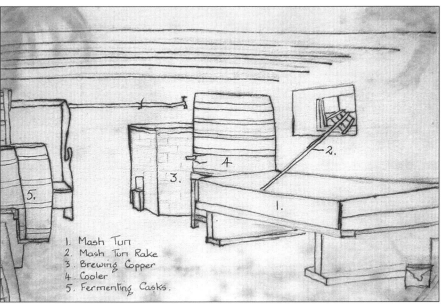

1. Mash Turn
2. Mash Turn Rake
3. Brewing Copper
4. Cooler
5. Fermenting Casks.

The Brewhouse in the Traveller's Rest — Llanthony Abbey, about 1900

narrow room with groin vaulting, thought to be a survival from the 13th century and to have been an outer parlour. Adjoining this is a building with a groin-vaulted undercroft, although the range above is thought to be a reconstruction of *c*.1800. The public bar is down several steps into the

An undated photograph of the kitchen at Llanthony Abbey

Locals in the bar at the Abbey Hotel in 2004

The Abbey Hotel sign at Llanthony

undercroft, but the vaulted ceiling appears curiously low, for the present floor level is built on top of much of the ruined material from the priory, the original floor being much lower. A short distance along the main road is another public house, no doubt established to cater for Kilvert's despised tourists. This is the **Half Moon**, which in 1852 was a beer house run by James Gwillim. Curiously, the 1861 census records Lewis Lewis here, although in the following year it reappeared in directories as a beer house run by James Gwillim. Elijah Williams, landlord in 1871, was described simply as an innkeeper, but Edward Whistance, recorded in the 1881 census, had to make ends meet by working as a cordwainer (shoemaker). The **Half Moon** was marked on the 1888 Ordnance Survey map as a public house and so had become fully licensed. As with other licensed premises in the valley, it has

The Half Moon Hotel

only remained open due to the flourishing holiday business, the economy of the valley being very much dependent on the sort of tourist that so upset Kilvert.

In recent years the image of the **Half Moon** has reached a much wider public, even if unacknowledged. The film, *An American Werewolf in London*, opens with scenes shot in and around the Black Mountains, purporting to be Yorkshire. The inn that the two young Americans reach towards the end of a good day's walking is called The Slaughtered Lamb — and it is the **Half Moon** that provides the backdrop for the film. Fortunately the script writer's dabbling with the reality of the locality is well ended by the time that the werewolf effects his attack in the subsequent mists and gloom of the evening.

Four miles up the valley from Llanthony Priory and just over the county boundary into Breconshire is Capel-y-ffin, formerly a chapelry of Llanigon. On 8 December 1870 Kilvert visited a sick man who told him stories of the Black Mountain where his forebears had lived for 300 years. One story was of Capel-y-ffin:

> Capel y Ffin is a third part of Llanigon parish. The Chapel was built partly for the convenience of the people on the Southern side of the Mountain. Owing to the snow and terrible storms these poor people were sometimes in the winter obliged to keep their putrefying dead in their cottages for weeks before they could carry them to Llanigon for burial.

Chapel House, near to the chapel, is said to have been a public house at some time in the remote past, but no direct evidence has so far been found.

From Capel-y-ffin the road continues to climb, reaching its highest point at Gospel Pass, with Twmpa or Lord Hereford's Knob on the left, and Hay Bluff on the right, before the descent over open moorland. The final stretch into Hay is down the left-hand bank of Cusop Dingle. Near the top of the dingle, the road from Craswall joins from the right-hand side and after the junction there is New Forest Farm. Here, in the 19th century, was a wooden building used as a canteen by soldiers practising at the firing range on Hay Bluff. This may have served alcoholic drinks, although it has not so far been traced in any directory or in surviving licensing records. There is now little trace of the building. From here the road winds down the valley until it reaches the western outskirts of Hay-on-Wye.

CHAPTER FIVE

The Ewyas Harold area

Ewyas Harold was fortified in the Norman manner before the Conquest of 1066, one of the earliest places in the kingdom to be so treated. In 1046 Edward the Confessor, that most Frenchified of English kings (1042-1066), granted the earldom of Hereford to his nephew Ralph — a Francophile — who took to Hereford a number of Frenchmen. Of these, two were rewarded with grants of land, Osbert Pentecost at what became called Ewyas Harold, and Richard fitz Scrob at Richard's Castle in north Herefordshire. Both men built motte-and-bailey castles in the style that was then current in Normandy. In 1051 Ralph was displaced in favour of a previous holder of the earldom, but was reinstated the following year. Subsequently, during Ralph's absence elsewhere, the Welsh invaded Herefordshire and the combined forces of the Saxons and Frenchmen were defeated. The castle at Ewyas Harold was dismantled. Ralph retained his earldom of Herefordshire, but it was again devastated by a Welsh raid in 1055. Earl Harold, subsequently to be the ill-fated king of England in 1066, was sent to Hereford where he refortified the city and punished the Welsh marauders who retreated to Wales. Earl Ralph died in 1057 and his heir was his five-year-old son Harold.

After the Conquest, William fitz Osbern was created Earl of Hereford, and he held the county by building castles in strategic places, including the rebuilding of the castle at Ewyas. In 1067 an invasion by the Welsh in support of Edric the Savage, who held the north of the county, was only put down with difficulty. During this revolt, Ewyas and Archenfield were laid waste, and only Hereford itself, and the castles at Ewyas and Richard's Castle were held by the Normans. Subsequently the castlry of Ewyas was granted to Alfred of Malmesbury, who held it at the time of the Domesday Survey in 1086. It was stated: 'The King himself granted him the lands which Earl William, who had refortified the castle, had given him'. Subsequently Harold, the son of Earl Ralph, became possessed of the land of Alfred of Malmesbury, and seems to have made Ewyas his main residence, as he began to call himself 'Harold of Ewias', leading to the present name.

The castle had a turbulent history in the earlier middle ages, and Robert, son of Harold, was a notable warrior. In 1135, during yet another Welsh revolt, the castle of Ewyas Harold was besieged, Robert could not relieve it in time, and it fell from famine. With the gradual settling down of the border area in later centuries, the necessity for the castle was reduced. Even so, when John Leland, the King's Antiquary, passed this way in the 1530s he saw considerable buildings, describing the castle as 'a notable thinge'. However, when Richard Symonds visited a century later he could not even find the foundations, all the walls having been taken down and used as a quarry for building materials. Evidence of this is still visible.

Despite the castle's prominence in years gone by, Ewyas Harold village has never been of great size and although it probably had a market by 1272 it was gone by 1500. In 1851 its population was 392, increasing to 507 by 1891. It dipped slightly to 476 in 1901 and by the time of the 1931 census it had declined further to 461. Now, however, as a result of the expansion that has happened to most villages around Hereford, the population of the civil parish was 847 in 2001. Interestingly, the number of licensed premises in years gone by did not directly relate to the size of the population, as in 1851

A photograph of the Red Lion in 1909. It was eventually rendered and painted white and finally demolished about 1990

```
┌─────────────────────────────────────────────────────────────┐
│                                                               │
│                        LOT  1.                                │
│   The substantially built and convenient and commodious       │
│                                                               │
│     Freehold Fully-Licensed Premises                          │
│                        known as                               │
│                                                               │
│             THE  RED  LION  INN.                              │
│                                                               │
│  Situate in the Parish of EWYAS HAROLD, within half-a-mile    │
│                   of Pontrilas Station.                       │
│                                                               │
│  THE HOUSE contains Bar, Smoke Room, Beer Cellar, Kitchen,    │
│                 5 Bedrooms and Sitting Room                   │
│                                                               │
│  THE OUTBUILDINGS consist of newly erected Club Room,         │
│  Washhouse and Stores, 2 Cart Sheds, 3-stall Stable with      │
│  loose box and loft over, Chaff House, Cowhouse for 2,        │
│             Engine House and Pigs Cot.                        │
│                                                               │
│  With a very Valuable and Productive Orchard and Garden       │
│                                                               │
│  with a long frontage to the main road, and having a          │
│       considerable element of building value.                 │
│                                                               │
│             The whole having an area of                       │
│                                                               │
│     2 acres,  1 rood,  30 perches  (or thereabouts).          │
│                                                               │
│  Let, with other lands, on a yearly tenancy to Mr. James      │
│  Cole, and the rent apportioned in respect of this lot is     │
│                                                               │
│               Per  £30  Annum.                                │
│                      ─────────                                │
│                                                               │
│               Commuted Tihe, 12/1.                            │
│                                                               │
└─────────────────────────────────────────────────────────────┘
```

Even in 1919 the development value of the Red Lion and its site was
appreciated as this sale notice indicates

there were only two public houses, whereas by 1902 there were five within the parish. It is, no doubt, more dependent on social factors, such as greater prosperity, which led to the increase, and, in more recent years, improvedmobility which has led to a decline back to two.

The main approach to Ewyas Harold is from the A465 at Pontrilas and along the B4347. Just under half a mile from the turning, opposite Morgan's Garage, was the **Red Lion.** This first appears in a directory in 1867 when it was run by James Lewis, but it was subsequently taken over by William Prosser who owned the property. At this period it appears in directories and in censuses as the **Lion**, without qualification. In 1881 William Prosser was aged 41 but he died 14 years later and the licence and ownership were transferred to his widow in 1895.

How it happened is not certain, but the **Red Lion** came to belong to the Bacton Estate and, when that was sold in lots by auction at the Green Dragon Hotel in Hereford on 14 May 1919, the first lot was the **Red Lion**. The tenant, James Cole, who had been there for at least ten years, bought the property for £825.

The last owner and publican was Harold Bishop, who has been met with in connection with the **Scudamore Arms** at Pontrilas, and during his time part of the car park was sold off for development. On 12 January 1989, an article about the **Red Lion** appeared in the *Hereford Times*, entitled 'Old pub may go'. Sadly this was only too true, and within a short while the inn was closed and the site was eventually developed for housing.

Bridge View was once the Prince of Wales beer house

Continuing past the site of the **Red Lion** towards the centre of the village, the road swings sharply right over a bridge across the Dulas Brook. On the left-hand side by the bridge is Bridge View, which was formerly the **Prince of Wales** beer house. The house was much remodelled in the 20th century and its age is not immediately apparent; the single-storey building on its north side was formerly much higher. In a directory of 1867, John Vaughan appears as a maltster and beer retailer, and the 1871 census, not too surprisingly, refers to his premises as the Malt House. He carried on his trade as a maltster in the building to the north of the house, which is evident on old photographs. It was not until 1876 that the licensing records give the name of the beer house as the **Prince of Wales**. On 10 September 1877 John Vaughan's son, another John Vaughan, took over the licence and, with the help of his older sister, Sarah, kept the beer house for some considerable time, the last mention being in a directory in 1914.

A number of stories are told of his time in charge. There was formerly a bannut (walnut) tree at the front of the pub, and the local boys used to pinch the walnuts when John Vaughan was not looking. His sister, Sarah, seems to have been a character also, and had a silver teapot, from which she would pour herself an amber liquid. This was, however, whisky!

In living memory there was a local character named Oliver Monkley, usually referred to as Monk. He slept rough where he could, and did odd jobs to keep body and soul together. On one occasion the local hunt met on the other side of the river in front of the pub. Now Monk had laid a trail from the meeting place through the front door of the **Prince of Wales** and out of the back door — which the hounds found and followed!

Leaving the former **Prince of Wales**, crossing the Dulas Brook and turning left, after a short distance there is the **Temple Bar** on the right-hand side. This is not recorded in the 1851 census and first appears in a directory in 1856, when Mrs. Ellery was in charge, perhaps taking advantage of the closure of the **New House Inn** (below). Mrs. Ellery seems to have had a lodger, as Cassey's *Directory* of 1858 records that James Payne, a farmer and butcher, was also resident at the **Temple Bar**. On 18 August 1862 the gentlemen of the Woolhope Naturalists' Field Club visited Pontrilas and area, and took their dinner in a tent at the **Temple Bar**. No doubt Mrs. Ellery, who was still in charge at that time, provided the food that they so much enjoyed. In the 1860s the licence was held by John Parmiter, who also appeared as a butcher and farmer. Alfred Prosser, here by the mid-1890s, was a busy man for not only was he the agent for Arnold, Perrett & Co.'s Gold Medal Ales & Stout, but he was also a baker, corn dealer and farmer. The 1903 printed list of public houses records that he was the tenant, the owner being the Rev. A.

Roadmen with their Aveling Porter road roller resurfacing the road in front of the Temple Bar early in the 20th century

The Temple Bar in 2004

Jones, who lived at White Rocks, Garway. Prosser was licensee at least until the beginning of the First World War. In the early 1970s the customers were often entertained by a four man band — gipsy violin, guitar, piano and a single-stringed box! One more recent owner was Doug Mountjoy, the world famous snooker player. It is now known as the **Temple Bar Inn and Restaurant**, with the restaurant specialising in home-cooked food.

In the 1820s there were two people who took out alehouse keeper's recognizances in Ewyas Harold, but where their establishments were located can only be deduced from other sources. Of the two James Powell was at the **Dog Inn** and John Jones was at the **Newhouse** or **New House Inn**. The **Dog**, only a short distance from the **Temple Bar**, claims pride of place among surviving establishments in Ewyas Harold; it is claimed that it was called the **Bell** in 1509, changed to the **Dog** in 1750, to the **Castle** in 1844 (actually somewhat later), and back to the **Dog** in the second half of the 20th century.

One early mention is in 1819, when an advertisement in the *Hereford Journal* of 15 December stated that coppice wood was to be sold by auction at the **Dog Inn**. James Powell of 'Ewias Harrold' took out alehouse keeper's recognizances between 1818 and 1828, and this sale must have been during his time. Directory entries start in 1851 and show that George Powell was at the **Dog Inn**. His relationship to James Powell is uncertain, however, as George Powell was born in Bacton in 1824, during the time that James Powell held the

The Dog/Castle almost adjoins the Temple Bar

Locals line up for a photograph outside the Castle (Dog) Inn around 1900

licence of the **Dog Inn**. George Powell was still at the **Dog Inn** in 1858, but by 1867 the name had disappeared being replaced by the **Castle Inn**, with John Goodyer as licensee. Perhaps there was not enough trade for a livelihood, as he was also a baker, flour and corn factor. By 1891 he had been succeeded as licensee by Thomas Prosser, who tenanted the pub, the 1903 printed list of licensed premises showing that the owner, a Mr. William Jones, could be contacted via a Hereford solicitor.

A story about the **Castle Inn** is told in *Yesterday in Ewyas Harold*, concerning Lionel Williams and his business partner Charles O'Gorman.

> In 1966, Lionel and Charles went to live in the Castle Inn (now known as the Dog) at Ewyas Harold whilst still having their workshop in Pontrilas and they were both well-known for their love of animals. They had reared many a wild animal and bird — the most famous being Foxy the dog fox and Tuppence the badger. Tuppence was very popular with the 'regulars' at The Castle going from table to table and generally rummaging around as badgers do. One day, Lionel and Charles returned from the workshop to find a trail of straw leading upstairs. They went to investigate and found that their beds had been filled with straw and a very contented badger lay there fast asleep! Both Tuppence and Foxy gradually went back into the wild of their own accord but they had given a lot of people immense pleasure before each found a mate and settled in the wild.

A later paragraph on Lionel Williams goes on to state:

> He was well-known as a part-time barman, firstly at the Scudamore Arms, Pontrilas for Harold Bishop, then at The Castle for Ernie Ireland and latterly at the Red Lion, Ewyas Harold for Horace Mudge and later Harold Bishop. He would chat for hours with the 'regulars' and was always ready for a laugh.

Lionel Williams died in 1973 at the age of 57.

Telephone : Ewyas Harold Post Office

THE CASTLE INN
Ewyas Harold

Free House, Fully Licensed, Parties Catered for

Proprietor : Ernest Revell

In the 1960s the Dog was still called the Castle Inn.
The telephone was still manual through the post office

*The changing face
of the Dog:*

Left and above: 2000

Below: 2005

The name of the pub was subsequently changed back to the **Dog**, and in 1985 CAMRA described it as

> A very old and excellent one-bar village local adjoining an antique shop, the Dog has an interesting and comfortable interior. Since 1509 the inn has changed its name no less than four times.

The **Dog**, like the nearby **Temple Bar**, offers food as well as liquid refreshment for locals and visitors alike.

At the end of the 18th century and the beginning of the 19th century the rival to the **Dog** was the **New House Inn**. This was on the site of what is now Down House, reached by turning up the lane between the **Temple Bar** and the **Dog** and bearing left, where it stood on the left-hand side.

Because of its situation, the **New House Inn** is more likely to have been the place referred to in a news report that appeared in the *Hereford Journal* on 17 August 1780:

> Yesterday se'nnight a barn and cot, belonging to a public house at Ewyas Harold in this county, were destroyed by lightening. A team from Mr. Purchas's, Brewer and Wine-merchant of Fownhope, had put up there that evening, and the horses were fortunately saved by having been turned out to grass a few minutes before the incident happened. Four pigs, near twenty fowls, a dog, and the geers [*sic*] of Mr. Purchas's horses were burnt; and about six dozen of glass bottles melted.

An advertisement in the *Hereford Journal* of 20 October 1802 stated that coppice wood was to be sold by auction 'At the dwelling-house of Mr. Samuel Jones, called and known by the name of the New House, in the parish of Ewyas Harold …'. This does not, of course, certainly identify this as a public house, but there is confirmatory evidence in the book *Farm and Furrow. A local farm study by Ewyas Harold and District WEA Research Group*. In a discussion about John Williams, who farmed at Walk Mill Farm at the very beginning of the 19th century, and his work in the parish as churchwarden it is stated:

> John Williams was no exception, attending many meetings, sometimes at the Church, but more often at the house of Samuel Jones, innkeeper at New House (now Down House).

There is a slightly earlier reference that may well apply to the **New House Inn** which, if it is to be believed, suggests the name of a possible predecessor to Samuel Jones. At that period it was the custom for strolling players to play in temporary theatres, and often these were at a licensed establishment as they had larger rooms which could be utilised. An announcement of about 1795 has been preserved, written in the following terms:

This is to give notice to all Gentlemen, ladies and others, for the diversion of the neighbouring Gentry, at Argus's Long Room in Ewyas Harold. Upon the first Monday in the new year will be performed a comedy called "The Old Doctor" or "The Antiquated Cuckold Unmask'd…" Price 2d. or 6d. the Pit. At which time all virgins in Ewyas Harold from 15 to 25 shall be entitled to each a ticket (*gratis*) provided they prove their virginity. To begin precisely at seven o'clock in the evening.

It almost reads as if it was a wind-up! Only three Land Tax Returns survive for the 1790s and in none of these does the name Argus occur, although this is not certain evidence. However, John Jones bought some premises occupied by Samuel Jones in 1799, and Samuel continued to occupy them until at least 1802, tying in with other evidence quoted above. After a gap in the returns, from 1809 onwards the premises were occupied by John Jones, whose name appears as taking out alehouse keeper's recognizances between 1818 and 1828, so clearly all this relates to the **New House Inn**. John Jones would thus have been landlord in 1821 when a sale of timber was advertised to take place at the inn. In 1833 Mary Jones was recorded as the occupier, and in 1834 she was stated to be the owner and occupier, inferring that her husband had died (although the return of the next year still has him as the owner). The 1841 census records her as innkeeper at the **New House Inn**, while a directory of 1851 records her as a victualler in Ewyas Harold. She was the last licensee of the **New House Inn** and the 1851 census shows that she was then a widow aged 64 and that she had been born in Ewyas Harold. Also living with her were two unmarried daughters, Elizabeth and Mary, and there was a general servant also resident. Cassey's *Directory* of 1858 records that the Misses Jones were resident at New House, but there was no suggestion that it was still an inn. Miss Mary Jones was still at

New House in 1867, when her name appears as a private resident there, but in 1871 New House was occupied by Mrs. Sarah Jones, a farmer's widow aged 83, her unmarried daughter Elizabeth and a lodger, Mary Jones, described as an annuitant. How they were related to the former residents is not known.

Down House, where the one-time New House Inn stood

The New House was demolished not long

afterwards and a new house was built on the same foundations, including the cellar. Because the previous building was said to have been only single storey, the foundations for the new building were inadequate, and it had to have buttresses erected against it. This house was called Harold Villa until 1951, when Colonel George Brown bought it and renamed it The Grange. He sold it to Mr. C.H. Smith in 1953 who promptly changed the name to Down House, which it has been called ever since.

During the 19th century there were two short-lived establishments in Ewyas Harold. In the licensing records from 1872 onwards there is an unnamed cider house run by James Watkins, but the licence was not renewed in 1882. In 1867 there were two persons of this name in Ewyas Harold, one a wheelwright by trade while the other ran a shop and post office, but as the name of the postman disappears before 1876, the wheelwright must have been the seller of cider — and very welcome it would have been during the warm work when a tyre was being shrunk on a wheel! The 1871 census shows that the wheelwright was then aged 47 and worked at the Prill where he employed one workman. His former workshop — and presumably place of refreshment — was a short way up the road opposite the **Temple Bar**.

Along the road past the **Dog** towards Dulas and Longtown, lay Walk Mill Farm. It was tenanted in the 1850s and into the '60s by John Griffiths who, as suggested by a single directory entry, in 1856, seems to have augmented his income by running the **Walk Mill** as a beer house.

However, there was one other longer-lived establishment close to Ewyas Harold. Continuing along the road through Dulas, there was the **New Inn**, standing well above the road on a sharp left-hand bend, just over the boundary in the parish of Longtown. This was already in existence in 1872 when the surviving licensing records start, and first appears in directories in the 1870s when it was run by William Gwillim. The 1881 census records that he was then aged 54 and a farmer of 93 acres, and that he had been born at Ewyas Harold. In the later 1880s his widow continued to run the **New Inn** for a while, and she was succeeded by Peter Watkins, who was a man of many parts as in 1902 he was described as a farmer, miller and shop-keeper, of Park road (Longtown) and Cwm Dulas mill, residing at the **New Inn**, Cwm Dulas. By the following year Matthew H. Meredith was running the **New Inn**, but he was a tenant and the inn was owned by a member of the Gwillim family. By 1905 Wilfred George Watkins was there, and within a few years his widow took over and brewed her own beer. She was still there in 1922, but by 1926 Edwin Powell had taken over both the pub and the brewhouse. He was still there in 1941, but by that time he had given up brewing.

The Trout (New Inn) in 2000, shortly after it closed as an inn

Like so many other pubs this one suffered a name change and some time after the Second World War became the **Trout**, normally referred to as the **Trout Found Out**. A story is told of one regular, within living memory, called Sid Powell. He farmed at Lower Newton and was in the habit of having a regular weekly night out at the **Trout**, which he enjoyed, not wisely but too well. However, he had no problem getting home as he travelled by horse and trap, and his horse could be relied on to find his way home unguided!

In the 1960s electricity had not reached this area, and when electric light was needed a generator was turned on, and all the lights, including those outside down the dingle, came on. When electricity finally arrived, there was a problem, as all the lights were on the same circuit, and there wasn't a light switch in the house! It was around that time that the **Trout** was run by Major Eggington — famous for serving his beer in quart glasses — the pints were reserved for the ladies!

The **Trout** was still open in 1985 when CAMRA described it in the following terms:

> A truly marvellous pub of about 1850, isolated and overlooking the beautiful Dulas valley, this is definitely worth a visit. The interior of the bar is full of interesting artefacts and pieces of bric-a-brac which, together with the locals, give it a very cheerful and homely atmosphere. The small lounge is a piece of history: it is set out as a Victorian 'front room' complete with gramophone and records.

Sad to relate, it closed within a few years, the last licensee being Bill Smith, who wrote a book on the Golden Valley Railway. The building is still prominent on the bend in the road, and the frame for hanging the inn sign is still in place on the corner of the house.

Finally, mention should be made of the **Griffin**, which was on Ewyas Harold Common. This was on the very edge of the parish, just off the road to Abbey Dore, and is discussed in chapter 8.

CHAPTER SIX

Clodock & the Monnow Valley

Running more or less parallel to the Vale of Ewyas are the valleys of the River Monnow and the Escley Brook. These, together with the smaller Olchon Brook, all join just south of Longtown, and wander south, past Clodock, joining the River Honddu a mile or so north of Pandy, by the great house of Alltyrynys (now an hotel and rather too grand for a book on pubs). The augmented river then turns north-east, forming the boundary of the area known as Ewyas Lacy. This was a major border holding after the Norman Conquest and was centred on a castle at Longtown. The first Norman lord was Hugh de Lacy, who gave his name to the whole area.

This important lordship covered a great swathe of country, bounded on the south-east by the river Monnow, on the west by the Black Mountains, and on the east by the Golden Valley, and extending as far as Cusop near Hay. While it was centred on Longtown, the ecclesiastical centre was Clodock, an early church dedicated to a murdered 6th-century king of the area, whilst Craswall, Llanveynoe, Longtown and Newton were all townships within the parish. This, together with parishes to the south-east and north-east of Clodock, made up the lordship. Because it was a border lordship, it was not part of Herefordshire until the Act of Union of 1536.

This remote area has always been sparsely populated, and is generally unspoilt, unlike other areas closer to Hereford. Surprisingly, the number of licensed premises is greater than would have been expected, but the majority were simple beer houses, and the licensee often had to make ends meet by having another trade. Thus the **Carpenters' Arms** at Walterstone, close to the church, may have been named in this way. In 1818 one Edward 'Llewelling' of Walterstone took out an alehouse keeper's recognizance, and most probably he was there. The **Carpenters' Arms** seems to have been in the hands of the same family for many years as Benjamin T. Llewellin of Walterstone took out an alehouse keeper's recognizance in 1828, and the 1841 census records that Benjamin Teague Llewellin was then at the inn, but described as a shoemaker. He had died by the time of the 1851 census, when his widow Mary was in charge. She was then aged 67 and within a few years she had left, as in 1856 Mary Teague was a beer retailer at an unnamed place in Walterstone, and as there was no other public house in the parish apart from the **Carpenters' Arms** she must have been there and a member of the same family.

By 1867 Mrs. Ann Parry was recorded as being a shoemaker and publican in Walterstone, and she was followed at the **Carpenters' Arms** by John Parry, her son, also a shoemaker. He was in charge by 1879 and the 1881 census records that he was then aged 35 and unmarried. Some years later he had a brush with the law, as on 29 March 1897 he was convicted and fined £1 with 8s. costs for keeping his house open after 10 o'clock at night on 22 March 1897. The magistrates ordered that the conviction should be endorsed on his licence. The 1903 printed list shows that John Parry was the owner of the **Carpenters' Arms** and he was there until the 1920s.

The Carpenters' Arms at Walterstone in 2005

In 1924 W.G. (Bill) Watkins married a daughter of the family, and subsequently took over the **Carpenters' Arms**, staying for about 9 years. When he moved on, his sister took over, and she ran the inn for 50 years, although the pre-war directories give her husband Allen Grenow as the licensee. The **Carpenters' Arms** is still flourishing in the hands of their daughter Vera, although the wheel has turned full circle and her married name is Watkins!

East of Walterstone is the small parish of Llancillo. No public house has been identified, nor is one likely to have ever existed, as in 1851 the population was only 70. Nor was the population of Rowlestone, the next parish to the east, much greater as it was only 125 in 1851. However, there has been a public house here in the past, as alehouse keeper's recognizances were taken out for 'Rollstone' by Philip Roberts in 1820 and 1821, and on 7 January 1822 by George Williams. The inference is that George Williams took over mid-year from Philip Roberts but clearly did not prosper as he did not renew his recognizance later in the year.

North of Walterstone is Clodock, and the delightful **Cornewall Arms**, close to the church. Indeed, this L-shaped 18th-century building forms the southern boundary of the churchyard. It must have been the place referred to in an advertisement in the *Hereford Journal* of 14 August 1788 which stated that the tolls of the Pandy turnpike were to be let by auction 'at the dwelling house of Thomas Gain, innholder, at Clodick'. Another advertisement of 6 May 1789 advised of a meeting of the turnpike trustees to be held at the dwelling-house of Thomas 'Gaine', near Clodock church. Mary Gane, no doubt either the widow or daughter of Thomas, took out alehouse keeper's recognizances between 1818 and 1822 and seems to have been succeeded by one William Jones.

In the middle of the 19th century trade directories usually gave the name as the **'Cornwall' Arms**, rather than **Cornewall Arms**. By 1841 William Farr was here, and in 1851 it was recorded that he was 65, had been born at Bacton, and was described as a wheelwright and innkeeper. By 1871 he had been succeeded by William Lewis, who was also a butcher. The licensee in 1881 was 65-year-old John Gwillim, who had been born in Clodock, and who was described in the census solely as an innkeeper, so presumably he didn't have another trade.

Surviving licensing records show that the **Cornewall Arms** was, not too surprisingly, part of the Moccas Estate which was owned by the Cornewall family, and a rent book from the 1870s, surviving in the Moccas estate papers, shows that William Lewis, mentioned above, paid an annual rent of £13 6s. 8d. Because it was rented property, there were a number of changes of licensee in the years leading up to the First World War.

There was also a change of ownership in 1893, caused by a distressing event that took place here in that year. On the cold and snowy evening of 12 January 1893 a large group who had attended a funeral assembled in the **Cornewall Arms**, drinking rum hot, which was hot beer spiced with rum. Later that night, six of them turned out of the pub, looking for mischief. A stonemason sleeping in a nearby barn was awakened and rolled in the snow, but fortunately he escaped and sought refuge in the **Cornewall Arms**, where he was warmed up. A local wheelwright was then dragged out of bed and ducked in the icy waters of the River Monnow. The third victim was William Prosser, who had played a wooden whistle in the **Cornewall Arms** earlier in the evening. He had gone home to his bachelor cottage where he lived alone except for a ferret. The drunken six smashed his windows, and the terrified Prosser attempted to get away half dressed. He was rolled in the snow, but escaped with the drunks in pursuit. Eventually the pursuit was given up, but Prosser did not know, and he kept going, losing his trousers and socks on the way. The next morning his body was found hanging from a cottage gate in which his clothing was entangled, he being too exhausted to free himself so that he had succumbed to a combination of terror and freezing temperatures. This event caused outrage, as well it might, stimulating the following observation:

THE CORNEWALL ARMS

Longtown, Hereford

———

Teas catered for   .   Fully Licensed   .   Free House

Proprietor : John Prosser

A 1960s' advertisement

The Cornewall Arms adjoins the churchyard

90

> Total abstinence from intoxicating liquors is not one of the cardinal virtues of the parish ... and a funeral is as good as a fair to the publicans.

At the Hereford Winter Assizes in March 1893 the six pleaded guilty to 'technical manslaughter' and the two ringleaders were sentenced to 12 months' hard labour, three to a four-month term each, while a youngster was imprisoned for three days.

As a consequence of this scandal, the **Cornewall Arms** was closed, and the Rev. Sir George Cornewall sold it to Messers Sladden and Collier Ltd., brewers, of Evesham. It reopened later in the year with a new licensee, Elizabeth Parry, taking over the licence on 27 November 1893. She had had much experience in the licensed trade in the area, both on her own account and with her two husbands, and was clearly highly respected. Her first husband was William Hyde, who became the licencee of the **Black Lion** in Longtown in March 1875 and, after his death in 1877, she took over the licence. In July 1881 she moved to the **Crown** also in Longtown, and, after her second marriage in 1885, the licence was transferred to her new husband, David Parry. Following his death in 1889, she resumed the licence. After she took over the licence of the **Cornewall Arms** she may have run both the **Crown** and the **Cornewall Arms** for a few months, as a new licence for the **Crown** was not granted until 28 May 1894. She was still tenant of the **Cornewall Arms** at the time of the 1901 census, and also resident was her son by her first marriage, Harry Hyde, his wife, a daughter, and five grandchildren. This was probably the George Henry Hyde who took over the licence of the **Cornewall Arms** on 15 July 1901. He was a tenant, as the 1903 printed list shows that Messers Sladden and Collier Ltd. still owned the premises, but he had gone by 1909.

The **Cornewall Arms**, now a free house, has been in the hands of members of the Prosser family since 1940, the first being Mrs. Lilian Prosser. Little has changed in that time, and the traditional pub interior is unspoilt. There is a settle on either side of a wood-burning stove which has replaced the open fire, with polished brass above and flagstones on the floor beneath. The lounge area is truly like someone's lounge at home, only with more and varied old-fashioned easy chairs. Truly a step back in time.

About a third of a mile north of Clodock the road crosses the Olchon Brook. On the left, just before the bridge, is a castle mound, thought to be the first castle in the area and the predecessor of the castle at Longtown. The first house on the right after the bridge is Upper Pont Hendre, described in 1931 in the following terms:

Upper Pont Hendre… was built in the first half of the 17th century and has a modern addition built on the E. side. On the W. front is a projecting porch and the entrance-doorway has an old battened door with strap-hinges. Farther N. is a three-light transomed window with an oak frame. On the E. front is a doorway with a chamfered frame and the doorway leading to the modern addition has a similar frame and a battened door. There is a rectangular stone projection in the middle of the front containing the staircase. Inside the building are some old battened doors; the staircase has stone steps.

Once the short-lived Anchor Inn

Upper Pont Hendre is also known as Anchor Cottage, and was the short-lived **Anchor Inn**. This was certainly a post-1830 establishment, and the first mention in a trade directory is in 1867 when William Pritchard was the licensee. By 1871 Pritchard was recorded simply as a farmer, there being no mention of the licensed trade, nor is the **Anchor Inn** recorded in existing licensing records from 1872 onwards. Thus the entry for the **Anchor Inn** in Mercer and Crocker's *Directory* of 1874 was out-of-date — unless, of course, it was operating without a licence!

Now a private house, this was once the Black Lion beer house

A few yards north of the former **Anchor Inn** the road forks, the left turn leading to Longtown and the right to Michaelchurch Escley. The house in the point of the junction was formerly Hillside Garage, but is now a private dwelling. In the 19th century it was the **Black Lion,** a beer house catering for tourists. It first appears in a directory in 1867, when run by John Burt, who was also a grocer, draper and butcher — it seems that beer selling was just part of a general business. At that time the Longtown Castle Court of the Ancient Order of Foresters met there. There was a succession of licensees in the late 19th century, including William Hyde who took over in 1875, followed by his widow, already met with in connection with the **Cornewall Arms**. She was succeeded in 1881 by Thomas Frederick Townsend and then John Penry. Catherine Miles took over from John Penry on 27 March 1899, the licensing records carefully stating that she was the wife of Leonard Miles — no equal rights at that time! In 1902 she advertised 'Comfortable accommodation for tourists and visitors. Refreshments. Good stabling'. The same directory records that her husband, Leonard Miles, was a machinist at Pontynys Farm, Longtown, described in the 1901 census as an engine driver. The 1903 printed list shows that while Catherine Miles ran the **Black Lion**, it was owned by George Prosser of Abergavenny. It closed before 1905.

Not many yards to the north of the former **Black Lion**, the Longtown and Michaelchurch Escley roads are connected, cutting off a triangular piece of land. On the cross-piece itself is the **Crown Inn**, which is one of the oldest inns in Longtown. A date-stone indicates that it was built in 1751, a date which is proudly marked on the inn sign. Whether it was a pub from the start is not known, but if not it became one within a comparatively short space of time as a notice appeared in the *Hereford Journal* of 23 March 1782 advising the trustees of the Longtown Turnpike Trust of a meeting to be

James Wathen's view of Longtown castle, March 1804

held 'at the house of Samuel Jones, at the Crown Inn, Longtown'. The **Crown Inn** may well have been the establishment in the parish for which Thomas Williams took out alehouse keeper's recognizances between 1818 and 1828. It is also marked on Bryant's map of 1835 and on the tithe map of 1840, when it was owned and occupied by Elizabeth Hubert, whose name was given in 1841 as 'Hybert'.

Henry Price, whose name appears as licensee in a directory of 1867, was also a carrier, advertising that he left the **Crown Inn** for Abergavenny at about 7 a.m. and returned the same day. In the 1890s the pub was run by Benjamin Price, who had taken over the licence from Elizabeth Parry on 28 May 1894. Within a few years George Bridgwater had taken over, the 1901 census showing that he was then aged 50 and had been born in Leintwardine. The 1903 list shows that while he held the licence, the premises were still owned by Benjamin Price.

Little seems to have happened to the **Crown** for the first three-quarters of the 20th century until 1973 when Mr. Ian Brymer took over. During his 15 years as licensee the **Crown** was restored and improved, with the necessary toilets being put inside rather than having to go across the garden at the back. A porch at the front helped to solve the problem of surface water, which, if the drains on the road outside were blocked, would run in through the front door and out at the back!

The Crown at Longtown in 2005

94

Ian Brymer left about 1988 and since then there have been a number of licensees. The *Longtown Millennium Domesday Book* stated that it was particularly popular with the younger generation. The pub changed hands again in 2004 when it was offered for sale at an asking price of £398,000 and was sold leasehold for an undisclosed figure in November of that year.

Taking the left-hand fork towards Longtown, on the left side a few hundred yards further on is the one-time **Greyhound Inn**, described in 1931 by the Royal Commission as:

> part timber-framed. The S. end of the building appears to have been a small timber-framed cottage of 16th-century date to which a large stone-built house was added early in the 17th century. The earlier building has been encased in stone on three of the sides. On the E. front the original timber-framing appears in the projecting upper storey. It has heavy studs with sloping struts between, forming a herring-bone pattern. In the lower storey is a central doorway with an old frame and, flanking it, small windows of two lights with a smaller diamond-shaped mullion in each light. In the ground floor of the later building is a window of four lights with an oak frame. Inside the building some of the timber-framing is exposed. In the southern wing is a central roof-truss of double collar-beam type filled in the square framing to form a partition. In the northern wing is a blocked original doorway with the soffit of the lintel cut in triangular form with an ogee apex. In the N. room is a wide, open fireplace with a chamfered lintel.

The **Greyhound** is still quite a prominent building and even if it was not, it can easily be found as, by the side of the building, there is a new development called Greyhound Close. The 1841 census makes no mention of this public house, but it had come into existence by 1851, when John Lewis,

Left: The one-time Greyhound Inn. Right: A 1928 photograph

the licensee, was described as a victualler and butcher. He was there for many years but his successor, Aaron Farr, had taken over by 1881. He was then aged 35, was local, having been born in Clodock, and had just done a spell as the licensee of the **New Inn** (see below). Indeed, his connections were closer than that, as his wife was John Lewis's daughter. In the early 1890s his widow, Sarah, took over and was there with her son John Farr, employed as a butcher. In 1902 she was advertising 'Best wines and spirits. Good stabling', while John Farr advertised that he was a family butcher at the **Greyhound Inn**. The 1903 printed list of licensed establishments shows that the **Greyhound Inn** was owned by William Protheroe of Longtown. It is difficult to identify the owner, as there were two persons of this name in Longtown at that time, one a boot manufacturer at Penthilia and the other a photographer and grocer, draper, ironmonger and patent medicine vendor at Chapel House.

Sarah Farr was at the **Greyhound Inn** until at least 1909, but by 1913 Mrs. Alice Addis had taken over. By 1922 Allen Proctor was in charge, and he was still there in 1941. It was during his time that the Royal Commission recorded the building, describing its condition as good, except for a smaller outbuilding. The inn finally closed about 1983. The old Greyhound has been recently renovated and was offered for sale in 2005 as having been 'the subject of a comprehensive scheme of upgrading works' at an asking price of £525,000. Its appearance has been much improved by the removal of a stone building that was in front of the older timbered section, evident in a photograph of 1928.

Continuing up the hill, on the right-hand side, just before Longtown castle, was the **New Inn**, another of the older establishments in Longtown. This is easily identified from the incised stone plaque on the front which states 'New Inn, Spiritous Liquors Sold Here, Thomas Penry'. However, this

The one-time New Inn and its plaque

is a modern copy of the former plaque which was gradually decaying away. The name of the establishment is not given in an advertisement that appeared in the *Hereford Journal* of 7 June 1797, which announced that certain property was to be sold by auction 'At the dwelling-house of Mr. Thomas Penry, Innholder, in Longtown, in the parish of Clodock ...'. Another advertisement on 25 February 1801 announced that a messuage and land was to be sold by auction at the **New Inn**, Longtown. Penry was at the **New Inn** as another advertisement of 11 January 1815 announced that a house was to be sold by auction 'At the House of Thomas Penry, called THE NEW INN, in Longtown'. A further advertisement of 10 May 1820 announced that the Commissioners for Longtown District of Turnpike Roads were to meet at the 'Dwelling-house of Thomas Penry, Innholder, situate in Longtown ...'.

Thomas Penry took out alehouse keeper's recognizances between 1818 and 1828, and the tithe map of 1840 indicates that Thomas Penry both owned and occupied the **New Inn**. By 1841 he was 60 years old, indicating that he was at least the second person of that name to run the **New Inn,** as he would have been only 16 in 1797. He is mentioned by name in a news report that appeared in the *Hereford Journal* of 28 February 1844:

> LONGTOWN. The officers and brothers of the Friend-in-Need Lodge of the Independent Order of Odd Fellows of the Kentchurch District, opened a new Lodge (to be called the Loyal Castle Inn) at the house of Mr. Thomas Pendry [*sic*], New Inn, Longtown, on Monday week, when twelve most respectable farmers and tradesmen were initiated members of the order, and several respectable persons were afterwards proposed, After partaking of an excellent dinner, provided by the worthy hostess in her usual good style, the officers and brothers returned to their respective homes at an early hour.

The **New Inn** was advertised for sale by private treaty by Thomas Penry in the *Hereford Times* of 5 December 1846. In the advertisement it was stated that 'The Proprietor, Mr. T. Penry, after a 50 years' career of business is anxious to retire into private life'. Unfortunately no sale took place, as the name of Thomas 'Penery', victualler and farmer, was recorded in Lascelle's *Directory* of 1851, and the census confirms that it was the same person. Thomas Penry's name occurs again in 1856, but by 1858 Henry 'Penery' was at the **New Inn**. He was almost certainly the son of Thomas Penry who had been christened in 1817. His tenure was short, as by 1861 William Farr was in charge, and he was followed by James Holley. When surviving licensing records begin in 1872 Aaron Farr was licensee; he had probably taken over after his marriage to Sarah Greenow (née Lewis) in 1871. He was still there in 1876 when the Pandy and Monnowside Ploughing and Agricultural Society held its meeting in Longtown, followed by a dinner at the **New Inn,** when about 70 sat down. In the late 1870s Farr moved on to the **Greyhound** and during the later years of the 19th century there was a succession of landlords and one landlady, who succeeded her husband (Louise Johnson in 1898), but in the early years of the 20th century the licensee was Benjamin Price. The 1901 census shows that he was then aged 34 and was a farmer as well as an innkeeper on his own account. However, the owner of the **New Inn** was Thomas Dalafield of Abergavenny, as the 1903 list shows.

All this is very curious, as the **Crown Inn** at Longtown was then owned by a Benjamin Price of Longtown. At the time of the 1901 census the only Benjamin Price in Longtown was the licensee of the **New Inn**, implying that he owned one pub but was a tenant in another!

The **New Inn** kept going during the first half of the 20th century, but with a change of landlord after the Second World War, when Major and Mrs. Greenwood took over and it became known as the **Court House**. This change of name was a reference to the fact that many years ago the Court Leet of the manor met here (nothing to do with a criminal court). It closed about the year 1962 and became an outdoor education centre, — a use which still continues.

Once the Sun Inn at Longtown

On the other side of the road from the **New Inn**, tucked in by the redundant church and overlooking the former market area, was the **Sun Inn**. No doubt the fairs that were held here until the last third of the 19th century helped boost its takings. Sheep and cattle fairs were held on 29 April and 22 June, a wool fair during the first week in July and a statute fair on 21 September. If the surname of the licensee is anything to go on, the **Sun Inn** may well have been the inn for which alehouse keeper's recognizances were taken by Elizabeth Parry between 1818 and 1828. On at least one occasion a parish meeting was held in her establishment, and the church accounts for 1823 record: 'Pd. Mrs. Parry of the Publick for Ale that was drunk at Mtg. May 16th £1'.

By 1841 Thomas Parry had taken over the **Sun Inn**; in 1851 he was aged 65, still unmarried and was there until at least 1872. The name of his premises were given as the **Sun Inn** in 1862, while in 1867 it was called the **Rising Sun**, a name that appears in directories for some years, although the licensing records from 1872 onwards still call it the **Sun Inn**. In the 1890s the licensee was William Cooper, and he was the last, as on 24 May 1897 he was convicted and fined £2 with 9s. costs for permitting drunkenness on the premises on 29 April 1897. As a consequence, on 30 August 1897, the magistrates refused to renew his licence. This property formerly belonged to the Herefordshire Estate of the Marquess of Abergavenny and when the estate was broken up and sold by auction in January 1920, Lot 162 was 'An excellent Holding, known as Sun Inn'. Of course, the licence had long since been withdrawn. Also part of the lot was the ruins of Longtown castle, and something over 3 acres of pasture, and pasture orchard.

After the loss of the licence it became Sun Inn Cottage, and is now a fine building essentially dating from the 17th century. The entrance is on the east side, which has a servery on the south side with a sliding sash and shelf through which drink was once served.

At the end of the long, straggling, main street of Longtown there is a fork in the road, with the left-hand road leading to Llanveynoe and the Olchon valley. About a mile or so along this road is a right turn and just down here on the left-hand side, at Upper Cwm Farm, was a former beer house. This may have started as the cider house run in 1856 by John Manister, but by 1867 beer was being retailed by William Greenow, who was also a farmer, and he was probably at the same building. He died soon after as his widow Sarah married Aaron Farr in January 1871 and in the registers she was described as an innkeeper. He was succeeded by James Davies, another farmer, whose name occurs in the licensing records from 1872 onwards, where the name of the establishment was given (probably in error) as the **Crown**. In 1871 James Davies, who was 33 years old, was a farmer and innkeeper at **Cwm**. The 1881 census adds the information that it was the **Cwm Inn**, and that James Davies farmed 10 acres, so evidently he had to supplement his income by selling beer. However, the licence was not renewed in 1887. Upper Cwm farmhouse was built of sandstone rubble in the early 17th century, and extended in the 18th century.

A precipitous drop past Upper Cwm Farm leads down to a crossroads where a left turn leads up the valley of the Monnow in the direction of Craswall. This settlement has more of interest than

Upper Cwm Farm in 2005

Forest Mill in 2005

FOREST MILL,

Situate in the Township of Llanveynoe, in the Parish of Clodock,

CONSISTING OF

A good accustomed Water Corn Grist Mill, well supplied with Water,

With a Public House, called the Golden Lion, attached to the same,

AND

THE FOLLOWING LANDS,

In the Occupation of ————

No. on Plan.	Names of Pieces.	State.	Quantity.
			A. R. P.
58	House, Mill, Gardens, Mill Stream, &c. - - -	- -	1 1 3
59	Mill Meadows - - - - - - - - -	*Meadow*	1 1 17
60	- - - - - - - - - -	*ditto*	0 3 38
61	Rough - - - - - - - - -	*Pasture*	1 1 10
	Total -	- - -	4 3 28

LOT VII.

A very neat COTTAGE and GARDEN, and Parcel of MEADOW LAND, containing together 1A. 0R. 13P. adjoining to the Church-yard of Michaelchurch, in the Occupation of THOMAS HUGHES, as yearly Tenant.

The 1815 sale of Forest Mill included the Golden Lion Inn

100

The Forest Mill sign

might be expected in such a remote placet. A few hundred yards along here, by the roadside on the right, is a small cottage, empty for many years, but at the time of writing being tidied up, which is called locally Tafarn Twlch (Cottage Inn) but which is properly called Tarren Twlch. Any use as an inn must have been a very long time ago as no documentary evidence has so far been found.

Somewhat over a mile further on there is road to the right leading to Michaelchurch Escley and a few yards down here on the left-hand side is Forest Mill. This was part of the Michaelchurch Court Estate, and was one of the lots that was offered for sale at the Green Dragon, Hereford, on 13 July 1815, when it was described as 'A good accustomed Water Corn Grist Mill, well supplied with Water, With a Public House, called the Golden Lion, attached to the same'. Curiously, the mill is stated in the sale particulars to have been in Llanveynoe, but the area is in Craswall. The public house was part of the same holding and was most likely the building on the roadside. No occupant was given, either in the sale particulars or in the advertisements in the *Hereford Journal*, and there is no further mention of the **Golden Lion**. Whether the parish boundaries have been changed is not known, but certainly no alehouse keeper's recognizance was taken out for Llanveynoe from 1818 until 1828 and the only one taken out for this

period for Craswall can be assigned to another establishment, so it is inferred that the **Golden Lion** closed at about this time. In 1851 Forest Mill was occupied by a shopkeeper, but Cassey's *Directory* of 1858, under Llanveynoe, records that William Goderich was operating it as a mill.

After the turn, a few yards farther along the Craswall road, on the left-hand side and overlooking

The Three Horse Shoes in 2005

The Old Public in 2005. Was it ever an inn?

Forest Mill, was the former **Three Horse Shoes**. Just past this was a smithy, the buildings of which are still evident. The 1841 census for Craswall lists Samuel Jones as a blacksmith, and ten years later he was recorded as being at the Three Horseshoes, but with no suggestion that it was a public house. In 1861 William Prosser, who had independent means, lived at the Three Horseshoes, while next door at what was noted as 'Publick' was William Lewis, described as 'Farmer of 30 Acres & Public'. The 'Publick' was what became the **Three Horse Shoes** which first appeared in a directory in 1867 when William Lewis was still the licensee, but by 1871 it had been taken over by David Watkins, and he and his son, also David, ran it until at least the First World War. In 1881 the older David Watkins was 77 and was described as a publican and farmer of 15 acres. He died in 1889 and his son took over the licence. The 1903 printed list records that he owned the premises, which he held until at least 1913. The **Three Horse Shoes** was still open in 1941, but closed its doors to the public about 1960, although it is still owned by the family of the last licensee.

A place somewhat further up the valley, on the right-hand side, has the very suggestive name of the **Old Public**, which was occupied in 1851 by Mary Jenkins, a widow, aged 66, but no trade was given. In 1881 her son, William Jenkins, was a farmer of five acres, while John Jenkins, resident in 1902, was a farmer at Ireland farm, but lived at the Old Public. John Jenkins was still tenant of the Old Public in 1920, when it was Lot 105 in the sale of the Marquess of Abergavenny's estate. At that time the property was just under three acres in extent, and John Jenkins paid a rent of £5 *per annum*, with a tithe of 2s. 3d. and Land Tax of 4s. 6d. Despite its name, no firm evidence has been found to confirm that this was indeed a public house, but there is a suggestion as to what the name may have been. The draft drawings made by the Ordnance Survey in 1814-5 mark the White Lion in this position, a name which is very suggestive of a public house but which is not known to occur again.

In view of its remote situation, it is remarkable that the **Bull's Head**, further on towards the head of the valley, is still open and flourishing. Between 1818 and 1828 George 'Brentall' took out alehouse keeper's recognizances in the parish and it is a natural assumption that he was here, as the 1841 census shows that George Bruntnell, then aged 75, was at the **Bull's Head**. The name Bruntnell later occurs in Hay in connection with the licensed trade, but no connection has so far been established. However, nothing is quite that simple and surviving Land Tax Returns tell a somewhat different picture. In 1813 George Bruntnell took over the tenancy of a property owned by Penry Williams Esq. and he held this until 1825, so this must have been where he carried on the licensed trade. Later entries shows that this property was **Fidler's**, a farm opposite the present **Bull's Head**. In 1825 Fidler's was taken over by David Jenkins, and George Bruntnell moved to another property called **Forest House**, which presumably became his public house, as he continued to take out alehouse keeper's recognizances until 1828. During 1828 David Jenkins took over **Forest House** as well and Bruntnell's name disappears from the surviving Land Tax Returns, the last of which is for 1836. There is no clue as to whether David Jenkins ran **Forest House** as a public house but this does seem likely, and indeed there is evidence to suggest that the name was changed. Now the 1840 tithe map marks the property rented by David Jenkins and the 1843 apportionment names the holding as the Bull's Head. Indeed, the **Bull's Head Inn** is marked on the tithe map where it is now, and the meadow around it, called Forest House Meadow, was part of the holding. In this meadow is a barn, marked on the tithe map, which has been recently converted into a dwelling, and is now called River Barn. All this suggests that **Forest House** was the earlier name for the **Bull's Head**.

The entry for the **Bull's Head** was the first in the census of 1841, with George Bruntnell in occupation. He seems to have been the person who earlier took out alehouse keeper's recognizances for the parish, but there is no clue as to where he had been living since 1828. By 1851 Thomas Gane, a native of Craswall and then aged 33 had taken over the **Bull's Head**. He also farmed 65 acres and employed two men, but there is no mention of the licensed trade although it would be surprising if he did not follow that as well. *Cassey's Directory* of 1858 records Thomas 'Gaine' as a farmer in Craswall, and although no place is specified, presumably he was still resident at the **Bull's Head**. In 1861 his widow, Mary Gane, was at the **Bull's Head**, and she seems to have married again, being the Mrs. Mary Rowley who was at the **Bull's Head Inn** in 1867 and who also farmed 100 acres. However, the licensing records from 1872 show that the licence was in the name of John Rowley, her husband, and that the owner

103

The Bull's Head in 2005

of the premises was Penry Williams Esq., no doubt a second person of that name. On 28 August 1878 a second Thomas Gane took out a licence for the **Bull's Head**, and in 1881 it was recorded that he was 36 years old and was farming 80 acres. He must have been the son of the first Thomas Gane who was living at home with his widowed mother in 1861, but he had moved out by the time of the 1871 census. Although the licensed trade was not mentioned, directories of the period show that this was part of his business. In 1902 he was advertising 'Good stabling. Refreshments supplied'.

The 1903 list records that the owner had become W.C.A. Williams, Esq., a solicitor from Monmouth. Thomas Gane was at the **Bull's Head** until at least 1905 after which it was run by his widow Mrs. H. Gane for a few more years. For most of the 20th century the **Bull's Head** remained a small pub in a remote area, but managed to keep going with a regular trade of tourists and pony trekkers throughout the summer season who appreciated the bread, cheese and pickles that was the standard fare. In 1985 CAMRA recommended that it was 'Worth a visit if you are passing

Interior of the Bull's Head in 1998

through — a really unspoilt, old-fashioned pub with a small bar, beamed ceiling and stone floor'. How they could imagine that one would be 'passing through' in that remote area beggars belief!

The most recent phase in the history of the **Bull's Head** started in 1997 when the pub was sold for £118,000 on the retirement of Beattie Lewis, who, with her husband Wilfred, had run the pub for 44 years. Under the new owner this remote inn was gradually renovated and extended within the existing building to include a dining room, restaurant and two letting bedrooms. When the new owner decided to sell in the autumn of 2004 the publicity material made great play of the unspoilt nature of the building and its character and atmosphere, which came with a price tag of £525,000. A report in the *Hereford Times* of 9 June 2005 stated that there had been interest in the property from a wide area, and that it had been sold. Soon afterwards, the new owners moved in and discovered an alleged ghost, called George! Said to be something to do with a local who died of a heart attack on the premises, he is not unfriendly but manifests himself by moving cutlery and other things about when there is nobody there!

By the side of the **Bull's Head** the road turns sharp right, drops down to the river bridge and climbs the other side, before turning left for Hay. This last bend is by the church, at the rear of which was formerly a cockpit in use until about 1840 — cockfighting taking place after the Sunday service. The game of fives also used to be played against the north wall of the church.

From here the road climbs up and out of the valley, past the drive on the right-hand side leading down to the ruins of Craswall Priory, before a precipitous descent to join the road from the Vale of Ewyas and the run down the left-hand side of the Cusop Dingle into Hay.

CHAPTER SEVEN

The Valley of the Escley Brook

Returning to the fork in the road at the **Crown Inn**, Longtown, the right-hand road follows the valley of the Escley Brook towards Michaelchurch Escley. A quarter of a mile along this road is Pont yr Ynys, near where there seems to have been a short-lived establishment, for the 1841 census records a James Pitt at the **Bell Inn**, an adjacent property being 'Pontagnas' Mill. However, there is no further mention of this inn in any available records.

After a right turn the road climbs steeply and, after a mile or so, a left turn heads north, along the high ground above the Escley brook. The first right turn off this road, after less than a mile, leads to the settlement of Lower Maes-coed, on the plateau between the valleys of the Escley and Dulas Brooks, the southern part of which is in Longtown parish. Here, surprisingly, were three places meriting attention. One was yet another **New Inn**, locally nick-named the **Kicking Donkey**, the only directory reference to which was in 1874, but which was already open in 1871. It appears as a beer house in the licensing records from 1872 onwards, and there were a number of licensees until 1887, when the licence was not renewed. It was marked as the **New Inn** on the 1891 six-inch Ordnance Survey map, no doubt having closed during its preparation, but in the next edition of 1904 it was marked as New Inn Farm. This was part of the estate of the Marquess of Abergavenny, being

The one-time New Inn at Lower Maes-coed

included in the 1920 sale. At that time it was just over three and a half acres in extent and was tenanted by Mr. H. Howells at a rent of £10 p.a. and tithe of 4s. 10d. There is still internal evidence of its former use in the shape of a blocked-up serving hatch between the front room on the left-hand side of the front door, and what must have been the tap-room behind.

Also in the licensing records is an un-named beer house at Lower Maes-coed, which does not seem to appear in any trade directories of the period. It, too, was already open in 1871 and appears in surviving licensing records from 1872, although no name is given there, and it was not until the 1881 census that the name was given as the **Ely Dawn Inn**. The licensee at this time was Thomas Lloyd, a local man, who was then aged 41 and whose trade was 'keeper of a beer and cider house'. He held the licence until the beer house closed in 1884. Its position has not been identified, but the entry in the 1881 census suggests that it was in the vicinity of Yew Tree Cottage, to the east of the **New Inn**.

North of Lower Maes-coed are the small parishes of Newton and St. Margaret's, Newton being formerly a chapelry of Longtown, and St. Margaret's a parish in its own right. Both of these parishes had small populations in 1851, Newton having 275 inhabitants and St. Margaret's 316. The northern part of Lower Maes-coed is just in the parish of Newton

Formerly the Sun Inn at Lower Maes-coed

where, in the first half of the 19th century, there was the **Sun Inn**. Surviving Land Tax Returns record a property that was held in 1782 by Anne Lewis and by Benjamin Lewis from 1795 until the end of the Land Tax in 1838. From 1823 until 1828 Benjamin Lewis took out alehouse keeper's recognizances, suggesting that either a new inn had been started in 1823 or a former inn had been revived. The inn is shown on the tithe map, the apportionment confirming that Benjamin Lewis was the owner. In 1851 Lewis, who had been born in Clodock, was still at the **Sun Inn** being then 55 years old. As he was described as a freeholder this suggests that the inn may have lapsed by this time, and certainly there are no later directory references to the **Sun Inn**.

His age indicates that there must have been more than one person of the same name at the inn, presumably father and son. The closure of the **Sun Inn** clearly left the way open for the later establishments in Lower Maes-coed. It was later called New House and is now Great House.

To get to the centre of the small parish of Newton, it is necessary to retrace the diversion to Lower Maes-coed, and then take the next right turn after about a mile and a half. This road drops down past the church to a cross-roads, where the left turn leads to Middle Maes-coed; the right turn leads towards Abbey Dore; whilst straight on is St. Margaret's.

First taking the left turn, after a quarter of a mile or so there is a small chapel on the left, opposite which is a rough track. Just here, on the opposite side of the track to the chapel, is a property which was formerly an inn. In the early 1840s this was the **Royal Oak Inn**, run by James Davis, a cooper. He made his will on 8 July 1844 and this was proved on 20 June 1845, being endorsed 'Estate under £200'. While he left his coopering tools to his father, the **Royal Oak Inn** went to his wife Jane who sold it in 1847 to Charles Davies of Ploughfield, Preston-upon-Wye, for £177 10s. No trace was found in the 1851 census, but in 1861 the **Oak** was occupied by Joseph Higley, a tailor, but there was no mention of the licensed trade. Its position in the census was next to Chapel House. The **Royal Oak** does not appear again until an entry in *Mercer and Crocker's Directory* of 1874 which records one Joseph Sanders at the **Royal Oak**, in a format that suggests this was a pub. However, as with the **Anchor Inn** at Longtown, there is no mention of it in

Little Green Farm may once have been a beer house

the licensing records from 1872, and this was either an error on the part of the compilers, or it had closed and the compilers had not caught up with the change. In 1871 the Oak was occupied by Samuel Jenkins, a retired farmer, and in a directory of 1876 Joseph Sanders was recorded as a shopkeeper at an unspecified place. In 1902 one Joseph Higley was a tailor and shopkeeper at Oak Cottage, and the 1910 Land Valuation demonstrates that this was another name for the **Royal Oak** which was owned by Joseph Higley. All this shows that this was not the unidentified beer house at Little Green Farm, nearly a mile to the north-west, which was remembered as an inn by Trevor Powell in the 1995 booklet *Memories of Newton*.

> My grandfather said that this house used to be a pub, and when he was about seven he used to come and mind the children for the people who were keeping it. Sometimes it was very dark when he went home and he had to go across the fields and he used to run all the way. A lot of it was rough grass and gorse bushes. That must have been in the 1860s.

No other evidence about this establishment has so far been found.

Bridge End, another possible inn

Turning right at the crossroads, the road drops and crosses the Dulas Brook, just over which is **Bridge End**, locally said to have been a beer house at some time in the past. However, no written record has so far been found and it does seem an unlikely spot. If it indeed was a beer house, then it was in a predecessor of the present building. Bridge End belonged to the Bacton Estate and was one of the lots in the auction of the estate in 1919, when it was described as being a 'newly erected and convenient brick-built and slated Dwelling House'. It was sold with a total of 31 acres of land.

Continuing straight ahead at the crossroads leads uphill to St. Margaret's where alehouse keeper's recognizances were taken out between 1818 and 1828, firstly by James Walter for 1818 and 1819, then Richard Powell for 1820 and 1821. On 26 December 1821 an advertisement in the *Hereford Journal* stated that the **Crown and Anchor** at St. Margaret's was to be let or sold by private contract, which identifies the inn. What happened is not recorded, but in 1822 and 1823 Thomas Griffiths took out alehouse keeper's recognizances. John Price took over on 29 March 1824 and renewed his recognizance later that year. There was then a gap before Edward Powell took out recognizances for 1827 and 1828. This can be interpreted as either a break in continuity in the licence or one establishment closing and another opening.

Whatever happened, the next reference in 1851 is to the **Sun Inn**, which was then in the hands of 82-year-old David Thomas, described as an innkeeper, who had been born in Vowchurch. The inn does not appear in a directory until 1867, when James Thomas, innkeeper and tailor, was in charge. A directory entry of

The well-placed Freehold Licensed Inn and Small Holding

known as

THE SUN INN, ST. MARGARETS.

Situate on the Road from Newton to Vowchurch, in the Parish of ST. MARGARETS.

It is a modern, brick-built house, slated, with a useful garden attached.

THE ACCOMMODATION in the house is as follows :

Bar, Bar Parlour, Kitchen, Cellar, Washhouse, Coal Cellar, 4 Bedrooms.

THE OUTBUILDINGS consist of Barn, Trap House, Cowshed, Stables and 2-bay Open Feeding Sheds.

With the Productive Orcharding, Pasture and Arable Land,

having an area of about 12 acres. Let to Mr. Wm. Jordan at a yearly rental of £30. Together with the Two Meadows Nos. 564 and 565 on the Ordnance Survey, let, with other land, to Mr. Geo. Powell, and the rent apportioned is £4 5s. ; also the Woodlands known as Rock Wood and part of Park Wood (in hand), having an area of about 14 acres, 1 rood, 25 perches, making a total area in respect of this lot of

32 acres,   2 roods,   17 perches   (or thereabouts.)

SCHEDULE.

ORDNANCE. NO.	DESCRIPTION.		AREA.		Tenant.		Rent.	
Pt. 534	House and Garden	...	.458					
560	Orchard	...	.820					
563	ditto	...	1.834		Mr. Wm. Jordan	...	£30 0 0	
566	Pasture and Arable	...	2 434					
567	ditto	...	2.049					
564	Pasture	...	4.380					
565	ditto	...	6.028		Mr. Geo. Powell	...	£4 5 0 (appd).	
574	Rock Wood (in hand)	...	5.687					
Pt. 597	Park Wood (in hand)	...	8.817					
			32.607				£34 5 0	

Commuted Tithe payable to Sir Geoffrey Cornwall, Bart, 11s. 7d.

,,   ,,   to the Rector of St: Margarets, 18s. 3d.

Land Tax, 10s. 5d.

This lot is sold subject to the owners of lot 19 having the right to haul timber from the Park Wood across field No. 565, making compensation for any unnecessary damage to the land and fences.   The purchaser of this lot shall erect and maintain a fence in the Wood between the points " F.G.H." on the Plan.

The Timber on this lot is valued at £51, which shall be paid for in addition to the purchase-money.

Sale of the Sun Inn at St. Margaret's by the Bacton Estate in 1919

1872 records that Mrs. Mary Preece was at an unnamed beer house in St. Margaret's and later entries demonstrate that this was the **Sun Inn**, with her name given correctly as Reece. She was still there in 1881, when she was recorded as a widow aged 78. Members of the family continued to run the **Sun Inn** until at least 1903 when the printed list records that landlord John William Reece was the owner of the premises. What happened subsequently is not known, but within a few years the licensee was William Jordan. By the end of the First World War the ownership

The Sun Inn was illustrated in the 1919 sale catalogue
(Photo: Derek Foxton collection)

had passed to the Bacton Estate, and it was one of the lots that was offered for sale on 14 May 1919. A hand-written note on the sale catalogue in Hereford Reference Library states that it was bought for £1,020 by 'Messrs. Jones'. However, it continued to be run by members of the Jordan family and it may be that 'Messrs Jones' refers to a solicitors' firm acting as an agent for the family. Certainly it was claimed to have been almost completely rebuilt in 1931, a fact made much of when it was auctioned on 2 August 1950 and sold for £3,900. In the 1960s the landlord was Edwin Hawk, a retired Thames River Policeman — quite a change to living on top of a hill! It appeared in the 1985 list of Herefordshire pubs issued by CAMRA, which was dismissive of the beer sold as it was not real ale, and it closed soon afterwards. It is still called the Sun and is just south of the parish church.

The old Sun Inn in 2005

ST. MARGARET'S, VOWCHURCH

About 14½ miles from Hereford and 3 miles from Bacton.

HILES-SMITH & SON

Have been favoured with instructions to OFFER FOR SALE BY AUCTION, at

The Law Society's Rooms, East Street, Hereford

On WEDNESDAY, AUGUST 2nd, 1950

Punctually at 3.30 in the afternoon

AN EXCELLENT COUNTRY INN

KNOWN AS

.THE SUN INN-

St. Margaret's, Vowchurch, Herefordshire

Well constructed of Red Brick, Stone and Slate Roof, this modernised Property comprises :—
First-class **B A R**, approximately 12ft. 6in. by 12ft., excluding counter space, with red tiled floor
and large windows at the front. Well-fitted Bar Counter and shelving, together with new ' Dalex '
double-pull Beer Engine and Piping, and modern 3-optic fitting.

BAR PARLOUR

at the front, approximately 12ft. by 9ft., fitted with servery and fireplace ; fully equipped Cellar ;
Kitchen with new ' Raeburn ' Cooker ; Outside ' Elsan ' sanitation. **On the FIRST FLOOR** is an
excellent Lounge, approximately 13ft. by 12ft. 6in., with fireplace ; Three large Bedrooms, one
having a fireplace and all in excellent condition.

At the side of the Inn there is a useful " Pull-in " and a large **PIECE OF GROUND**,
eminently suitable for the erection of a Hall, if required, and in addition there is approximately

TWO ACRES OF GROUND

approx. 1. acre

including a fully-planted **KITCHEN GARDEN**.

The Property was almost entirely re-built in 1931 and is in first-class condition throughout.
Rates approximately £5 per half year.

The situation of the Property is first-class as it stands on high ground with an excellent
outlook all the way round.

FREEHOLD

VACANT POSSESSION

Solicitors : MESSRS. HUMFRYS & SYMONDS, 8, St. John Street, Hereford.

For further particulars and Orders to View, apply : THE AUCTIONEERS, Imperial Chambers,
138, Widemarsh Street, Hereford. Tel. 2413.

N.B.—This Property may be viewed by ORDER to View only.

The Hereford Times Ltd., Printers.

Sale of the Sun Inn in 1950

(Derek Foxton collection)

113

Crossway was a pub until about 1884

After the **Sun**, the road loops around the church, and heads north-west across Upper Maes-coed, to meet the road joining Turnastone and Michaelchurch Escley. A short distance to the left is a crossroads called Crossways where there is a boundary between St. Margaret's parish and that of Michaelchurch Escley. On the junction was a beer house, just in St. Margaret's parish, which may have been the **Cross Keys**, recorded in the 1851 census, when it was run by Elizabeth Williams, a 45-year-old widow. If so, the licence possibly lapsed for a while, as in 1858 James Thomas, tailor, was at Crossways, but with no mention of the licensed trade. However, this had been recommenced by 1867 and in the records from 1872 the licence was held by Edmund Harper, later described as a beer retailer, farmer and shopkeeper, and the records refer to the premises as **Crossway**. In 1881 the then licensee, Henry Cousins, who was 28 years old, also farmed 28 acres. The licence was not renewed in 1884. This is the building on the left-hand corner as the crossroads is reached, which is now divided into two cottages. Locally it is known as Bob's Shop, a name it has been called for many years. This may refer to William Robert Howard, a ladies and gents' tailor at Crossway House, whose name appears in a directory in 1902 — members of whose family continued at Crossway for many years.

Turning right at the crossroads, after a few hundred yards there is a derelict building on the left-hand side. This was formerly a beer and cider house, which is un-named in directories and in the licensing records from 1872 onwards, but which the census records as the **Victoria Inn**. In 1851,

This ruinous building was once the Victoria Inn

David Pritchard, the innkeeper, was 35 years old. He continued there until it closed in 1887. In recent years it has been used for agricultural purposes.

Somewhere about here there may have been another public house, for on Bryant's map of 1835 is marked the **Cock**. This is very suggestive of licensed premises and in 1841 the occupier of the **Cock** was James Smith, a 39-year-old labourer, but no other evidence has so far come to light.

Above: The 1990 excavation at the King's Arms
Left: The cruck timber that dated the remains of the King's Arms

About a mile and half further along there is a fork, with an even smaller road to the left. The left fork leads in a short distance to the **King's Arms** while the right fork carries on to the **New Inn**, both on Urishay Common. The **King's Arms** was another place marked on Bryant's map and is in the parish of Michaelchurch Escley. There are no recognizances from the period 1818 to 1828 that can be ascribed to it and later records all describe it as a farm,

Sale of Clothier's and King's Arms farms in 1913

so that if it was a public house, then this usage must predate 1818 or have been unlicensed. In 1841 it was occupied by Daniel Watkins, stated to be a farmer aged 60, but by 1851 it was occupied by his 49-year-old widow Elizabeth Watkins, who was also described as a farmer. Samuel Wright, here in 1862, was a farmer as well as innkeeper. On 24 September 1913 the sale of the Urishay Estate had Clothier's and King's Arms Farms as Lot 45, but this was withdrawn at £1,325.

By the 1980s the **King's Arms** was reduced to an isolated barn in a poor state of repair, a single bay of which was of cruck construction, which, because of its interest, was listed in October 1988. The owners, Mr. & Mrs. Pritchard, of Clothier's Farm, obtained planning permission to convert it into a residence, but the size was restricted because of planning considerations. In order to provide evidence that the barn had previously been larger, they commissioned an evaluation excavation to determine the length of the original building. This indicated that the building was previously some 12m. longer, analysis suggesting that this demolished section probably consisted of two 6 m. bays. The barn is shown full length on the tithe map of the 1840s, but was probably partly demolished in the early 20th century. With this evidence, planning permission was reapplied for and permission was given for a larger building within the footprint of the former barn. This has now been built, and the building retains its historic name.

On the east side of Urishay Common was yet another **New Inn**, the earliest name of which was the **Gate**. This was also in the parish of Michael-church Escley, but only just, and while most directories record it under the correct parish heading, it is occasionally given under Peterchurch. The entries can, however, be linked by the licensing records. It first appears in the 1841 census, when William Williams was stated to be a publican at the **Gate**. Ten years later, 37-year-old Richard Ball was recorded as a tailor at the **Gate**, and although the

The rebuilt King's Arms in 2005

The one-time Gate Inn on Urishay Common

census does not record it, no doubt he was selling beer as well. By 1858 it was advertised in a directory, being first named as the **New Inn** in 1867. The surviving licensing records from 1872 use this name, although directories of 1876 and 1879 still refer to it as the **Gate**. Richard Ball ran this beer house until 9 September 1878 when his successor, John Allen, took out a licence. He was followed in turn by Thomas Harris in 1882, William Pugh in 1895 and Joshua Jenkins in 1898. Jenkins died in 1902 and his widow Elizabeth took over. The printed list of 1903 records that the **New Inn** was rented from Lewis Williams of Kingstone, who is recorded in a directory as a farmer at Smallbrook. Elizabeth Jenkins carried on for a number of years, but by 1910 Henry G. Price was in charge, renting it from Lewis Williams. The 1910 Land Valuation calls it the **Gate Inn**, although there is a pencilled alteration to the **New Inn**. As such it survived for a number of years, although it was still referred locally as the **Gate**.

It was last mentioned in a directory in 1929, but had closed by 1934. It is now a private residence but still called the Gate. A reference to the pub appeared in the pages of the *Hereford Times* on 4 November 2004 in a report on a campaign to save a telephone kiosk at Urishay. In the report it was stated that 'They voted to put it there because it was a little hamlet, and there used to be a pub next door'.

Returning to Crossways, after a right turn the road drops down and crosses the Escley Brook, and swings left on the other side. Down here is Michaelchurch church, and behind it and over the brook is the **Bridge Inn**, which was not, however, the first inn in the village. In the *Hereford Journal* of 11 July 1771 there is an advertisement for an auction that would take place 'at the dwelling house of Nicholas Johnson, Innholder, Michaelchurch Escley'. No name is given to Johnson's house, but on 28 September 1786 an estate was advertised to be sold by auction 'at the White-Hart, in the parish of Michaelchurch Escley'.

Eventually, however, the **White Hart** gave way to the **Sun Inn**, and when Lower Maes-coed, on the boundary between Newton and St. Margaret's, was enclosed, meetings were held there. Thus a meeting about the St. Margaret's 'Inclosure' was held at the **Sun Inn** in Michaelchurch Escley, on 19 June 1816, and a similar meeting about the Newton 'Inclosure' the following day. After the allocation of land, the spare allotments on Lower Maes-coed Common, four in Newton and sixteen in St. Margaret's, were advertised in the *Hereford Journal* to be sold by auction on 16 September 1816 'at the Dwelling-house of James Johnson, called THE SUN INN, in the Village of Michaelchurch'. The surname of the licensee suggests that this was a name change rather than one establishment closing and another opening. James Johnson took out alehouse keeper's recognizances between 1818 and 1828, the only person in Michaelchurch Escley to do so, so his was the only licensed establishment in the parish at that time.

On 12 September 1844 a meeting about the tithe was held at the **Sun Inn**, which was occupied in 1851 by Samuel Smith, a 66-year-old landed proprietor who had been recorded as running an un-named establishment in Michaelchurch Escley in the 1841 census. The **Sun Inn** was part of the Michaelchurch Estate that was offered for sale in 1862 and 1863. It is assumed that for some reason a sale did not take place on the first occasion. In the first set of sale particulars it was stated that the **Sun Inn** was in the occupation of the representatives of the late Mrs. Smith — presumably Samuel's widow — while in 1863 it was in the occupation of Mrs. Ann Jenkins. More importantly, the map of the estate contained with the sale particulars shows that the **Sun Inn** was directly opposite the church. Ann Jenkins was still at the inn in 1867, but by 1871 Isaac Pugh had taken over. The census of 1871 records that he was at the **Bridge Inn Public**, that he was then aged 35, and was a mason as well as an innkeeper. The details

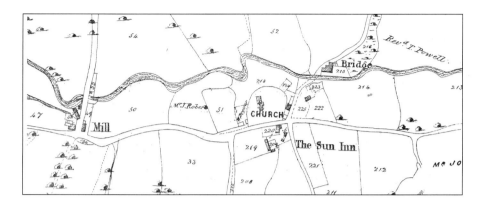

The BRIDGE FARM,

In the occupation of Mr. Alexander Gordon, as tenant from year to year, at the annual Rent, including interest on draining, of £73 4s. 6d. The tenant holds under an agreement of the terms of the tenancy.

No. on Plan.	DESCRIPTION.	STATE.	A.	R.	P.
194	... ...	Arable ...	0	3	36
195	... ...	Do. ...	2	0	9
196	... ...	Do. ...	2	3	20
197	... ...	Do. ...	4	1	14
198	... ...	Do. ...	0	1	13
199	... ...	Wood ...	2	2	10
200	... ...	Arable ...	0	3	5
201	John Jones's Pasture	Do. ...	6	2	35
202	Thistley Piece	Grass ...	4	3	12
203	John Jones's Pasture	Arable ...	8	0	14
204	Cae Glwyd	Grass ..	3	1	36
205	... ...	Arable ...	1	2	17
206	... ...	Do. ...	0	1	8
207	Lug Meadow	Grass ...	0	2	13
208	... ...	Do. ...	2	0	4
209	Buildings and Fold	... ...	0	0	20
210	John Jones's Meadow	Arable ...	4	3	8
211	... ...	Do. ...	4	2	32
212	... ...	Do. ...	3	2	33
213	... ...	Grass ...	6	2	33
214	... ...	Arable ...	3	2	33
215	House and Garden	... ...	0	1	0
216	... ...	Rough Grass ...	1	0	22
217	... ...	Grass ...	2	1	8
218	... ...	Do. ...	1	1	33
			70	1	18

The Bridge Farm Homestead comprises a Dwelling-house, Shed, Granary, and Piggeries, with detached Fold Yards, Barn, Stables, Cattle-houses, and Sheds.

The SUN INN,

Consisting of a conveniently situated Public House, Stables, Yard, Cattle-house, and Piggeries, with Garden in the occupation of the Representatives of the late Mrs. Smith, and also a Cottage and Garden in the occupation of George Watkins, the whole being of the estimated annual value of £25.

			A.	R.	P.
219	Meadow	Grass ...	0	3	0
220	Sun Inn, House, Garden, and Yard	... ...	0	2	15
221	... ...	Grass ...	1	0	38
222	... ...	Ditto ...	0	2	25
223	Cottage and Garden	... ...	0	0	39
			3	1	37

Map and details of Bridge Farm and the Sun Inn

The romantic setting of the Bridge Inn in the early 20th century

are given in the part of the census relating to the east bank of the Escley Brook, and so the **Sun Inn** had closed and Isaac Pugh had opened the present inn, based on the then Bridge Farm, down the road by the church and over the Escley Brook. Curiously, the name of the **Sun Inn** continued to appear in both licensing records and directories until 1876, so it seems that the licensing authorities had not caught up with the change of name and premises. The former **Sun Inn** became the farmhouse for the new Bridge Farm.

Isaac Pugh was still at the **Bridge Inn** in 1881, and he was also farming 23 acres. He stayed there until the late 1890s, when John Challoner took over as manager, the property being owned by the Trafford family of Michaelchurch Court. By 1909 Arthur Challoner was in charge and he remained there until the late 1930s. The 1880s series six-inch Ordnance Survey map shows that there was then a ford across the Escley Brook to reach the **Bridge Inn** and also a foot bridge, presumably the bridge after which the farm was named. The ford was in use until 1976 when a road bridge was built to give better access to the pub's picnic and camp site.

CAMRA gave an idyllic description in 1985:

> An excellent 16th century house in a very beautiful setting, off the road and over Escley brook, which is teeming with trout, and over which the pub has fishing rights.

However, all was not well in 2002, for in February of that year the landlady of the **Bridge Inn** appeared on a television news item saying that she was having to give up due to losses from lack of trade owing to the foot and mouth epidemic. Sadly this happened, and new landlords took over towards the end of

The Bridge Inn at Michaelchurch Escley in 2005

the year. The pub was subsequently offered for sale at an asking price of £380,000, and the freehold was sold in April 2005 for an undisclosed sum.

Returning past the church from the **Bridge Inn** and carrying on up the valley of the Escley Brook, after a couple of miles or so, a private track on the left climbs up to Little Cefn Farm. This was formerly a copyhold property held from the manor of Ewyas Lacy, and its history is given in the court rolls of the manor. It was leased for three lives to David Smyth on 11 October 1708, when it was stated to be of 12 acres customary Welsh Measure. Under this system, the lease was for the longest of three named lives, so it was important that one of those was of a young person. The lease was surrendered on 26 April 1739 and regranted to Ann Smyth, the daughter of David. She married James Harris and surrendered the lease on 19 February 1767 which was regranted at a fine of £52 10s., although the rent was only 3s. p.a. One of the three lives on that occasion must have been long, as there was no further grant of a lease until 27

Little Cefn Farm

November 1837, 70 years later, when it was granted to Thomas Powell and his heirs. It was subsequently sold, Little Cefn being the first of six lots in a sale which took place at the **Swan Hotel** in Hay on 14 June 1841. It was described in the notice of the auction in the *Hereford Times* as:

> All that newly-erected and substantial DWELLING-HOUSE, formerly known as the 'Carpenters' Arms Inn', otherwise styled 'The Little Keven Farm House', with the Barn, Stables, Outbuildings, and about 27 Acres of sound and very productive Arable, Meadow, Pasture, and Wood LAND (well stocked with thriving oak and Ash Timber) thereunto belonging, as the same now is in the possession of Proprietor, Mr. JAMES BEAVAN, having highly valuable and extensive Rights of Common, of Pasture and Turbary, on the Hatterell, Vagar, and Keven Hills.

The Anglicized spelling of Cefn was used as long ago as 1777 when both the Upper and Lower Keven were advertised for sale in the *Hereford Journal*. It seems remarkable that there should have been an inn in such an isolated place, and even more remarkable when it is realised that in 1841 the property was accessed from above, from a road from Hay to Michaelchurch Escley that ran along the ridge line of Cefn Hill. The implication is that the road was much more used in years gone by. This is the only mention of the **Carpenters' Arms** which must have been in business for a very short period up to 1841. Certainly it was not licensed in the 1820s, and its position suggests that drovers may have been the main customers, although this was not on one of their main routes to England.

Once the New House Inn at Cusop

Returning to the public road, another couple of miles further on, by the side of a wood is **New House**, just in the parish of Cusop. This is claimed to have been a pub at one period, and locally it is said that one frosty night a prostitute was here plying her trade when she died! However, no documentary evidence of licensed premises has so far been found, but this is not enough to dismiss the story. It could either have been a very long time ago or have been an illegal drinking place.

Nearly half a mile past the New House a track leads off to the right, and somewhere along here local folk memory recalls a pub called the **Bull's Tail** — a complement to the **Bull's Head** at Craswall. This is almost too good to be true! If it is correct, it must also have been a very long time ago.

From here the road drops sharply down to join the B4348 outside Cusop.

CHAPTER EIGHT

Up the Golden Valley:
Abbey Dore to Peterchurch

On the outskirts of Ewyas Harold, after crossing the Dulas Brook, the B4347 turns back on itself to skirt a promontory of high ground before heading north-west up the Golden Valley. This name is thought to be due to the mistranslation of the Welsh word *Dwr* by the Normans, who assumed that it was the Norman-French word *D'or* (of gold) and translated accordingly. However, the first certain time it was used was on Saxton's map of 1577 when it was marked as 'The gilden vale'.

The valley was also the course of the Golden Valley Railway, built on light railway principles, which had a junction with the main line at Pontrilas, and meandered up the Golden Valley to Dorstone and then on to Hay-on-Wye. The section of the railway up to Dorstone was opened on 1 September 1881 and on 25 May 1882 the gentlemen of the Woolhope Club availed themselves of the railway to visit the Golden Valley, travelling its length up to Dorstone where they met the rector, the Rev. Thomas Powell. He was one of the supporters of the railway and indeed in 1875 had chaired the inaugural meeting that led to the formation of the Golden Valley Railway Company. Early in 1882, to promote the railway, he wrote a booklet on the Golden Valley, based on a day trip on the railway, pointing out the objects of interest to be seen. Most of the

A £10 share in the Golden Valley Railway Company

gentlemen of the Woolhope Club on the outing had obtained a copy. Unfortunately the booklet, having being written by a 19th-century cleric, fails to mention any of the licensed establishments in existence at the time!

The Golden Valley Railway had intermediate stations at Abbey Dore, Bacton (a later addition), Vowchurch, Peterchurch and Dorstone, and, after the extension to Hay-on-Wye was opened in 1889, there were also stations at Westbrook and Clifford, both outside the Golden Valley. Writing in 1892, H. Thornhill Timmins well describes the rural nature of the line, and the financial difficulties that were experienced. He writes of Pontrilas, where

> we will retrace out steps after we have explored the country 'served' by that most eccentric of lines, the Golden Valley Railway; where we have seen *the* linesman, when not engaged in haymaking on the railway-bank, deeply engrossed over his occupation of weeding between the rails, as we waited for the train which, if we are to believe the tongue of rumour, sometimes fails to put in an appearance, the company's only locomotive having been seized for distraint of rent.

It is not surprising that the line was taken over by the Great Western Railway in 1901, but even then it was not financially successful and was finally closed to passenger traffic late in 1941. The last through train from Hay to Pontrilas was on 31 December 1949 and in 1950 the extension to Hay was dismantled, leaving Dorstone as the terminus for the limited traffic of local goods trains and occasional excursions. The rest of the line was closed piecemeal and by 1957 the only part left was the short section connecting to the Second World War Royal Ordnance Factory at Elm Bridge, which finally closed in 1969.

The first inn up the Golden Valley was the old **Griffin Inn**, a few yards up a track on the left-hand side of the road, a mile or so north of Ewyas Harold, but still just within the parish boundary. This was the premises of James Edwards, recorded in 1867 as a carpenter and beer retailer on Common Pitch. His name appears in the surviving licensing records from 1872 onwards, but these do not record the name of his beer house as being the **Griffin** until 1876. Mrs. Edwards, his widow, took over in 1883 and was still there in 1903 when the printed list shows that she owned the premises. The 1910 Land Valuation records the **Griffin Inn**, which was tenanted by John Gwillim, as being part of the estate of the Marquess of Abergavenny. Soon after this the **Neville Arms** was built on the south side and attached to the old **Griffin**.

The **Neville Arms** first appears by implication, but not by name, in 1913 when William Thomas Morgan was recorded as a beer retailer in Ewyas Harold parish. This was confirmed in 1914 when Jakeman and Carver's *Directory* states that he was an innkeeper at the **Neville Arms**. Directories after the First World War give the **Neville Arms** as being in Abbey Dore, but modern maps show that it is still in the civil parish of Ewyas Harold. However, an address in Abbey Dore is perhaps more logical as it is on the very edge of the parish and much closer to Abbey Dore village. The **Neville Arms** was built by the Neville family, Marquesses of Abergavenny, from whom it takes its name. It was part of the 2,670 acre Herefordshire estate of the Marquess that was sold by auction on 22 and 23 January 1920. The **Neville Arms** was lot 19 in the sale, and was described as an 'Excellent Roadside Inn' that had been newly built. The tenant was still Mr. W.T. Morgan who paid a rent of £40 per annum and tithe of 2s. 2d. Despite the property being new, Mr. Morgan had improved it, as it was noted: 'The Bath and Fittings, also the Bell Fittings, are the property of the tenant'. Curiously, the map used in the sale particulars marks the property as the **Griffin Inn**, confused by the fact that the map was based on the 1904 Ordnance Survey map, which was published before the **Neville Arms** was built. It took many years before the name of the **Griffin Inn** was finally removed from the maps! In 1941 the licensee was the splendidly named Leoline Gwyn Llewellyn. Things have changed since then and in December 2004 a new restaurant was opened at the inn, called the Dore River Restaurant. Another new departure over the Spring Bank Holiday weekend in 2005 was the Neville Arms beer festival, with 15 real ales on offer, as well as five different ciders.

The Neville Arms in 1999

Not far past the **Neville Arms** is Dore Abbey, after which the parish takes its name. This was founded in 1147; the main part of the church being built during the period 1180-1220 during the abbacies of Adam I and Adam II. During the abbacy of Adam I the abbey was subjected to virulent attacks from the pens of Gerald of Wales (*Giraldus Cambrensis*), archdeacon of Brecon, and Walter Map, archdeacon of Oxford. Among other things, they alleged that the monks broke their vows, eating meat when they should not, and that drink was also a problem in the abbey. These charges were rebutted by Abbot Adam II, but his reply has not survived. After the Dissolution in the 16th century Dore Abbey fell into decay, but was restored by Lord Scudamore from 1633 onwards. The nave was either too far gone to restore or too large for parochial purposes, and only the choir and transepts were repaired, the arch to the former nave being walled off, and a new tower built in a corner. The woodwork, including the roofs and bell frame, was undertaken by John Abel, that most famous of Herefordshire carpenters, and remains a monument to his skill.

Just to the north of the church, the road dog-legs to the left, while a minor road leads to the right. Here was the Abbey Dore station on the Golden Valley line. It was in the station yard that a stretch of Roman road was excavated in the summer of 1907. The road to the right leads past Abbey Dore Court in the general direction of Hereford.

Cottages on the site of the Red Lion Inn, Abbey Dore

The parish of Abbey Dore had a greater population than perhaps might have been expected. In 1851 this was 588, and there was thus enough trade to support a licensed establishment possibly before the **Griffin** was opened. This was the **Red Lion** and an advertisement in the *Hereford Journal* of 12 January 1820 announced a sale of timber was to be held there. In the 1820s Mary Harper took out alehouse keeper's recognizances in the parish, no doubt for the **Red Lion**, and the position of the pub was marked clearly on Bryant's map of 1835. It was on the opposite side of the road to Abbey Dore Court, where there is now a pair of brick-built cottages which probably post-date the licensed premises. Trade in this slightly out-of-the-way place may well have been limited, as William Gough, whose name appears in trade directories from 1851, was not only the landlord but also an auctioneer and appraiser. In addition he would have had to abide strictly by the conditions of his licence, for over the road was the local lock-up! After the Parish Constables Act of 1842 ten lock-ups were built in Herefordshire, the first at Bromyard, opened in 1844 and the tenth and last at Abbey Dore, completed in 1856. The Abbey Dore lock-up included a room for the magistrates, and cost some £470. Gough may have done better as an auctioneer than a publican, for a directory of 1867 shows that he had given up the licensed trade and so the parish of Abbey Dore was without a pub. In 1882 the Rev. Thomas Powell commented that 'It may be peculiar to Abbey Dore to have in it a union poor house, a police station, and not a public house'.

This statement is still strictly correct as regards a public house, the **Griffin/Neville Arms** being in Ewyas Harold, but the union poor house has now been converted into housing as has the police station. One of the brick cottages became the village post office (now the Old Post Office), and the lock-up is now called, not surprisingly, the Old Magistrates Court. The Poor Law Union, mentioned by the Rev. Thomas Powell, served more than 25 parishes and was the basis of the Dore Union Friendly Society whose rules were enrolled in 1854 and which met in the school-room in Abbey Dore. Friendly societies were normally based in licensed premises, but there must have been some reason why it did not meet at the **Red Lion**.

A mile or so north of Abbey Dore the main road takes a sharp right turn, while off to the left is the turn to Bacton, best known for the monument in the church to Blanche Parry, handmaid to Queen Elizabeth I. This has always been a sparsely populated area, and in 1861 the parish of Bacton had only 154 inhabitants. Despite this it then supported two public houses. In the 1820s one William Hughes took out alehouse keeper's recognizances and although the records do not give the name of his establishment, it was probably the **New Inn**, which was the only licensed establishment in the parish when the 1841 census was taken. At that time it was kept by Joseph Cooke, aged 35, who was recorded as a carpenter, but by 1851 Samuel Hughes had taken over. He was then described simply as a victualler, but trade must have declined, as in 1891 he had become an agricultural labourer. The licence was not renewed in the following year — not too surprising as he was then about 80. The building is described by the Royal Commission on Historical Monuments as being:

> of two storeys with attics. It is partly timber-framed and in modern times has had the N. and S. walls rebuilt in stone and brick respectively. Later additions have been made on the E. and N. sides. On the W. side is a projecting chimney-stack which is original up to the weathered offset.

The building has been restored in recent years and is now called Church Cottage. During the restoration it was discovered that one corner of the cottage had been built over an old well, and this had to be capped off and the corner of the cottage rebuilt.

The one-time New Inn at Bacton

In the 1850s the **Oak Inn**, run by Richard Holl(e)y, was a competitor of the **New Inn**. In the 1851 census Richard Holly was described as a mole catcher — a specialised, but presumably not full-time job as he also ran the **Oak Inn**. The position in the census record indicates that the **Oak Inn** was not far from the **New Inn**. By the 1860s the **Oak Inn** had disappeared, to be replaced by the **Apple**

Once the Apple Tree Inn, then the local Post Office, now a private house

Tree Inn, recorded in 1867 as being a few yards along the road from the **New Inn**. This was doubtless a name change, probably with the change of licensee, who was now James Wheale. Like the **New Inn**, the **Apple Tree** survived until 1892, but with several changes of licensee. In that year the magistrates refused an application for the renewal of the licence and it closed as an inn. In 1902 it was described as Apple Tree Cottage, and was occupied by Emmanuel Evans, a wheelwright and carpenter. This was another property that belonged to the Bacton Estate, and was also auctioned in 1919. It was then run as a smallholding, and was auctioned with just over 32 acres of land, being described as 'Apple Tree and Post Office'. The tenant was Mr. William Kedward. The successful bidder at the auction was Captain Partridge, who bought it for £1,000. He seems to have been a member of the family that was auctioning the estate

The Valuable and Convenient Freehold Small Holding

situate in the Parish of BACTON, and adjoining a good road, and known as

APPLE TREE AND POST OFFICE.

Comprising: substantial stone-built and tiled Dwelling House and Shop, containing Parlour, Kitchen, Back Kitchen, Washhouse, 3 Bedrooms, and Shop to which is attached the Post Office.

THE OUTBUILDINGS comprise large Wood and Iron Cowshed, 2-stall Stable and Trap House, Pigscot.

The Land consists of excellent Garden, Orcharding and Useful Pasture, having an area of 20 acres, 3 roods, 29 perches.

Let with other land to Mr. Wm. Kedward on an annual tenancy, and the rent apportioned on this portion is £27 per annum. Together with the Grazing Land and Limestone Quarry known as

THE KILN FIELD

(in hand), and a portion of Pasture, part of Lower Grange Farm, No. 153, at the apportioned rent of 10s. per annum, and making a total area in respect of this lot of

32 acres, 1 rood, 13 perches.

SCHEDULE.

ORDNANCE NO.	DESCRIPTION.				AREA.			Rent.
105	Pasture	...	...	...	9.510			
144	ditto	...	...	...	5.243			
145	Orchard	...	...	...	1.454			
148	ditto	...	...	...	.653			
150	House and Garden		...	...	.340	... Mr. W. Kedward	... £27 0 0	(appd.
151	Pasture	...	...	...	2.777			
149	Orchard	...	...	...	1.021			
153	Pasture	...	...	...	.684	... Mr. H. Patrick	... 0 10 0	
152	Kiln Field	...	...	...	10.150	... In hand		
203	Orchard	...	...	...	.324			
Pt. 147	Pasture	...	...	...	.175	... Mr. W. Kedward.		

32.331

Commuted Tithe, £3 0s. 4d. (apportioned).   *Land Tax, 6/9.*

NOTE.—This lot is sold subject to the owner of The Cwm having an agricultural right of way from the main road across fields Nos. 144 and 145.

The water supply to this holding is obtained from the Maerdy Farm, and the lot is sold subject to the owner of The Lower Grange Farm being entitled to collect an annual water rent of £2 from the owner of this lot, and the owner of this lot shall be responsible for the maintenance of the water pipes from the boundary fence of The Lower Grange land.

Sale of the Apple Tree, then the Post Office, in 1919

and bought back a number of the properties on offer. In 1941 Mrs. Eva Kedward was running a grocer's shop and post office at Appletree, Bacton, and the name of the house survives today. The post office was in use until recently and was run from premises at the rear of the house. During repairs and renovations to the house some years ago a hatchway was found in the wall between a rear room and a front room. The ceiling beams of this rear room had many nails driven in, as if for hanging mugs, suggesting that this was the former tap-room. However, as the floor of this room is lower than the floor of the other room, the hatch was close to the ground in the front room and the locals would have had to stoop down to collect their pints!

Returning to the B4347, the road crosses the river Dore close to the site of the former Bacton station and then, after a sharp left-handed bend, runs parallel to the river. On the other side of the valley is Newcourt Farm, formerly the residence of that interesting character Rowland Vaughan, whose influence spread well beyond Herefordshire. What he did from about 1585 onwards is described in a book that he published in 1610. Noticing that grass grew better where it had been flooded by a spring, he devised a system of irrigation whereby he could 'drown' or flood meadows. This was based on what he called his 'Trench Royal', which was nearly three miles long, ten feet broad and four feet deep. He claimed an astronomical increase in the value of the

The cover of Vaughan's book

produce of such ground, particularly if it was otherwise dry. He also claimed to have set up a commonwealth of 'mechanicals' at New Court — workmen who included many trades — and housed them all, feeding them with his own produce. However, he was selective as to who he allowed to join, stating that 'no common *Swearer*, *Drunkard* nor *Swaggerer* shall live within the limits of my allowance'. Even so, there is mention in his writings of an 'Inholder', but no further details survive. There are no physical remains that might point to where he housed his commonwealth and it is reluctantly concluded that it was just a figment of his imagination, or at the least very exaggerated. As for his 'drownings', there are surviving trenches from his irrigation works, including the Trench Royal, so this at least did happen, and was later copied in many places, the trade of 'drowner' being known into the 19th century.

The B4347 joins the B4348 near Vowchurch, and a right turn here leads towards Kingstone. Somewhat over a mile in this direction, on the right-hand side, was formerly yet another **New Inn**. This was marked on the draft drawings made by the Ordnance Survey in 1814-15, but surviving alehouse keepers' recognizances for the period 1818 to 1828 do not record any for Vowchurch, so it had lapsed by that time. When the one-inch Ordnance Survey map was published in 1831 it was just marked as a cottage, while Bryant's map of 1835 calls it Yew Tree Cottage.

Turning left instead of right, about a third of a mile along the B4348 another left turn leads down to Vowchurch church. John Lewis Smith had a draper's and provision shop in Vowchurch in the late 19th century, to which he later added

The old shop in Vowchurch was also an off-licence as the sign on the gable shows

an off licence. This no doubt was the business run in 1913 by William Edwin Booker, who was a grocer and tea dealer, and a beer and wine retailer. The shop premises and off-licence were in use until about 1980 when Mrs. Wilding, the then proprietor, ceased trading; she died in 1985. Nothing has been touched since then, and the shop and adjoining cottage, along a short track on the left-hand side of the road, before the church, are just as they were, complete with fine, enamelled-metal advertising plaques. It is said that this was something of a social centre for the village and that 50 years or more ago, in the absence of a pub, the men of the village used to buy their drink at the off-licence and drink it sitting on a bench outside the shop.

Over the river is Vowchurch's twin settlement of Turnastone. This, though small, evidently had need of liquid sustenance for its residents and presumably those of Vowchurch, and there was a pub there at the beginning of the 19th century. In 1803 J.P. Malcolm toured the area, looking at places of interest, and for part of the time stayed with the Rev. Mr. Vaughan, a clerical friend, who looked after, among others, the parishes of Turnastone and Vowchurch. Prior to a service at 'Turmaston' the parish clerk asked the Rev. Mr. Vaughan to give Holy Communion to a local cottager who was at the point of death. Malcolm recorded the following conversation:

As the dying man's bedside is a scene for his relatives only, I chose to wait under the shelter of the church porch for my friend's return. The sexton in answer to my inquiries, said, that 'John Mathews was a little koind of puublican, as sold yeale [ale] and cyder', and was an industrious well-disposed man; that he had a wife equally industrious, who was the mother of two children, one a year and a half, the other but three weeks of age. A fever seized Mathews, and a delirium followed. He now lay exhausted, quiet, and sensible.

Cross House, Turnastone, once the Red Cross Inn

Turnastone petrol station

This sad story indicates that there was a pub within the village at that time, but the name is not known, nor are any details. However, Malcolm was wrong about the first name of the 'publican' as the burial register records that his name was James and that he died on 21 June 1803 at the age of 48.

Certainly in the period 1818 to 1828 there was a licensed establishment, run from 1818 by Thomas Hancorn jun., then by Matthew Gough from 9 January 1823 until Charles Vaughan took over later that year. This may well have been the unnamed establishment recorded in the 1841 census, when 25-year-old John Wilson was the publican. The tithe map of 1842 marks the **Red Cross Inn** and the apportionment shows that it was held by William Garrett. His name appears as a publican in the 1851 census, but directories of 1851 and 1856 state that James Garrett was then at the **Red Cross Inn**, and that he was a victualler and carrier to Hereford. The name of William Garrett appears again in a directory of 1858. Although his name appears in Morris & Co.'s *Directory* of 1862, he had probably moved on to the **Boughton Arms** in Peterchurch by that time, and his son-in-law James Seaborne had taken over. Seaborne's name is recorded in a directory of 1863, but the **Red Cross Inn** seems to have closed soon after as it does not appear in Littlebury's *Directory* of 1867 — perhaps not too surprising as there were then only ten houses in the village. The premises became known as Turnastone Cottage and subsequently Cross House, by which name it is known today.

Cross House is directly opposite the old garage and stores. The garage was started by James Wilding, who made the first wireless set in the area in 1923. In 1948 it was taken over by his sons Hedley and Percy. The following year the post office on the main road closed and the business was transferred here, still called Vowchurch Post Office! It closed in 1985 after the death of Mary Wilding, wife of Hedley. However, the petrol station continues in business, despite a scare a few years ago when regulations drafted by the European Union threatened it with closure, but it survived and is still run by Hedley Wilding with occasional help from his son, Robert. The premises were part of the 246-acre Turnastone Court Farm that was sold to the Countryside Restoration Trust in February 2003 for a figure in the region of £1.2 million. When sale particulars were published, it was stated that the house and shop were formerly known as the **Coach and Horses**, a complete surprise to the Wildings who have been there for a very long time. No record of this has so far come to light, but it may be where James Mathews carried on his trade, or perhaps some of the earlier references quoted above refer to this establishment and not to the **Red Cross Inn**.

Returning to the B4349 and turning north-west towards Peterchurch, after about half a mile or so is Poston Mill, marked with a sign on the roadside for The Mill with every appearance of a pub. However, this is a licensed restaurant, and so not really within the scope of this book, but it is used as a local by the residents of the adjoining caravan park. A little further along and across the other side of the valley is Poston Court where, in the early 18th century, Lord Arthur Somerset had his residence. Tradition says that he always kept a barrel of beer on tap outside his door, with a cup attached by a chain, for any passing traveller to quench his thirst. He was the youngest son of the 1st Duke of Somerset, and died on 21 June 1743 at the age of 72 when a small brass to his memory was placed in the chancel of Vowchurch church. Later, Shuckburgh Boughton lived at Poston Court, and his son Edward succeeded to a baronetcy after the death by poisoning of the seventh baronet, Sir Theophilus Boughton, of Loughton, on 21 August 1780. Sir Edward built a circular summer shooting box on the estate, under the direction of Sir William Chambers, in which every fitting followed the curve of the room. In the 19th century the estate passed by inheritance from the Boughton family to the Robinson family, and the shooting box was extended into what is now Poston House, on the east side of the road. The former house at Poston Court has long since been replaced.

Peterchurch, the next settlement up the valley, is a place of some antiquity. It has a Norman church, to which a tower was added in the late 13th century, and a spire in the 14th. However, for safety reasons the spire had to be taken down in 1946 at a cost of about £6,000. At that time it would have cost about £7,000 to rebuild it in stone, but there was no money, and subsequent fund raising could not keep up with the rising costs. Eventually, in 1972, it was replaced with a fibreglass construction at a cost of £32,000. Not too long afterwards the weathercock blew down, damaging the nave roof in the process, but could not be replaced as erecting the necessary steeplejack's ladders would have damaged the fibreglass, and the spire remains without its weathercock.

An early 20th-century cast-iron milestone in the Golden Valley

Peterchurch seems to have been a rough and ready place in the past, with the local bellringers taking a leading role. At the beginning of the 20th century, while Mrs. E.M. Leather was collecting material for her book on Herefordshire folklore, an 80-year-old woman told her a story about the bellringers, which must have happened in the middle of the 19th century. Apparently the ringers at Peterchurch rang for a wedding, but not having received any recompense for their services went again to the belfry and rang the bells backwards in revenge. The idea seems to have been that this would bring bad luck! In the late 1880s the Hereford Diocesan Guild of Bell-ringers employed a person called William Fussell to act as an instructor to novice bellringers. In the course of his employment, Bill Fussell travelled around the diocese and, fortunately, kept a diary of his activities. In his diary for 1888 there is a vivid description of the carryings on at Peterchurch:

> Mr. C. Garretts father was a farmer & a ringer — if he happened to be ploughing & heard the Bells go up for a wedding or, anything else, he wd. take in the horses leave the plough & at once go up & ring for the rest of the day & night. He it was who saw Peterchurch Bells arrive in the Village — six bells all at once.
>
> Mr. Garretts grandfather & his great Uncle were the two who arranged to get the bells home from Gloucester by Road & provide Cart & horses for the purpose. Up till within very recently — parts of the old farm wagon — which actually carried the Bells to Peterchurch would be seen laying about near the Chyard wall when disused & no longer of use. C Garretts Father had it stowed away in a field close under the Ch:yard wall, where old Villagers would often come with pride & point out to a friend or visitor the wagon 'what had brought our bells here'.
>
> A flight of House block stone steps led up to the Ringing Room from the outside (North) where a door is still to be seen. Cider & smoking was carried on here & a fire lit somewhat after Lugwardine — but water was made behind the door leading up stone stairs to the Bells. — until the place began to smell very strong & foul. The Vicar in Mr. C Garretts father's time was not so particular — & evidently, one of the old sort of gentlemen. He wd. come into the Chyard when a company of farmers from miles around wd. play at Ball against the Ch walls & caution a boy to see the shutters were closed for fear of breaking a window occasionally saying 'well done' — & 'good' when an exciting game was on.
>
> As soon as the service hour was up (his big watch was referred to) he wd. say 'now lads lets get in & have it over — open the Shutters boys — tell the ringers to set up a bit'.
>
> Peterchurch was a notorious place for fighting then adays. Farmers usually met on Sundays at 'The Crown' & if they quarrelled or disagreed — generally arranged to fight it out 'after dinner' or 'after Church'. A Village policeman was seldom seen & if there both farmer & policeman wd. say let them fight it out. As many as 2 or 3 stand up fights have taken place in the field between the Church & the river — on the south side.
>
> The Crown is now occupied by a dissenter named Lane who is a teetotaller, but sells some spirits & ales & yet proposes strong temperance principals [*sic*].

Fussell was somewhat dismissive of Charles Edwin Lane, perhaps somewhat unfairly as he was a prominent local personage and took a deep interest in local affairs. A letter by Lane that appeared in the *Hereford*

Times on 21 August 1875 promoted the idea of the Golden Valley Railway, although the initial suggestion was to connect with the Hereford to Brecon railway at Eardisley and not Hay. This letter led to a discussion and the eventual formation of the railway. Lane's store at Albion House in Peterchurch was reputedly the largest general store in

Albion House, Peterchurch, once the Crown Inn

Herefordshire and it was claimed that it could supply all its customers' requirements from the cradle to the grave. The stock included some 3,000 pairs of boots and shoes.

The **Crown Inn** occupied the right-hand half of the pair of cottages, now No. 2 Albion House, on the left when approaching the centre of the village from the south. These cottages are set back and old photographs show that Lane built a shop in front of them, but this has since been demolished, as has the upper story of Albion House itself. The **Crown** first appeared in a directory in 1851, when John Howard jun. was described as a victualler, but it is likely to be older that that date.

By about 1870 it had been taken over by Charles Lane and although it continued to be licensed, it disappears from directories. From 1876 the licence was a six-day one. This was not renewed in 1892, possibly connected with a reaffirmation of Lane's principles, for after his death on 9 December 1916, his obituary in the *Hereford Times* told the story of how he poured his shop's entire stock of wines and spirits down the nearest drain!

The earliest licensed establishment in Peterchurch, of which information is known, was the **Sun Inn**. An advertisement in the *Hereford Journal* of 16 July 1778 mentions a sale by auction that would take place 'at the dwelling-house of Thomas Price, known by the sign of the Sun in Peterchurch'. By 1791 it had been taken over by Charles Garrett. An attempt to sell the **Sun Inn** by private contract was made in January 1819, when it was described in the following terms:

All that well-accustomed INN, called The SUN; consisting of a good roomy Kitchen, Bar, Pantry, Two large Parlours, Under Ground Cellars, Seven Bed Chambers, Malt-house, and Brew-house, Stabling, Barn, and other Buildings; with an excellent Garden, Two Orchards, and Five Acres of Tillage.

An 1882 sale at the Boughton Arms

This seems to have been unsuccessful, and in June 1820 it was advertised that the inn would be sold by auction on the premises. Again, this seems to have been unsuccessful and in May 1821 it was advertised that it would be sold by auction at the **Boughton Arms Inn**, Peterchurch — 'for a view apply to Mr. Gwynne, at the Boughton Arms'. This suggests that the **Sun Inn** was the licensed premises for which James Brown took out alehouse keeper's recognizances in 1818 and 1819, and Charles Garrett in 1823 and 1824. No more recognizances were taken out and the **Sun Inn** must have finally closed, as in the later 1820s John Gwyn of the **Boughton Arms** took out the only alehouse keeper's recognizances in Peterchurch. It seems likely that the **Sun Inn** was in the village centre and Sun Cottage, formerly opposite the post office and demolished recently for redevelopment, may well have been the location.

The **Boughton Arms** is in a prime position in the middle of the village and no doubt received its name from the notable Boughton family, which held property in Peterchurch and nearby Vowchurch until the middle of the 19th century. In the 18th century the field behind the inn was used for cockfighting, the story of which is told in the Woolhope Club *Transactions* for 1914:

The Boughton Arms provides an end-piece to this 1930s street scene
(Photo: Derek Foxton collection)

The Boughton Arms, Peterchurch, shortly after the First World War

In the churchyard is a tombstone to one John Andrews, who died in 1799, and who owned a famous cock named 'Captain', in the days when cock fighting took place in the field behind the Boughton Arms, and he was nicknamed after his famous bird. The epitaph reads:

Alas poor Captain winged by cruel death,
He pek'd in vain, o'er matched resigns his breath;
Loves social mirth, none dare his word distrust,
Sincere in friendship, and was truly just.

By 1818 the **Boughton Arms** was being run by John Gwyn, and this surname continues until 1861. There must have been two of the same name, as the 1851 census records that the then occupier of the **Boughton Arms** was aged 45 and that he was a saddler as well as an innkeeper. He owned a copy of Cassey's *Directory of Herefordshire*, published in 1858, which is now in the possession of one of the authors of this book. Curiously, the name of this establishment is occasionally given in advertisements and in directories as the **Bo(u)lton Arms**. John Gwyn left the **Boughton Arms** in 1861 and an auction of his household furniture and other effects was held there on 22 April in that year. He was succeeded by William Garrett, who was still there 25 years later.

The Boughton Arms in 2005, resplendent in its coat of white paint

In the mid 1890s the **Boughton Arms** was taken over by James Thomas jun. and he was landlord at the time of the death of Robert Jones VC. Jones was a regular at the **Boughton Arms** and earlier in the week of his death in 1898 he had had a 'tiff' with his wife over the fact that he had been sent home drunk. A few days later his body was found with gunshot wounds at the house

139

of his employer at Crossways, Peterchurch. An inquest was held at the **Boughton Arms** and a verdict of suicide was recorded. However, in modern times it has been claimed that the verdict may have done him an injustice and that his death could have been the result of a tragic accident. A campaign to have the verdict quashed was mounted by the Rev. J.C. de la Tour Davies, for many years rector of Peterchurch, but the then Lord Chief Justice stated that it would not be possible to change a verdict after so many years had elapsed.

In the earlier part of the 20th century there were 33 shops and other businesses in Peterchurch, including the pubs. The latter were well supported and in the early 1960s there was still enough support for the **Boughton Arms** to field three darts teams. While there are now only a few businesses left in Peterchurch, the **Boughton Arms** continues to dispense food and hospitality and seems set to stay open well into the 21st century.

CHAPTER NINE

Up the Golden Valley:
Peterchurch to Dorstone & Hardwick

The Portway; was this once the New Inn?

On the east side of the road leading north from the centre of Peterchurch is a small stone cottage called the **Portway** which was formerly a cider house run by Thomas Ball. The tithe apportionment of the 1840s describes it as a public house, and although the 1851 directory describes him as a cider retailer, the census of the same year records him simply as a shoemaker. His name then disappears, but the 1861 census records a John Rubery as an innkeeper at the **New Inn**, which was in this area, and may well be a name change. It was offered for sale by auction on 31 May 1861 as:

> The New Inn situated in or near the Village of Peterchurch consisting of a substantial Dwelling-house and a detached Shop in Front, suitable for a Butcher or Saddler, with back Premises and Stable, and a small productive Orchard and Garden, containing about half an Acre.

This **New Inn** cannot be identified in the 1871 census and it may well have closed after the auction.

The **Nag's Head** is on the corner of the B4348 and the unclassified road leading in a south-westerly direction to Hinton Cross. The pub car

The Nag's Head at the beginning of the 20th century
(Photo: Derek Foxton collection)

THE "NAG'S HEAD,"

a brick-built and slated House, containing front Kitchen, Parlour, back Kitchen, Dairy and Cellar, and Four Bedrooms, and licensed as a Beer-house, on the main road from Peterchurch to Dorstone, and in the Village of **Peterchurch**; with a good Garden and piece of Pasture Land adjoining, containing about **5 acres.**

ALSO

Several Pieces of Land, containing between **4** and **5 acres,** situate near the Baptist Chapel and School, in the same Parish, all Pasture with the exception of rather less than an acre of Arable; the whole lot containing nearly **10 acres.**

THE FOLLOWING ARE MORE DETAILED PARTICULARS:—

No. on Ordnance Map.	DESCRIPTION.				State.			Quantity.
866	"Nag's Head" Inn and Garden	...	...	...				·211
507	Meadow adjoining	...	...	...	Meadow	...	...	5·010
883	IN PETERCHURCH FIELD ...	...	...	...	Arable	...	...	·589
882	Do.	...	...	...	Pasture	...	...	2·000
887	Do.	...	...	...	Do.			·487
Part of 886	Do.	...	...	...	Arable	...	...	·308
879	Do.	...	...	...	Pasture	...	...	·899
888	Do.	...	...	...	Do.	...	...	·335
								A. 9·839

The Property is all Freehold, and is now in the occupation of GEORGE MORGAN, and possession can be had on the 2nd February next.

The Tithe Rent-charge payable for this Lot in 1904 was { To the Vicar ... £1 3 5 / To the Impropriator 13 11

The Land Tax paid is 3s. 6d.

Lot VIII — The Nag's Head — in the 1905 sale

The Nag's Head in 2005

park is to the south-west of the inn and is accessed off the unclassified road. It seems to have started as an inn about 1870 and by the time of the 1871 census was occupied by John Probert, who was then aged 46 and had been born at Clifford. Curiously, his profession on the census return was given simply as an agricultural labourer. However, by the time that the surviving licensing records start in 1872 the inn had been taken over by George Morgan jun., who had moved his wheelwright's business from Crossway. He owned the premises, and was still recorded there in the 1903 printed list of licensed establishments. However, it seems that Morgan sold the business soon afterwards, for in 1905 the **Nag's Head** was offered for sale by auction by the executors of the late Thomas Llanwarne, a prominent Hereford solicitor. The sale details for Lot VIII indicate that the Nag's Head was licensed as a beer house and included some 10 acres and the adjoining cottage. The property was occupied by Mr. George Morgan, but possession could be had on 2 February next. The result of the sale was not reported, but in 1910 Rees Williams, successor to George Morgan, was recorded as the owner. He was running this beer house until at least 1929, but a full licence was not obtained until the late 1930s.

In the early 1960s the **Nag's Head** was run by Bob Bowyer, a member of a well-known local family, and it then fielded three darts teams — the same number as the **Boughton Arms**.

From the **Nag's Head** a road leads south-west through Hinton and over a crossroads. About half a mile further along, on the left-hand side, is the former **Plough Inn**. In 1851 John Howard sen. was a beer retailer, a wheelwright, clerk and sexton at the premises, while the census in the same year shows that he lived at Court Field, Long Lane, and was a carpenter.

By 1861 the establishment had become the **Plough and Harrow**; living at home was William Howard, John's son, also a carpenter, and within a few

The Plough in 2005

years he had succeeded to the pub and had also become the parish clerk. The earliest directory reference, in 1867, calls it the **Plough and Harrow**, but the licensing records from 1872 onwards just called it the **Plough**. The licensing records also show that William Howard owned the premises in 1872. On 26 March 1883, after the death of his father, the licence was transferred to William Howard jun. John Charles Jones took over the following year, when the owner had become William Prosser. Jones was also described as a farmer in 1885, and it was not until 1900 that the licensing records list him as the owner of the premises. However, he apparently bought them in 1887 for £316 from the then owners, James Medlicott of Mowbage and James Pearce of Snodhill Court. John Charles Jones died on 8 November 1902 and the licence was transferred to Mary Jones, his widow, on 1 December 1902. He left most of his property to her and the printed list of January 1903 had already caught up with this change of ownership, although it does call the inn the **Plough and Arrow**!

One interesting piece of ephemera from this time survives. On Saturday 18 June 1904 Mary Jones sent a postcard from Peterchurch to the solicitor R.T. Griffiths in Hay. Posted in Peterchurch, it arrived in Hay on Sunday morning, in time for the message to be effective, for Mary Jones informed Mr. Griffiths that she wanted to see him at 2 p.m. in Hay on Monday! Her faith in the efficiency of the post and rail network was clearly justified!

Mr. R. Graves, writing in 1986 about this time, had the following to say:

> The pub was run by Edgar Jones' mother Mary for 52 years and was known as a lively and friendly establishment. On a Saturday night the whole staff of C.E. Lane's store including the young delivery boys used to meet there for a sing-song when either Mrs. Lloyd or Mrs. Hallard played the piano.

Towards the end of Mary Jones's time at the **Plough**, she sold the premises to the Alton Court Brewery for £1,900, the conveyance being dated 28 March 1946. Eight years later the Alton Court Brewery sold the inn to Ernest Vincent Bowyer for £1,800, the Brewery holding a mortgage on the property. It does seem to have been well patronised at this time as it was able to field two darts teams, but financially all was not well and Ernie Bowyer could not keep up with his mortgage payments and pay for his stock from the Stroud Brewery. Despite warnings about what would happen he was taken to the High Court in 1960. Ernie Bowyer was the last landlord, and the inn closed in the late 1960s.

On past the **Plough** is the **Temple Bar**, which was said to have been a public house with a spirits licence, although this has not yet been identified. The list of drinking establishments up Long Lane is not yet complete, for there is Vine Cottage, apparently at one time a cider house, and what is now called Mount Pleasant used to be a drinking house called the **Drum and Monkey**. Although these names have not been found in the licensing records, there is evidence to suggest that the proper name of the **Drum and Monkey** was the **New Inn**, which was run in 1867 by Charles Maddox, farmer and beer retailer. The building cannot be traced in the 1871 census, but in 1881 the only Charles Maddox in the parish lived in Long Lane, and the entry is in the correct position in relation to the **Temple Bar** and **Vine Cottage**. He was recorded as a farmer of 25 acres, but as there is no mention of the licensed trade it was probably only a minor part of his activities. He apparently ran the inn until 1892 at which date the licence was not renewed

The next village after Peterchurch is Dorstone, in the vicinity of which men have lived, presumably drank, and died for thousands of years. On the top of the hill to the east of Dorstone is Arthur's Stone, a prehistoric burial chamber said to date from about 3,500 B.C.

Dorstone village in the early 20th century. The Pandy Inn is on the right
(Photo: Derek Foxton collection)

The Pandy Inn about 1904

Dorstone village has a history that goes back before the Norman Conquest when the manor belonged to Earl Harold Godwinsson. At the time of the Domesday survey it was held by Drogo, son of Poyntz. On the west side of the village is a prominent motte and bailey castle.

The Pandy Inn about 1920
(Photo: Derek Foxton collection)

146

In the centre of the village sits the **Pandy Inn**, which is said to have been built to house Richard de Brito's workmen when they were working on a chapel, since demolished, that was originally attached to the parish church. He is said to have been one of the four knights who murdered Thomas à Becket in 1170, and built the chapel in expiation of his sins. However, there is good evidence that the chapel was not built until 1256, which rather throws doubt on the whole story. Neither is the inn of such antiquity.

Fairs were held in front of the **Pandy Inn** until the last third of the 19th century. Cooke's *Topographical Description of the County of Hereford*, published about 1830, states that there were fairs on 27 April, 18 May, 27 September and 18 November 'for horned cattle, horses, sheep, and pigs'.

An early reference to the **Pandy Inn** is in the *Hereford Journal* of 28 December 1780 when it was advertised that coppice wood and timber was to be sold by auction 'at the Public-House called The Pandy, in Dorston'; a similar advertisement appeared in the *Hereford Journal* on 14 March 1810. The **Pandy** first appeared in a directory in 1851, although John Reece, who took out alehouse keeper's recognizances in this parish in the 1820s, must have been there.

The **Pandy Inn** was the venue for an annual assembly which took place on 9 January 1845, and was presided over by Colonel Powell of Hardwick, when 'upwards of 160 sat down to supper, which consisted of every delicacy of the season'. The company was entertained afterwards with songs, and dancing took place until a late hour. The report in the *Hereford Journal* concluded by stating:

> We have heard that it is the intention of the gallant Colonel, who is the owner of the Pandy Inn, to build, by next season, a new and more commodious room for the accommodation of his numerous friends.

The visit of the gentlemen of the Woolhope Club to the Golden Valley on 25 May 1882 has already been mentioned. A favourable impression of the **Pandy Inn** was gained, as the report of the meeting the *Transactions* of the Club records:

> Assembled at the Pandy Inn (Pandee – a tannery – we are in the midst of old Welsh memories), with appetites sharpened by the journey and the weather, such a dinner was waiting that showed that the resources of the Golden Valley are quite equal to entertaining all the visitors that it can reasonably expect.

The attractions of the Golden Valley around Dorstone had not been exhausted by the Woolhope Club members and on 28 June 1888 another visit was made. Peterchurch was visited again, as was Snodhill Castle, and then a walk through to Dorstone — with a short stop at the rectory, from which they were summoned by the sound of a bugle — and then a climb up to Arthur's Stone, and a return by Scotland Bank. Dinner was no doubt very welcome after such an energetic day:

> Dinner was the next business, served *al fresco* by the landlady of Pandy Inn, Dorstone, under the trees growing upon the adjacent ancient mound, misnamed Dorstone Castle.

The day finished with scientific papers read in the schoolroom, and then a return by the Golden Valley Railway.

By 1890 the landlord of the **Pandy Inn** was George Probert — who is remembered as having a tame jackdaw — and in 1902 he advertised 'Every accommodation for cyclists and visitors. Good beds. First-class wines and spirits'. George Probert was a mason on the Moccas estate, and the **Pandy** was actually run by his wife.

The 1903 printed list indicates that the premises were owned by the Rev. Thomas Prosser Powell, rector of Dorstone and the son of the protagonist of the Golden Valley Railway. The elder Thomas had served as a surgeon with the East India Company, and then, on his father's advice, had come home and taken holy orders. He married Clara Prosser, daughter of the then rector of Dorstone, whose family had held the living since the 17th century. He served as rector from 1843 until 1886, and in 1887 his son, Thomas, who had been vicar of Peterchurch from 1875, took over the family living which he held

---

An Old Established Fully Licensed and Highly Popular Free House

KNOWN AS

"THE PANDY INN"

practically the only house of call within a road radius of about 3 miles. Situate in the Village of Dorstone within 5 minutes of Station. The accommodation represents Entrance Passage through to back, Tap Room with Bar, Sitting Room, Club Room, Spirit Store, Private Sitting Room, Kitchen with Baking Oven, and good Cellar having yard approach. Above are large Landing, 4 good Bedrooms, Bathroom, Box and Servants Bedrooms. In close proximity to the House are Dairy, 3-Stall Cart Stable and Coach House with Lofting over, 2 Piggeries with yards, Open Wainhouse, and Cowhouse for 3. There is an excellent supply of water to the premises, and the area, which includes a valuable though small Orchard, represents

0a. 2r. 36p. (or thereabouts).

For many years past this house has been in the occupation of Mr. G. Probert on yearly Candlemas taking at an arranged Rental as between Owner and Tenant.

The commuted Tithe Rent charges amount to 3s. 5d., and the Land Tax to 2s. 10d.

The 1919 sale of the Pandy Inn

148

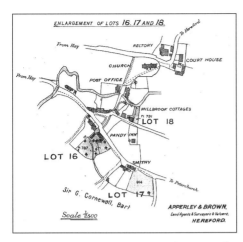

The map showing the Pandy grounds — lot 16 — in the 1919 sale

until his death in 1905; the following year his son George took the living in his turn. It is assumed that Colonel Powell of Hardwick was a member of the same family and that the **Pandy Inn** was inherited from him.

In 1919, what were described as the outlying portions of the Dorstone Estate were sold by auction. They were then in the possession of T.P.P. Powell, the older brother of George, described as a 'well-known barrister, who has been serving in the Army'. The **Pandy Inn** was 16th of the 18 lots, and the report in the *Hereford Times* stated that:

> There was some spirited bidding for the Pandy Inn, at Dorstone, a first offer of £500 rapidly rising to £1,300 in hundreds, when Mr. Pikes secured it, amid applause.

The purchaser was Ephraim Pikes, the wheelwright and carpenter at Penpound, Dorstone, and he ran the **Pandy Inn** for a short while, but it was said that 'It interfered with his business, and so he gave it up'. As well as being a wheelwright, he was also the village undertaker, and when he died in the later 1930s his grandson, Mr. Reg Dawe, was encouraged by local people to take over that side of the business. This he did — at the age of 17— and went on to found the well-known Hereford undertaking business of Dawe Brothers.

Tel.: PETERCHURCH 273

PANDY INN
(J. T. PAINTER)
DORSTONE — HEREFORDSHIRE

A 1960s advertisement for the Pandy Inn

The Pandy at Dorstone in 2005

In 1922 the licensee of the **Pandy Inn** was Robert McCann, who advertised 'good accommodation for commercial and cyclists; within five minutes of station; centre of village'. He owned the premises, having presumably bought them from Ephraim Pikes. On 16 June 1924 the licence was taken over by Richard Arthur Palethorpe, and Robert McCann moved on, later being at the **Red Lion Inn** at Bredwardine. The ownership of the **Pandy** also changed, as McCann sold it to Arnold, Perrett & Co. of Wickwar. However, in May 1925 it was sold on to the Cheltenham Original Brewery, and then in 1927 back to Arnold, Perrett & Co. by then with offices in Broad Street, Hereford. Meanwhile on 14 September 1925 the licence was taken over by Evan Evans who was at the **Pandy** until at least 1941.

At this period and later, one of the regulars was Leonard Lewis, who had served in the First World War and liked to wear his medals and sash as a member of the Royal and Ancient Order of Foresters at any celebration. He was also a good story-teller with a fine voice and, on coach trips and in the **Pandy Inn**, he and his brother would entertain with old soldiers' songs and songs of the day. He and his wife lived in one of the last houses in Dorstone to be modernised, even lacking electricity, and at the end without part of the roof. He died in 1985 at the age of 93.

A good description of the **Pandy Inn** was given by CAMRA in 1985:

> Marvellous 17th century timber-framed village inn, well worth a visit, consisting of one large but comfortable bar with a huge old fireplace which, in winter, had a large warm and welcoming wood fire ... The original inn on the site was said to have been built in 1185 by Richard le Breton, one of the four knights who killed Thomas a Becket in 1170. The inn was built to accommodate workers for a local cloth mill – Pandy being the name for a machine used in the mill.

In February 1999 the new owners of the **Pandy**, Paul and Marja Gardner, had an unusual house warming. On the day that they received their first licence they lit the fire for the first time but, because the chimney was in poor condition, the whole of the upstairs was filled with smoke and firefighters, one of whom was a regular at the pub, had to be called to deal with the blaze. Fortunately, not too much damage was done. Despite this rather warm welcome to the **Pandy**, the Gardners moved on in 2004.

The short-lived Pear Tree Inn, Dorstone

In the mid-19th century there were two other licensed premises in Dorstone parish. One was, not too surprisingly, attached to a blacksmith's shop. At this time there were two blacksmiths in Dorstone, one having a smithy on the west side of the minor road leading south to Hinton, while the other lived near the church in a cottage that is now part of Church House. It was formerly one of a pair of buildings called Penbont Cottages, belonging to the wife of Rev. T.P. Powell, and in 1895 the left-hand one was rebuilt as a reading room at her expense. The right-hand half included a smithy and it was here that the blacksmith, Thomas Lewis, ran the short-lived **Pear Tree Inn**, having only a single directory entry in 1867. The blacksmith's shop continued for many years and in 1906 was taken over by John Hendy. He had settled in the village after service in the South African War, and in that year married Sarah Moseley from the **Pandy Inn**. She was an orphan who had been taken in at the **Pandy** by her aunt, Mrs. Probert. John and Sarah Hendy settled in at Penbont Cottage, he working as the village blacksmith and both acting as Reading Room caretakers. The premises were bought by the Hendys about 1930, but they continued to allow the free use of the Reading Room. After the death of John Hendy in 1931 Sarah Hendy continued in the business, employing a number of blacksmiths for the practical side. She finally gave up the blacksmith's shop in 1943. The premises are still owned by a descendant.

On the north side of the village, at the junction of the village road and the main road, there is a minor road signposted to Mynnydd Brith. Folk memory in Dorstone recalls a drinking place there, although it has not yet been traced in any official records.

The head of the Golden Valley lies just to the north of Dorstone, and both the road and the former railway leave the valley at Bage or Bach, a mile or so north-west of Dorstone. This is thought to be the place called Becce, recorded in Domesday in 1086, when it was held by Gilbert, son of Thorold. Bryant's map of 1835 marks this area as Bridge End, while modern maps mark it as Bage. Here was the **Bridge (End) Inn**, which was also part of the Powell estate. Its use as a public house seems to date from 1824, when John Higgins took out the first of several annual alehouse keeper's recognizances. In 1841 60-year-old William Price was innkeeper of the **Bridge End Inn**, but by 1851 the licence was held by James Farr Higgins, presumably a relative of the earlier landlord. He was still there in the early 1860s after which he was succeeded by his widow. James Hammond, also a blacksmith, had taken over by 1867 and his widow,

---

An Excellent Small Holding

KNOWN AS

"BAGE BRIDGE"

situate in the Parish of Dorstone, about 1¾ miles from Dorstone Station and 4¼ from Hay, and on the main road Peterchurch to Hay.

The House contains Sitting Room, Kitchen, Back Kitchen, Dairy, Lean-to Scullery and Coal House, 4 Bedrooms and 2 good Attics. The Buildings comprise Cowhouse to tie 2, Barn with a further Cow House to tie 2 and Calves Cot with Loft over; Cart Stable for 2 with lean-to Chaff House at end; lean-to Fowl House and a range of 2 Piggeries. The foregoing together with the Land which is all very useful Pasture, extends to an area of

16a. 1r. 29p.

or thereabouts. There is a plentiful supply of water laid on to the House and Buildings which gravitates from a spring on the Lands.

The whole with the exception of No. 130, is in the occupation of Mr. William Tompkins on yearly Candlemas taking at the Annual Rent of

£25.

No. 130 is in the occupation of Mr. J. Owen Davies on yearly Candlemas taking at the apportioned Annual Rent of £5. The commuted Tithe Rent charges amount to £2 13s. 8d., and the Land Tax to 14s.

Sale of the Bridge End in 1919

The Bridge End in 2005

Ann, had succeeded him by the mid-1870s. By 1895 George Page had taken over and he was probably the last publican as the **Bridge End Inn** had closed by 1901.

The census of that year records that Felix Fencott, a 73-year-old market gardener was resident at the Bage Bridge. He had been a coachman to Rev. T.P. Powell, who owned the premises and who had put him in there rent free, dependent on him providing meals for travellers. This was another property that was auctioned on 17 September 1919. It included just over 16 acres of land and was described as 'An Excellent Small Holding'. It was tenanted by Mr. J. Owen Davies, but occupied by William Tomkins, who was a tailor. Owen Davies purchased the former Bridge End as sitting tenant before the sale. The building is now called Glenside.

From Bach the road carries on through Hardwick, formerly part of Clifford parish where, until recently, was the **Royal Oak** — a pub of some antiquity as it was marked on Bryant's 1835 map, but was probably post-1828. George Daniels, recorded as landlord in 1867, was still there at the beginning of the 20th century; he was also a brewer and farmer and in 1901 was 76 years old. The 1903 list of licensed premises shows that it was owned by a Miss F. Hall (*sic*) of Rock Villa, Winforton, and so George Daniels was a tenant. The owner then and into the late 1920s was actually one of the Misses Holl of Winforton.

William Ballinger was there just before the First World War, and was still there at the beginning of the second one when the inn had been dignified by being called the **Royal Oak Hotel**, although in the 1920s it was only licensed as a beer house. Members of the same family were there until the 1960s. In 1985 CAMRA described it as 'A well-kept 16th-century timber-framed pub set in beautiful countryside high above the Wye'.

On 18 May 2000 the *Hereford Times* reported that the **Royal Oak**, which was about to close and become an ordinary house instead of a public house, had been bought and was to remain licensed premises. Regretfully, this only lasted for about 12 months, after which it closed again, perhaps not too surprising considering its remote situation and lack of neighbouring houses. It has now been converted into a private house.

The Royal Oak is now a private house

About a mile past Hardwick, the B4348 joins the B4352 and a left turn along it continues to Hay-on-Wye. The area around this junction was marked on Bryant's map as Hardwick, but the centre has clearly shifted since then. Near the junction is the former **Unicorn** (chapter 11).

On the outskirts of Hay is the parish of Cusop, which adjoins Hay and is virtually indistinguishable from it. Just before crossing the Dulas Brook, the boundary between England and Wales, there is a left turn and just over a quarter of a mile up this road, on the right-hand side, is the former **Sun Inn**. This was probably one of the two establishments in Cusop for which alehouse keeper's recognizances were taken out in the 1820s. Joseph Prothero, there in 1841, was described as a simple publican, but John Howells, recorded in the 1851 census, was also a blacksmith.

An inquest took place at the **Sun Inn** on Wednesday 16 June 1850. Stephen Nicholls, a blacksmith of Talgarth, was found in a distressed state near Nant-y-glaster gate at about half-past four in the morning by Anne Kerriotts, whilst on her way to work at Hay. The gate-keeper could not help, so she summoned the police from Hay and the superintendent constable carried Nicholls to the gate-house and then to a cottage 150 yards away, where he soon expired. At the inquest Nicholls' father said that his son was at home at one o'clock on Sunday and then only had 2s. 6d. in his pocket. He heard afterwards that his son was in the Bridge-End in Talgarth with one Henry Prosser, and that they left that house at half-past ten that night for Hay, where he expected work. Both were said to be tipsy, and he knew his son was much addicted to drink. With the surgeon reporting nothing untoward, the jury was satisfied that Nicholls died from intoxication and exposure to weather, but the coroner admonished the gate-keeper for his conduct.

Later licensees also had mason's businesses. The first directory entry was in 1856 when George Price, mason, was there and stayed until the early 1890s. John Pugh then took over for a while, but by 1900 George Watkins, a monumental sculptor and mason, was there and the 1903 printed list shows that he was the owner. The last time the **Sun Inn** appeared in a directory was in 1905 and it had closed by 1909. It is now called, rather appropriately, Rising Sun Cottage.

CHAPTER TEN

Hereford to Bredwardine

Belmont Abbey is on the west side of the main A465 road, about two miles south of Hereford; the B4352 is a right-hand turn just after the abbey. This is locally described as the back road to Hay-on-Wye but, during the 19th century and no doubt earlier as well, this was one of the routes used by the drovers bringing Welsh cattle to the English markets, long before that trade ceased with the widespread introduction of the railways. This particular drovers' route came from the collecting point at Lampeter, through Llandovery to Trecastle, then on to Talgarth and through Hay and Bredwardine to Hereford.

The Seven Stars
(Photo: Derek Foxton collection)

The centre of Clehonger is to the south of the B4352, about a mile after turning off the main road. For most of the first part of the 20th century this was home for the cider manufactory of Ridler and Son Ltd., based at Clehonger Manor Farm. The business started in the early 20th century and after the Second World War it became Evans and Ridler Ltd., finally closing in 1950. There were no licenced premises down here, the only pub in the parish being a little further along the B4352 at Gorsty Common. This is

Above: The Seven Stars in 2005
Left: The unusual sign

the **Seven Stars**, the first directory reference being in 1851 when James Berrow was landlord; he, and later his widow, held the licence for more than 25 years. At the beginning of the 20th century William Ariss was licensee for a few years and in 1902 he advertised that he was 'agent for Arnold, Perrett & Co's Gold Medal Ales & Stout'. The position of the pub on the roadside has no doubt helped in its survival, and it now boasts a sign indicating that it is the home for the Seven Stars and Golden Valley Petanque Club.

Eaton Bishop is the next parish, and is signposted off to the right at Honeymoor Common, the sign encouraging the visitor to see the 14th-century stained glass in the parish church. It is said that a man called John Ruck, who once lived on Honeymoor Common, wrote his own epitaph before he died:

Who lies here? Who d'you think?
Old John Ruck – gie 'im a drink.
Gie a drink to a dead man?
Ah, and I'll tell you the reason why,
For when I was alive, I was always dry.

Beyond Honeymoor Common is the centre of the village, laid out around the parish church and churchyard. An early reference to drink in the parish is in 1716 when the churchwardens' accounts record a payment of 2s. 6d. to Stephen Payne jun. for drink for the ringers on 5 November. The road through the village wanders gently to Lower Eaton, and down a small road to the right is a large house which, due to its recent history, more-or-less qualifies for inclusion in this book. This property was bought in 1866 by Joseph – later Sir Joseph – Pulley, who set about enlarging it, and the 1887 O.S. map shows that it was lit by gas, for there was a gasometer near the river. It was inherited by Sir Joseph's nephew, Charles Pulley, in 1901 and he ran it as a luxurious country residence, but after his death in 1947 the contents were sold and the property was bought by Mrs. Daisy Bishop. She modernised the building and opened it as the Mansion Hotel, but was unsuccessful in gaining a drinks licence and a few years later the building was sold again, to be divided into three residences.

At Lower Eaton there was a ferry across the Wye, to the manor of Sugwas which was formerly part of the parish of Eaton Bishop. From remote times this was a private ferry for the benefit of the Lords of the Manor of Sugwas, and in a lease of 1533 it was valued at 6s. per annum. As there was often an inn by the side of a ford or ferry, it comes as no surprise that on the Sugwas side of the river there was a licensed house called the **Sugwas Boat**, which may well have been of considerable antiquity.

The Boat Inn, on the north side of the Wye at Stretton Sugwas
(Photo: Derek Foxton collection)

157

The fading sign for the Boat Inn in 1999

The list of persons taking out alehouse keeper's recognizances in the period 1818 to 1828 includes Joseph Be(a)van of the parish of Eaton Bishop, and in 1818 he was stated to be at the **Sugwas Boat**. The inn was sometimes called the **Boat House** or just the **Boat**. In 1861 it was being run by Richard Morris who, as well as being an innkeeper, was also described as a hat manufacturer; by 1867 he was also a shopkeeper. This part of Eaton Bishop parish was transferred to the parish of Stretton Sugwas under the Divided Parishes Act of 1884 and subsequent directory entries for the **Boat** come under that parish. Jakeman and Carver's *Directory* of 1902 refers to it as the **Sugwas Boat Inn** and the 1903 list of licensed premises shows that it was then owned by His Honour Judge James T. Ingham. He lived at Sugwas Court and for more than 30 years he used the ferry to cross the river to attend services at Eaton Bishop church, never missing no matter how high the level of the water. The **Sugwas Boat** was still recorded in Kelly's *Directory* of 1941, but it finally closed in 1948.

At Breinton Manor lived George Marshall, the noted local antiquarian, and he made a passing reference to the **Boat Inn** in the *Transactions* of the Woolhope Club in 1947:

> A few years ago my attention was drawn to a heap of stones on the left bank of the river Wye about half a mile above the 'Boat Inn' at Sugwas. They had been put there to act as a breakwater to the save the bank from being cut away. The stones had been set roughly in cement in any order and upon examination proved to be a wheel-stone and sections of the troughs of several cider mills. On enquiry I could trace the stones as having been placed there about the year 1860. It is impossible at present to say the number of pieces of cider mills of which the heap is composed, many being submerged in the water or underground in the bank, but they evidently formed the unfinished troughs of at least three or four. This is proved by the ends of the troughs never having been cut out but left in this unfinished state to save damage in transit.

The stones probably came by a river barge and most likely were wrecked on the journey. No doubt this was the usual condition in which they were delivered from the place where they were quarried, the solid ends dividing the troughs being cut away after the stones had been placed in position for use. I do not think that this has been noted before.

However, the river Wye is the strict northern limit for this book and the excursion to the opposite bank is purely for historical purposes as the present parish lies only on the south side of the river. Over the years there were several establishments on Ruckhall Common, north-east of Eaton Bishop centre. In 1851 William Silvester, a tailor, was supplementing his income by selling cider. His widow Elizabeth had taken over this un-named cider house by the late 1850s, and she continued with the business until at least the early 1860s.

The 1861 census shows that Charles Perfrement, who had been born in Kent, also lived on Ruckhall Common and that he was a bookseller. This was a change in career as he had previously been a silversmith. Clearly there was little demand for books and for silver on Ruckhall Common, and by 1867 Perfrement had become a cider retailer, and then later a beer retailer. The 1871 census shows that his establishment was called the **Apple Tree Inn**. After his death in 1885 at the age of 81, the inn was taken over by Benjamin Morris, described in 1891 as an innkeeper and boot maker. The 1901 census records the name as the **Pine Apple Inn**, and indicates that Morris had become the assistant overseer for the parish. However, this new name may have been a mistake on the part of the enumerator as the 1903 list of licensed premises still records it as the **Apple Tree**. Ben Morris is said to have been something of a character who collected copies of the *Hereford Times* and sold them as far afield as Stoke Edith. Sometime he hawked fish around as well; any left-over stock being fried up for his customers at the **Apple Tree**! His name appears in directories for a few more years and then disappears, and it is assumed that the **Apple Tree** closed at that time. There is at present no certain evidence about the location of the **Apple Tree**, but it has been suggested that it was close to the present house called Green Briar. To complete the story, after the death of Charles Perfrement it seems that his widow and two of his sons moved from the **Apple Tree** to another cottage on Ruckhall Common, and that Tom Perfrement continued to sell cider there for a few years. They were still living there in 1901, when Mrs. Perfrement was 92 years of age. However, the cottage where they then lived has since been demolished and a new house called Beth Car built on the site.

The best-known licensed establishment on Ruckhall Common is the **Camp Inn**, now called the **Ancient Camp Inn**, well hidden down very minor roads and only to be found with a map. It is in a prominent position

The Ancient Camp Inn in 2005

overlooking the Wye, close to Eaton Camp and was built about 1837, originally as a shop, then a forge and, in the 1880s, when it was held by James Holder, it became a licensed beer and cider house. The 1891 census records him as a blacksmith, which must have been his main occupation. Like most of the working people in Eaton Bishop, James Holder had a donkey, and these animals were sometimes named after their master's trade. Thus the postman's donkey was called Letter Bag, while James Holder's donkey was called Beer Barrel! The name James Holder also occurs in an advertisement of 29 December 1894 which states that:

> The annual pigeon match will take place on Tuesday 1st January 1895 when a fat pig will be shot for. Pigeons in trap 11.30 sharp. Dinner 2s. each. James Holder, landlord.

In 1898 the premises were bought by Arnold, Perrett & Co. who also owned the **Apple Tree**. It was about this time that Walter Manning from Somerset became the licensee. However, by 1902 William Eyles had taken over and he held the licence until at least the beginning of the First World War. During this period there were many more visitors to Eaton Bishop than

160

might have been thought. At weekends during the summer many Hereford people would walk out along the north river bank, and cross the river either by the ferry or punt to the **Camp Inn**, where they could have ham and egg teas, or picnic by the river.

The situation of the **Camp Inn** was well described in the *Transactions* of the Woolhope Club in 1922:

> Below Sugwas 'Island', a short distance, at Bogwell Pool, formed by a weir of stones, there was formerly a ford, not now in use. Commanding these crossings, on the right or south bank, there are the remains of a large entrenched fortress of British origin, with ditch and rampart, known as Eaton Camp. The 'Camp Inn' (well known to the rivermen as 'Betty Phillips') is on the site, and perpetuates the old-time facts. Cannon ball and iron bullets have been turned up by the plough on the adjacent farm, indicating fighting in the past, possibly during the Commonwealth wars.

It is stated that Betty Phillips was the licensee for many years, but as her name does not occur in trade directories she may have been just a barmaid.

At the beginning of 1998 the **Ancient Camp Inn** was taken over by a husband and wife team, and he used his skills as a chef in an effort to develop both the cuisine and the accommodation. However, this did not last and there was a very real risk that this well-known establishment would close. Fortunately, at the beginning of 2004 the pub changed hands again and the catering side of the business has now become predominant, with a bistro-style restaurant, and accommodation. Visitors will note on the front of the bar various levels, stated to be the flood levels of the river Wye in the years given. In view of the elevated position of the **Ancient Camp** above the river, if you believe that you will believe anything!

Returning to the main road and continuing towards Hay, at Woodyatt's Cross, the crossroads just before Madley, is the **Comet Inn**. The sign depicts a man gazing at a comet, but there was a time in the 1950s when it showed the ill-fated Comet airliner. This inn was established some time after 1828, and probably came about after the 1830 Act. The *Hereford Journal* of 22 July 1846 reported that the Good Intent Lodge of Odd Fellows (Manchester Unity) held its second anniversary meeting at the **Comet Inn**, Madley, on 16 July and that 'nearly fifty brothers and friends sat down to dinner, and justly deserved encomiums were passed on the catering of host Merrick'. The evening was enlivened by Mr. Robbob's brass band.

The **Comet Inn** first appears in a trade directory in 1850 as the **Corner Inn**, and in the following year as the **Cornett** — probably both mistakes as subsequent entries all refer to the **Comet** — and Thomas Merrick, who was already in charge in 1846, was still there more than 20 years later. The 1861 census indicates that he was a local man from Kingstone, then aged 64,

The Comet Inn in 1999

and that he was a victualler and carpenter. His services as a wood-turner and cabinet-maker were advertised, and this may have been his main line of business.

In the late 19th century the **Comet Inn** was the centre of some lively activity. One Sunday in May or June the members of the Ancient Order of Foresters from surrounding parishes attended service in Madley church and then went to a field near the **Comet Inn** where sports were held, generally ending up with a bit of a fight!

By 1904 Solomon Porter was landlord, and his widow Rosa was still there in 1941. But of course, things move on, and when the **Comet Inn** was offered for sale in May 2005, it was priced at £375,000. The publicity material pointed out that the **Comet** had more than 1½ acres of land, and that it also offered two separate units of owners' accommodation, perhaps appealing to a family partnership.

Woodyatt's Cross is where the B4352 cuts across Stone Street, the line of a Roman road that once joined Kenchester (*Magnis*) to Abbey Dore and Abergavenny. A detour to the south-west along this Roman road brings the traveller to the former Madley airfield. This was established in 1941 as a training base, but was decommissioned not long after the end of the war. In 1978, 110 acres at Street House Farm was purchased by the Post Office to establish a satellite communications centre (now part of B.T.) and, by 1980 several dishes had been built at a cost of £12 million. These are visible for miles around, the largest being 120 ft. high and 102 ft. in diameter.

Madley is a short distance along the B4352 from the **Comet**, where the **Red Lion** continues to serve travellers as it has done since the 18th century, and perhaps before. In 1931 the Royal Commission described it as a timber-framed building 'of T-shaped plan with the cross-wing at the

W. end. The front had been refaced in brick, but the timber-framing is exposed

Collected in style from the Red Lion at Madley
(Photo: Derek Foxton collection)

on the W. and on part of the N. sides'.

An early reference to its use as a public house is in an advertisement in the *Hereford Journal* of 11 August 1774:

> Whereas JOHN FARR, of the parish of Kington, waggoner and hauler, lately left at the house of John Payn, the Red Lion, in the parish of Madley, in this county, where he boarded and lodged, divers horse-geers (*sic*) and chains, not having satisfied the said John Payn, for his board and lodging, &c. this is to give notice, that if he does not claim the above articles within three weeks, from the date hereof, they will be publicly sold for the benefit of his said landlord.

In the 18th century the **Red Lion** was a centre of 'sporting' activity, and on 15 June 1775 the *Hereford Journal* advertised that a Main of Cocks would be held there. John Marsh, a later landlord of the **Red Lion** who died in 1793, took up boxing and this is referred to in a verse inscribed on his tombstone in the churchyard, which is still just about visible.

> Famed little John a terror to many a boxing blade,
> But now alas an insult brooks from sexton's dirty spade,
> For coward death waiting the time till Jack was weak and low,
> The moment seized and spite of art put in his favourite blow.

In the 1820s the licensee was Philip Lewis, but by 1851 the census refers to the pub as the **Lion** and records that John Powell, then aged 28, was a farmer as well as an innkeeper. He must have been busy for he farmed no less than 60 acres and employed two men. Mrs. Catherine Preece, there in the late 1860s and most of the '70s, was also described as a farmer. By 1879 William Pritchard had taken over, and he also followed in the farming tradition. All these were tenant licensees, as the 1903 list shows that William Pritchard's landlord was C.B. Lee Warner Esq. of Tyberton. By 1905 Henry Pritchard, William's son, had taken over and he was still there at the outbreak of the First World War.

A 1960s advertisement

One well-travelled local who visited the pub in 1957, brought a python skin with him, and the story that a man had lost his life in trying to wrestle the python! The skin was displayed in the bar for many years.

As with most country pubs, the **Red Lion** has had to change with time from a simple pub to a place where food is a main attraction. This is shown by publicity material that appeared in the *Hereford Times* of 15 March 2001, which stated that the heart of the pub was the non-smoking restaurant, and that the business had expanded by the conversion of a next door granary into residential accommodation. Fortunately however, the building in general and the bar in particular have not been spoilt. The bar still retains its flagstone floor and would be immediately recognisable to the customers and publicans of a hundred years ago.

The Red Lion at Madley in 2005

Not surprisingly for a rural area, there were one or two cider retailers in the parish of Madley. A directory of 1851 records the name of Wm. Thomas, a tailor, cider retailer and shopkeeper. He was recorded in the census of the same year, which shows that he was aged 38, that he had been born locally in Blakemere, and that he was resident at **Castlebury**. This establishment was taken over by Thomas Cross, recorded in another directory of 1858 as a cider retailer and shoemaker. The surviving licensing records give Harriet Cross as the licensee of a beer house called the **Castlebury** in 1872; it was last licensed in 1875, but so far it has not been possible to locate this establishment.

A couple of miles past Madley, a road off to the right leads to Ploughfields Green and Preston-on-Wye. The former has a long history, for the 13th-century accounts of the Chapter Estates of Hereford Cathedral describe it as a borough and it had a bailiff, market and fairs. However, the only outward sign is the few houses around the triangular green which must have been the market place for a town that never grew. Here is the **Yew Tree**, which has a history dating back about a hundred years. However, it had a predecessor. On 4 January 1781 an advertisement in the *Hereford Journal* stated that the public house at 'Plowfields' Green in the parish of Preston-on-Wye was to be sold. In January 1791, another advertisement said that a messuage was to be sold by auction 'at the dwelling-house of Mr. James Mathews, Innholder, at Ploughfields-green, in the parish of Preston-on-Wye…'. James Matthews was still there in the early 1820s, but by 1828 he had been succeeded by Mary Matthews, perhaps his wife or widow.

The Yew Tree at Preston-on-Wye having a face lift in 2005

In 1841 the census recorded that Richard Matthews, aged 45, was at the **Board Inn**, and that he was a butcher. It has been suggested that this curious name refers to the mould-board on a plough. A directory of 1851 records Eleanor, yet another member of the Matthews family, as being a beer retailer in Preston-on-Wye at an un-named beerhouse. However, in 1862 William Prosser was described as an innkeeper in Preston-on-Wye, a directory of 1867 recording that he was at the '**Boar' Inn**. In 1871 he was 59, a publican and a labourer, who had been born locally in Kingstone. By 1876 he had changed the name of the inn to the **Preston Arms**, but by 1879 it had been changed back to the **Board Inn**, no doubt by George Preece who had taken over from him. In 1881 Preece, who had been born in the village and was then aged 42, acted as a haulier as well as a publican. The **Board Inn** is clearly marked on the 1890/1 O.S. map as being on a site behind the present **Yew Tree**. Locally it was known as the **Old Thatched House**, a name descriptive of the premises for old photographs show a half-timbered house that was more than half thatched. James Lewis, landlord from at least 1891, reverted to the old (mis)spelling of **Boar** by 1902, when he advertised that he was an agent for Arnold, Perrett, & Co.'s Gold Medal Ales & Stout.

The **Board Inn** was still marked on the 1904 edition of the O.S. map, but it was subsequently damaged by fire and, by 1909, the **Yew Tree** had made its appearance and the **Board Inn** disappeared from the record. This no doubt marked the transfer of the licence to the present premises, which were converted from a pair of cottages. The **Yew Tree** has been updated to some extent over the last 19 years, but still retains its atmosphere and acts as a centre for the village. The rolling programme of repairs has yet to be completed. The licensee also provides food as a service, but it is not a trendy 'foodie' place, and in 2005 only opened in the evenings.

As for the **Board Inn**, its remains were still visible in the 1960s and about ten or fifteen years ago, when the site was being developed, foundations of the old pub were discovered, but are now lost under Old Thatch Close.

Just past the turn leading to Preston-on-Wye, the main road makes a sharp right-hand bend, where a side road leads ahead towards Peterchurch. This minor road, which is the most direct route from Hereford to Peterchurch, is mentioned in a draft Bill for repairing roads around the city which was presented to Parliament. It includes the road 'from the said City to a Place called *Stockley-Hill*, in [the] Parish of *Peter Church*, (which are the great Roads leading into South *Wales*) being about eight Miles or thereabouts'. The Bill received Royal Assent in 1726, but the final form omitted the reference to Stockley Hill, and it seems that the more southern route through Vowchurch was adopted. In view of the severe gradient over Stockley Hill this would seem more prudent, and so this minor route carried only local traffic. Walking up this hill would have been thirsty work and just before the summit was a small beer house where the weary traveller could quench his thirst. This was the **Mason's Arms** which first appears in a directory in 1863; the landlord, William Pritchard, was also a carpenter. He was succeeded by William Morgan and then, in 1883, Robert Ireland took over, promptly changing the name to the **Brydges Arms**. In 1903, the printed list records that, while Robert Ireland was still the licensee, the building was owned by C.B. Lee-Warner Esq. of Tyberton Court. Robert Ireland was still licensee in 1905 but by 1909 the **Brydges Arms** had closed. The building was recorded by the Royal Commission in 1931, when it was described as timber-framed and of the 17th century. The condition of the building was then said to be poor, but it has since been renovated and extended and is called Barn Cottage.

Returning to the B4352, Tyberton is the next parish, but there does not seem to have been another licensed establishment there, the **Brydges Arms** being the only one within the parish — and that only just! Tyberton Court was formerly the home of the Brydges family, who had the church rebuilt in 1720, and the **Brydges Arms** was named after them.

After Tyberton is Blakemere, where there was a licensed premises called the **Plough**. This was on the right-hand side of the road, about a quarter of a mile before the church, and the building is still called by that name. On 11 September 1820 the *Hereford Journal* carried an advertisement for some land that was to be sold by auction at the **Plough**. At the time this was being run by Philip Bethell, and he was succeeded in the middle 1820s by Sarah Bethell. The **Plough** was of sufficient note for Bryant to mark it on his map of 1835. It continued in the hands of the Bethell family through the 1850s and '60s, but in 1867 William Reece was recorded as running an inn called the **Raven** in Blakemere. The 1871 census records that 62-year-old Joseph Sanders was at the **Raven** and states that he had retired from farming, but makes no mention of the licensed trade nor does it record the **Plough**, suggesting a name change. The **Raven** then disappears, and the **Plough** reappears again in a

Two long-lost pubs.
Left: The Brydges Inn at Tyberton   Right: The Plough at Blakemere

Once the Daw Inn at Moccas

directory of 1876 only to close shortly after. Curiously, a plough from this establishment was deposited in Hereford museum in 1972, and it would have been nice to think that this was the plough which gave the public house its name; unfortunately it dates from *c.*1900, long after the pub had closed.

Although there are few houses in Blakemere, there are even fewer in Moccas, the next settlement to the west, but there was still enough support for a licensed house called the **Daw Inn**. The road to Woodbury is to the left at the crossroads in Moccas, and the **Daw Inn** was on the crossroads, with the entrance facing the Woodbury road and the smithy on the main road. It was certainly run for the period 1818 to 1828 by John Price and possibly longer. In the 1858 directory the blacksmith in Moccas was Josiah Price; he was succeeded by William Price, who ran the **Daw Inn** as well as the smithy. In 1871 William Price was aged 38 and, as he had been born in Moccas, he was probably of the same family. By 1881 he had been succeeded by Benjamin Rudge, rather younger at 27, although he had an apprentice blacksmith to work with him. James Moreton, landlord in 1891, seems to have been the person who let the licence lapse, as the pub had closed by 1896. In 1902 James Moreton, blacksmith and farmer, was at the Daw and Woodbury farms, and although the name remained, there was no suggestion that the Daw was still licensed.

Less than half a mile past the crossroads, on the left-hand side, is Moccas deer park. This dates from mediaeval times, and is now a Site of Special Scientific Interest. The oak trees are of particular notice, and were commented on by the Rev. Francis Kilvert, vicar of Bredwardine from November 1877 until his untimely death in September 1879:

> I fear those grey old men of Moccas, those grey, gnarled, low-browed, knock-kneed, bowed, bent, huge, strange, long-armed, deformed, hunchbacked, mis-shapen oak men that stand waiting century after century ... No human hand set those oaks. They are 'the trees which the Lord hath planted'. They look as if they had been at the beginning and making of the world, and they will probably see its end.

CHAPTER ELEVEN

Bredwardine to Hay

Bredwardine is at a junction of roads with the B4352 continuing towards Hay and a north-eastern minor road, crossing the river Wye by a fine, red-brick bridge, leading towards Letton and Staunton-on-Wye on the main A438 Hereford to Kington and Brecon road. Two other minor roads lead westwards from the village over a steep hill to Dorstone and the Golden Valley. Bredwardine was the home of the Rev. Francis Kilvert, best known for his diary, a number of extracts from which have already been quoted. The church where he ministered is near the road leading to the bridge and in a prominent position above the river. The bridge was built in 1769 and was the only one above

Bredwardine Bridge toll cottage 2005

Hereford to survive the great flood of February 1795. On the near bank is a toll cottage, built in 1817, at one time let to the Hay Union for £40 per annum. Part of the income from the tolls was used for the upkeep and repair of the structure but, after tolls were abolished in the late 1870s, no repairs were carried out until 1920-1. By this time the bridge was in poor condition, and to put it in good order cost £4,124 9s.

On the far bank, at the Brobury end of the bridge, was a small beer house called the **Trap**, which was run in 1867 by Thomas Parsons. He is mentioned in Kilvert's *Diary* on 2 September 1878 — Kilvert had crossed the bridge to go to Brobury, a parish which was annexed to Bredwardine, and on his return noted:

> At the Trap end of the bridge some men were sitting and leaning over the bridge parapet while old Parsons brought up a stirrup cup to a horseman who had drawn reign there.

A visit, said to have taken place in the winter of 1880 or 1881, was recorded in the *Transactions* of the Woolhope Club in 1914:

> There was a small inn at the north end of Bredwardine Bridge, and an old woman named Parsons who lived there showed me a mark on the wall of her room where the flood of 1795 came up to, and which she stated was higher than that of 1852.

The 1881 census records that Thomas Parsons was still at the **Trap Inn**, that he was aged 76 and had been born in the parish. Keeping house for him was his widowed sister, Mary Evans, and it was probably her that was referred to above. The inn closed some time before 1885, and was subsequently demolished.

The **Red Lion** is a splendid building facing the road from the bridge and in 1931 was described by the Royal Commission as being:

> of two storeys with attics. The front walls are of red brick on a stone plinth and the other walls are of rubble; the roof is covered with stone slabs. It was built probably early in the 18th century. The N.E. front has a projecting band at the first-floor level and a dentilled brick cornice, above which rises a central gablet pierced by a round-headed window and flanked by two hipped dormers. The windows have plain keystones and are divided into two or three lights with oak mullions and transoms; two have been filled with later sashes. Inside the building some of the rooms have exposed ceiling-beams.

The size of the **Red Lion** is due to its one-time position on the main road from Hereford to Brecon. Paterson's road book of the early 19th century (p. 254) shows that the main route from Hereford went through Whitecross and out

All ready for an excursion from the Red Lion
(Photo: Derek Foxton collection)

A peaceful country scene outside the Red Lion at Bredwardine
(Photo: Derek Foxton collection)

past Portway, then rose over Tin Hill and across Bredwardine bridge, past the **Red Lion** and on to Hay. The road book records that Bredwardine was 148³/₄ miles from Tyburn Turnpike in London (now Marble Arch). However, before the construction of the bridge in 1769 the road would not have been so easy, as there was previously only a ferry, owned by Velters Cornewall of Moccas.

Bredwardine bridge was constructed under an Act of 1759, with the long title of: *An Act for repairing the Roads from the Town of Brecon to the Parish of Brobury and to Whitney Passage in the County of Hereford, and for building a Bridge over the River Wye at Bredwardine Passage in the same County.* The first meeting of the trustees for the turnpike — there was a separate set of trustees for the bridge — took place on 1 July 1760 'at the House known by the Sign of the **Three Horse-Shoes**, now kept by Richard Hancock in Bredwardine aforesaid …'. This suggests either that the present **Red Lion** had a predecessor elsewhere in the village or, more likely, that it was previously known as the **Three Horse Shoes**. If this was the case, the name was soon changed. The **Red Lion** was part of the Moccas Estate and a fine atlas of maps of the estate, with the accompanying terrier, made in 1772, shows that it was then tenanted by Henry Maddox. It was not

171

mentioned by name, being only described as a 'House, Yard &c.', although it was licensed at the time. Maddox also rented an adjoining patch of ground.

In the late 18th century the **Red Lion** was occasionally mentioned in newspaper advertisements. The *Hereford Journal* of 11 October 1771 mentions three cyder hogsheads that had been left at the inn, while notice of timber to be sold by auction at the **Red Lion** was given in an advertisement on 16 March 1791. At that time timber was hauled to the banks of the river Wye and was then floated down-river in large rafts.

In 1815 the **Red Lion** was taken over by Joseph Powell, who advertised his local connections in the *Hereford Journal* of 8 March 1815:

RED LION, BREDWARDINE BRIDGE.
TO GENTLEMEN TRAVELLERS & OTHERS
JOSEPH POWELL, (late servant in Sir George Cornewall's Family for
near Twenty Years), begs leave to inform Gentlemen Travellers from
Hereford to South Wales, and the Public in general, that he has taken
the above Inn, and laid in a good Stock of choice liquors, &c. with good
Accommodation and excellent Stables. Will endeavour to merit the
Approbation of a Generous Public. – Bredwardine, Feb. 21, 1815.

The social scene was not neglected by Joseph Powell, with regular balls, such as that advertised in the *Hereford Journal* of 7 April 1819:

RED LION INN, BREDWARDINE
JOSEPH POWELL,
Begs leave to inform his Friends, that his next BALL is fixed for
Tuesday, April the Thirteenth.
Tickets, Tea, Coffee and Music included, 5*s.*

Bredwardine also features in surviving accounts of 19th-century drovers, and it was no doubt at the **Red Lion** that they obtained their refreshment, liquid and otherwise. A triangular piece of ground opposite the toll house by the bridge was formerly a pound for cattle and sheep, and those using it paid for the use at the toll house. No doubt it was mainly used by the drovers, who were good business for such places, and licensees would take every advantage. Thus on 17 October 1831 John Watkins advertised in the *Hereford Journal* that he had opened a public house called the Oak Inn at Mansel Lacy 'as an INN and BAITING-HOUSE, for Gentlemen, Travellers, and Drovers'. This was on a drovers' route on the opposite side of the river Wye, but the **Red Lion** at Bredwardine would have benefited in a similar way. Indeed, it was a landmark on the route, and as such was marked on Bryant's map of 1835.

The 1867 directory records that the Petty Sessions were held at the **Red Lion** on the first Friday in every month, and that the inn was the base for the

The Red Lion in 1961
(Photo: Derek Foxton collection)

carrier to Hereford every Wednesday and Saturday. Trade directories also record that, from at least the middle of the 19th century to the beginning of the 20th century, several of the landlords of the **Red Lion** supplemented their income with farming.

The **Red Lion** — usually referred to as the **Lion** — features in the Kilvert Diaries after his appointment as vicar of Bredwardine in 1877. On 23 August 1878 he recorded an amusing story:

> Dinner with Dora at the Cottage at 7.30 to meet the Pooles and Mr. Bewton and passed a pleasant evening. I saw Sophy Poole to the Lion as we went home. It was very dark and neither of us could see the door and in groping along the wall for it I put my head through a pane of the bar window with a crash. What a story could be made out of this circumstantial evidence. The clergyman of the parish having dined is seen walking about in the dark with a young lady. He then goes to the public house and breaks the bar window.

Other entries about the **Red Lion** in the diaries show how it was the centre of village life. Thus, on Wednesday 18 September 1878, Kilvert recorded that an inquest was held at the **Lion** on the body of John Davies, who fell dead out of an apple tree on Monday evening; he had apparently died of heart disease. On 18 November 1878 Kilvert was laid up and spent all the day on a sofa in his library, reading. Parochial duties were not forgotten, however, and he noted:

> I sent Mrs. Wall three bunches of white muscat grapes from the Vicarage vinery for the Ploughing Match dinner at the Lion tomorrow.

On 10 December he visited the **Lion**.

> At 11 a.m. according to notice received I went to the Lion to attend a
> meeting of the Trustees of Bredwardine Bridge, I having lately been made
> a Trustee. Mr. Giles was there too. We waited an hour and then went
> away. After noon Sir George and Lady Cornewall called and then went to
> the Cottage. Sir George and I went to the Bridge meeting at 3 o'clock. No
> other Trustees came. Charles Griffiths put up the Bridge at £20 by 3-
> minute sand glass. Powell, James Davies of Fine St., and Mrs. Powell bid
> up to £25. Then Charles Griffiths bid £34 for the Trustees. Powell gave a
> deep sigh and bid £35. The last grains of the sand ran out and it was
> knocked down to him.

On 23 January 1879 he recorded that he 'went to the Lion to make
enquiries of Mrs. Wall about the scandal there. She was in great trouble
and perplexity'. The following day he recorded that he 'expelled William
--- from the Church Choir on account of the scandal at the Lion', tactfully
omitting the surname. The scandal was not reported in the *Hereford Times*
and seems to have been of a domestic nature.

Margaret Hall's name as licensee first appears in a directory in 1875,
that of Edmund Wall in 1876, and then Margaret Powell's name from 1879
until 1891. The 1903 list records that the
Red Lion was still part of the Moccas
Estate, being owned by the Rev. Sir
George Cornewall, Bart., when William
Hughes was licensee. By 1905 Joseph
Wilson had taken over, and surviving
licensing records covering the period
1923 to 1928 show that it had been
inherited by Sir Geoffrey Cornewall,
Bart., and that Robert McCann had taken
over the licence on 14 March 1927. He
may well have been the person of the
same name who had been at the **Pandy
Inn** at Dorstone a few years earlier. He
was still at the **Red Lion** in 1941.

An advertisement in 1964 shows that
there were five letting rooms, with bed
and breakfast at 18s. 6d., lunch from 3s.
6d. and dinner at 8s. 6d.

Renovation work in the late 1980s
was recorded in an advertisement in the
Hereford Times of 17 May 1990:

Telephone : Moccas 286

RED LION INN

BREDWARDINE

HEREFORDSHIRE

Red Lion, Bredwardine.

Board Residence
Bed and Breakfast
Picnic Lunches
Evening Meals

———

*Approx. one mile Salmon and Trout Fishing on
River Wye*

———

Proprietress : Mrs D. PAYNE

*A 1960s advertisement for
the Red Lion*

The Red Lion in 2005

> Michael and Lyn Taylor have kept the Red Lion for eight years now, and have been steadily making it into a nicer and nicer place to visit. Their task is almost complete. For their most recent accomplishment has been the refitting of the old Bredwardine Court Room, now called the Leaper's Bar. It is, after all, still a fishing inn, with its own waters along the Wye. There is some beautiful panelling and soft carpeting to complement the old building which dates back to around 1700.

The advertisement goes on to say that there were by then ten bedrooms to let, each with those essential modern requirements, colour television and en suite bathroom facilities.

Now, as with most progressive businesses, the Red Lion has its own web-site, although the claim that the court-room was where the judge of assizes sat must be treated with some scepticism!

From Bredwardine the road towards Hay gradually swings around Bredwardine Hill and Merbach Hill, with the wide flood plain of the River Wye on the right. The little settlement of Merbach, comprising two or three houses, was no doubt the location of the **Marbach Inn**, the first record of which is in the 1861 census, which records that Henry Hopton, of Meerbach Cottage, was an innkeeper. He was not local, having been born in Slimbridge, Gloucestershire. The only other mention of the **Marbach Inn** is in a trade directory of 1875, when James Meredith was in charge, and then nothing more.

On a sharp bend about a mile further on is the **Castlefield Inn**, in the area called Middlewood. Inns are commonly found near bridges, fords and ferries over a river, and this may well be the reason for the existence of this one, for the Clock Mill Ford is nearby, with a right-of-way path from Winforton on the other side of the river. A boat to cross the river was formerly available here and, in 1922, it was stated that the tenant of Clock Mill Farm had charge of the ferry. Although it may be of earlier origin, the first reference to the **Castlefield** is in the 1871 census when it was recorded that George Watkins of the **Castle Field Inn** was then aged 23, had been born in Staunton-on-Wye, and earned his living as an innkeeper and shoemaker. The 1903 printed list records that he was still licensee and that he owned the premises. By 1909 his son Frederick Watkins had taken over and he was still there in 1917. In 1923 the licensee and owner was George R.J. West, but when he renewed his licence in February 1924 the owner was stated to be William Frederick Lowe, who lived on the premises and took over the licence himself on 16 June 1924. Lowe had a brush with the law in 1925, for on 9 March he was fined £5 including costs for supplying intoxicating liquor other than during permitted hours. When he bought the property he had a mortgage with the National Provincial Bank and when he ran into financial difficulties he sold the pub

The Castlefield in 2003

to the Alton Court Brewery of Ross for £750 on 31 March 1926. The agreement was that this money would be paid direct to the National Provincial Bank to discharge the debt owing, so that Mr. Lowe ended up with nothing. On the same day that the completion of the sale took place, the licence was transferred to William Williams.

On 26 February 1960 the **Castlefield** was sold by the Alton Court Brewery to Ralph Clifford Edwards for £2,000 and he also entered into a covenant with the brewery to take his supplies from them for the next three years. The legal work was made more complicated by the fact that a small patch of ground across the road, which was included in the sale, actually belonged to the Stroud Brewery Company, and so there were two separate conveyances. The correspondence includes a statement of the sales for the year 1959. These were 25 barrels of beer, 225 dozen bottles of beer, 27 bottles of wines and spirits, 5^1/$_2$ gallons and 20 flagons of cider and 481^1/$_2$ doz. 'AW' (aerated water or pop).

At the time of writing the **Castlefield** is closed while renovation work is being carried out. However, it is intended to reopen it in due course, together with a site for caravans in an adjoining field.

From Middlewood the road meanders in a general direction slightly south of east towards Hay-on-Wye, and at Hardwick the B4348 from Dorstone joins from the left. The area around the junction is marked as Hardwick on old maps, but modern road maps mark the centre as the area around Hardwick church, a short distance back along the B4348. On the north side of the road, a few yards past the junction and down a drive, is the former **Unicorn Inn**. This was in existence in the 18th century, and on 19 February 1784 an advertisement appeared for the sale by auction of a messuage 'at the sign of the Unicorn, in the village of Hardwick …'. The position of the **Unicorn** was marked on Bryant's map of 1835.

This seems to have been in the hands of the Price family for many years in the 19th century. From 1826 John Price of Hardwick took out alehouse keeper's recognizances, and it seems most likely that he was there. Earlier members

The one-time Unicorn at Hardwick

of the Price family, who took out recognizances for Clifford from 1818 onwards, were likely to have been there also, for Hardwick was only formed into a separate ecclesiastical parish from part of the parish of Clifford in 1853. There may have been a name change, as in 1841 Anne Price was a publican at **Tan House** in Hardwick, the only one in the census of that year. If so, it was only temporary, as by 1851 Thomas Price was at the **Unicorn**. James Davies, recorded there in a directory of 1867, was also a 'thrashing' machine proprietor, as was Thomas Davies, there by 1868. He had been born in Moccas in 1832. His name appears until 1880, but the inn must have closed soon after.

A few hundred yards past the **Unicorn** a right turn leads to the old centre of Clifford around the church, and then down to a second, later, centre on the main road from Whitney toll bridge to Hay-on-Wye. Here, overlooking the river, are the remains of Clifford castle, once the home of Rosamund Clifford; the 'Fair Rosamund' who was mistress of Henry II. At the end of the 17th century there was, somewhere in Clifford, perhaps in one of these centres, an unlicensed alehouse. The following entry appears in the Court Rolls for the Manor of Clifford for 1699:

TWO STONE-BUILT COTTAGES,
KNOWN AS

" Clifford Castle Inn,"

Situate at CLIFFORD, adjoining the main road from Whitney to Hay, the one in the occupation of Mrs. DAVIES contains : Sitting Room, Kitchen, Back Kitchen (with Furnace and Sink), Pantry and 3 Bedrooms ; and the other (in the occupation of Mr. J. PROSSER) : Sitting Room, Large Kitchen, Back Kitchen (with Furnace and Baking Oven), Pantry, Underground Cellar and 3 Bedrooms.

WATER from Tap on opposite side of road.

FARM BUILDINGS,

including :—Stable with Loft over, Small Wainhouse, Piggeries and Small Open Shed.

The foregoing, together with the
GARDENS AND PASTURE ORCHARDING,
extends to an area of about
1 acre 2 roods 16 perches,
Viz. :—

O.S. No.	Description.	Acreage.
Pt. 296 ..	PART GARDEN	Estd. .030
360 ..	COTTAGES AND GARDEN	.372
361 ..	PASTURE ORCHARD	1.198
	TOTAL	A. 1.600

Let to Mrs. DAVIES and Mr. JOHN PROSSER at Rentals amounting to
£19 0s. 0d. per annum (Landlord paying Rates).

| Tithe, 8s. 0d. | Land Tax, 10s. 10½d. | Chief Rent, 8s. 2½d. |

Sale of the Castle Inn at Clifford in 1921

We present Mary … and Walter Knill for selling Ale without license and for keeping and harbouring people to play Cards for Cakes and Geese on the Saturday night and Sunday morning, and we, the Jurors, do lay a fine of 20s. on each of them if they do sell any ale without license for the future, or keep any disorders whatsoever.

Compared to the recently introduced unrestricted opening hours, this seems very small beer!

In the part of the village on the A438, on the corner of the road leading to the common, was the **Castle Inn**. The first mention of this that has so far been found is an agreement of 2 February 1809, by which Aneas (*sic*) Walter, of the Bwlch, Clifford, agreed to lease the **Castle Inn** to James Walter of St. Margaret's for 14 years at an annual rent of £40. James Walter's name does not occur in the list of alehouse keeper's recognizances for the period 1818 – 1828, so he must have died or moved on by that time. On 1 October 1825 James Spencer, a Hay solicitor and steward of the Honour and Manor of Clifford, wrote to the bailiff of the manor, Henry Saunders, notifying him of a Court Leet of the manor that was to be held on 24 October 1825 'at the Dwelling house of John Williams known by the name or sign of the Castle situate in the parish of Clifford'. John Williams took out alehouse keeper's recognizances between 1824 and 1826, but did not renew the licence in 1827. At the time of the 1841 census the licensee was William Morgan, who was aged 30. Thefirst mention of the **Castle Inn** occurred in a directory in 1851, when Mrs. Catherine Vernon Gough was the licensee. By 1867 James Watkins had taken over; he was aged 42 in 1871 and had been born in Clyro just across the river. He was there until 1881 (although there is an odd directory entry of 1875 that gives the licensee's name as William H. Wilce). In 1881 the **Castle Inn** was bought by Evan Howells, who was described in the 1891 census as a shepherd and innkeeper. He was still there in July 1899,

but presumably died soon afterwards as his widow Ann appears as the publican in a directory of the following year. The 1903 printed list of licensed premises records that she owned the pub as well as running it. However, it soon closed as a public house, a reason being given in *The Herefordshire Village Book*:

At one time the Castle Inn at Clifford

179

The Old Castle Inn was said to have been closed when the irate wives of the estate workers complained that their menfolk were spending most of their wages on the way home.

This must have been in 1904, as in that year the **Castle Inn** was bought by Mr. Peter Coats. He had moved down from Paisley and, having bought the recently-built Whitney Court, was trying to build up an estate in the area.

Over the road from the **Castle Inn** was the less well-known **Well Inn**. This was almost certainly the un-named beer house run by Walter Hill in 1851, and in 1867 by Benjamin Hill, who was also recorded as a farmer. At the time of the 1871 census, when the name was given as the **Well Inn**, he was aged 47, had been born in Clifford, and was described as a labourer and innkeeper. A directory of 1876 states, almost certainly incorrectly, that Benjamin Hill was at the **Bell Inn**, all other references being to the **Well Inn**. By 1891 James Hill, son of Benjamin, had taken over. He was then aged 33 and, like his father, was a farmer as well as running the beer house. Curiously, the 1871 census states that he was born in Clifford, while that of 1891 states that he was born in the adjoining parish of Dorstone! By 1900 Thomas Parry was in charge — a native of Llanstephan, Radnorshire, in 1901 he was aged 60. The 1903 printed list records that he owned the **Well Inn**, which seems to have closed as a public house about the year 1910.

By the time that the Clifford Estate was offered for sale by auction on 11 August 1921, the Well Inn was in ruins. Despite this, by the time the final sale details were printed it had already been sold. There is now nothing left, but local memory places it in the field opposite the **Castle Inn**, somewhat

SOLD	LOT 15.

(Coloured Green on Plan.)

" Well Inn " Ruins and Pasture Orchard

Situate at CLIFFORD, adjoining the main road and Lot 1, and comprising an area of about

1 acre 3 roods 32 perches,

Viz. :—

O.S. No.	Description.	Acreage.
383 ..	RUINS, &c.	.252
384 ..	PASTURE ORCHARD	.870
399 ..	Do. Do. AND SHED	.831
	TOTAL	A. 1.953

Tenant : Mr. WM. LEWIS.   Rent, £10 0s. 0d.

Tithe, 5s. 2d.   Land Tax, 7s. 4½d.   Chief Rent 2s. 0d.

The ruins of the Well Inn were sold before the auction in 1921

180

along the road towards Hay, on the corner of the road leading up to Clifford church. This is confirmed by Bryant's map of 1835, which marks Well House in this position, proving the source of the name. There is an unnamed complex of buildings on this corner, on the 1903 O.S. map, but these have all now gone. The name of the pub suggests that there was plenty of water there, and indeed there is still a small, constantly-running, water spout on the opposite corner to the site of the **Well Inn**.

The Nelson Inn, on the boundary between Cusop and Hay
(centre left, behind telegraph pole)

From Clifford the road to Hay crosses the northern part of the parish of Cusop, and just on the boundary between Cusop and Hay — and hence the county boundary — was the **Nelson Inn**, then on the edge of Hay-on-Wye. Whether the opening of the **Nelson Inn** was stimulated by its position opposite the coal wharf of the Brecon to Hay tramway is not known. The first section of the tramway, from Brecon to Hay Bridge, was opened in May 1816, and the section from Hay to Eardisley followed in December 1818. The wharf was just over the Dulas Brook in Cusop. In 1863 the tramway was bought by the Hereford, Hay and Brecon railway, which built its track as far as possible along the line of the tramway, the wharf being replaced by Hay Station, which was directly opposite the **Nelson Inn**. This was almost certainly the second of the two establishments in Cusop for which alehouse keeper's recognizances were taken out in the 1820s, and it must have been the un-named establishment of which John Probert was the innkeeper in 1841. It is first mentioned in a directory in 1844, but under Hay, and a directory of 1868 notes its advantageous position directly opposite the railway station. In the late 1870s the licence was taken out by Alfred Henry

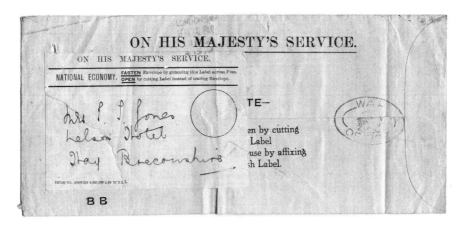

ON HIS MAJESTY'S SERVICE.

ON HIS MAJESTY'S SERVICE.

NATIONAL ECONOMY. **FASTEN** Envelope by gumming this Label across Flap.
OPEN by cutting Label instead of tearing Envelope.

Mrs P. S. Jones
Nelson Hotel
Hay Breconshire

TE—

en by cutting
Label
use by affixing
sh Label.

B B

War time economy re-use of envelopes

Stephens, but by 1891 his widow Elizabeth Thirza Stephens was in charge. She married again within a few years, and John Jones, recorded in directories between 1895 and 1900, was no doubt her new husband. However, from 1901 she was in charge again, and the census of that year records that Isabella Thirza Jones was the innkeeper, and her husband, resident at the **Nelson Inn**, was a woolstapler.

Surviving licensing records covering the years 1923 to 1928 show that the licensee was then Mrs. Alice Susan Davies, but that she actually lived at Llowes Court, over the river in Radnorshire. On 9 February 1925 the licence was taken over by James Henry Morgan, but Mrs. Davies retained the ownership

The licensing records also show that the licence was for six days only. At the beginning of the 20th century it was open on a Sunday while pubs in adjoining Hay were closed. However, the Salvation Army started to hold its Sunday evening services opposite the inn and the owner eventually decided to voluntarily give up his Sunday licence. Later in the century two attempts were made to re-obtain a Sunday licence, but each

The Nelson is now a private house

received opposition and the licence was not granted. But in 1960 an application was made which received no objection and was passed, the licensee stating that they 'did not foresee raids from wild and thirsty Welshmen from over the border'. The first Sunday lunchtime pint under the new licence was drawn by Lt. Col. Harry Llewellyn, of Foxhunter fame, who was then chairman of Rhymney Breweries. The first Sunday's clientele included a group of S.A.S. territorials who came down from the hills to quench their thirst. But despite all this, the **Nelson** finally closed in recent years, and is now a guest house called the Kingfisher.

The position of the **Nelson** was advantageous, as it was opposite what had been a coal wharf on the Hay tramroad, which subsequently became the railway station. However, somewhere near the station in the 19th century was a refreshment room, certainly licensed in the 1870s and '80s for 'sweets' which included 'weak' wines, mead and metheglin. Later such licenses included British wines.

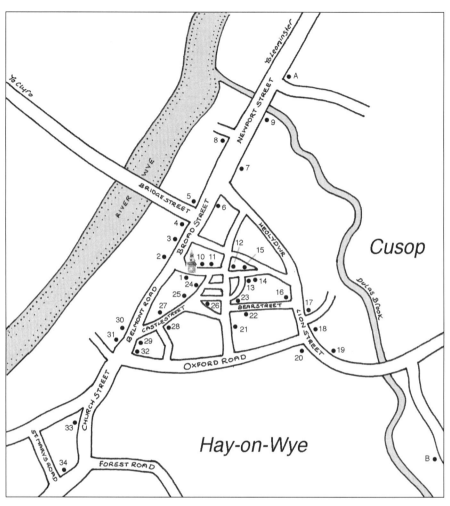

Cusop

Hay-on-Wye

CHAPTER 12	CHAPTER 13	CHAPTER 14
1. King's Head	10. Mitre	24. Three Horseshoes
2. Seven Stars	11. Red Lion	25. Fountain
3. Rose and Crown	12. Wheatsheaf	26. Market Tavern/George
4. Black Swan	13. Castle	27. Talbot
5. Three Tuns	14. Harp	28. Mason's Arms
6. Tanner's Arms	15. Half Moon	29. Golden Lion
7. Ship	16. New Inn	30. Wine Vaults/Grapes
8. Lamb	17. Black Lion	31. Cock/ Cock & Hen
9. Bridge End	18. Drill Hall	32. Blue Boar
	19. Drovers' Arms	33. Swan
	20. Traveller's Trap	34. Sun
	21. Bell	
	22. Bear	CUSOP
	23. Kilvert's	A. Nelson
		B. Sun

CHAPTER TWELVE

Hay-on-Wye:
Broad St.

Hay-on-Wye (Y Gelli) is at the junction of three old counties —
Herefordshire, Radnorshire & Breconshire. It sits on a triangular site with the
river Wye on the north-west and the Dulas brook on the east. The town
overlooks an early ford which crossed the Wye, but this has been bridged for
many years. It is over a mile from the present main road from Hereford to
Brecon and mid-Wales, which runs well to the north of the river through
Clyro. In the town one minor road leads eastwards to the toll bridge across
the Wye at Whitney; a second passes through Bredwardine to Madley and
Hereford (Chapters 10 and 11) and a third through Dorstone to the Golden
Valley (Chapters 8 and 9). A minor road, now much used by tourists, leads
towards the Black Mountains, passing through the Gospel Pass on its way to
Capel-y-ffin and the Vale of Ewyas (Chapter 4) — a track, for it was little
more for much of its life, which was once used extensively by drovers.

Surprisingly, considering its rather remote situation, Hay was a railway
junction for about 100 years — the main line came from Hereford and led

Hay railway station

185

Hay looking north-eastwards from the castle

to Brecon and Swansea, whilst the Golden Valley Railway led to Pontrilas (Chapter 8).

The name Hay is derived from the Norman French *haie,* which comes from the old German *haga* meaning enclosure. The original Norman settlement may have been around St. Mary's church to the south-west of the main centre of the present town, where there is also a small motte — perhaps the earliest castle. By the middle of the 13th century the central part of the town was walled and had a new castle — the old motte and the parish church being left completely outside these new defences.

The walled town had three gates in the circuit, one situated in Newport Street, close to the **Lamb Inn** (The Watergate), a second in Church Street, by the junction with Castle Street (The West or Carles Gate), and the third called the Black Lion Gate near the lower end of Bear Street. There may also have been some protection (or toll collecting point) associated with the crossing of the Wye. The gates and most of the town wall have all been demolished, but the overall course is still reasonably evident.

The street plan is relatively simple, following the triangular shape of the town defences with the castle mid-way along the southern defensive line and a market place positioned centrally. The main streets forming the triangle are Broad Street, Oxford Road and Heol y Dwr (Water Street). Within the triangle thus formed and central to the triangle are Chancery Lane, Castle Street and Bear Street. The large medieval market place

186

Hay castle from the north about 1910

would once have been completely open with temporary stalls, but now comprises a collection of buildings and several streets including the Bull Ring and High Town. Here for many years a small chapel dedicated to St. John graced the market place; it fell down in 1700.

Hay was a successful market town in the late medieval period with 183 burgages, but suffered much destruction at the hands of Owain Glyndwr in 1400 and never seems really to have recovered from this, and possibly the Black Death, until the latter part of the 20th century. With considerable help from Richard Booth, the self-proclaimed King of Hay, it became a world centre for second-hand books and the venue for an internationally recognised annual festival.

In 1878 Hay, or as it is sometimes designated *Welsh Hay*, was described as 'a parish and market town in the hundred of Talgarth and county of Brecknock, situated upon the borders of Herefordshire and Radnorshire'.

The best known landmark in the town is the castle — partly bookshop and partly ruined — which stands towards the south, high above the centre of the town. It is not certain when this castle was built, but it is supposed to have been erected during the reign of William Rufus by Sir Philip Walwyn, who received a grant of the manor of Hay from Bernard Newmarch, the Norman conqueror of Breconshire.

187

Nowadays one of the central landmarks in Hay is the clock tower at the top end of Broad Street which was built by J.C. Haddon of Hereford. The finance was provided by the estate of a Captain Brown, who left a legacy in his will for a clock for the church tower. His executors originally decided to expand this legacy to include a town clock, public hall and corn exchange, but in the event only the tower was built at a cost of £600.

Hay, like many other towns on the borders of Wales, was for several centuries engaged in the flannel trade. Geoffrey Fairs in his *History of the Hay* gives the following trades and industries around 1770 — saddler, wig maker, tailor, carpenter, blacksmith, mercer, flax dresser, watchmaker, brazier, carrier, cooper, and shoemaker. In addition there would have been builders, and employment in connection with the food industry, such as butchers and bakers. Some of these trades were operated in addition to that of owner or licensee of a public house, the wife often dealing with the customers of the inn.

The King's Head, next but one to the clock tower, used every available space to advertise the Hereford Brewery and its best-selling ales in the late 19th century

In 1782 the population of Hay parish was 1,100, decreasing to 882 by 1801. This must have been a particularly low spot, for by 1871 the population had more than doubled to 2,011. In the 1961 census the population was down again, being only 1,321, but by 1991 it had once more increased, to 1,407.

One of the main reasons for the numerous public houses in Hay in relation to its population was the weekly market and hiring fairs. The sale of cattle took place in Broad Street, right in the middle of the town, until 1919 when the new cattle market was opened. On market day, the town, despite its small population, was invaded by many hill-farmers and others from all the outlying districts. They came on horseback and on foot, and many of their favourite hostelries provided stabling and, for those who had perhaps over-imbibed during their visit, mounting blocks outside the door to help them clamber onto their horses for the trek home. There have at various times been at least 40 public houses in Hay. Indeed, quite a few of the streets, such as Bear Street, New Street, Lion Street, Ship Pitch and Bell Bank, were named after the inns, giving a firm impression of continuity to the town and its hostelries. Some street names have changed over time, pehaps due to changing use. Thus part of Horsefair became Bell Bank, perhaps because the **Bell Inn** was situated half way down Bell Bank on the right-hand side going towards Bear Street. The once appropriately named Coal Market became The Square then Broad Street, and Wyebridge Street became part of Broad Street. New Street became Bear Street, the lower part of Chancery Lane was called Gravel Lane and the former name for Church Street was George Street.

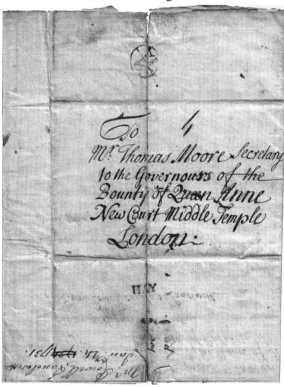

This 1731 letter probably came via the Swan Inn

There is some evidence of the postal system to and from Hay from the early part of the 18th century, the earliest known item to have left Hay via a recognised postal system being dated 24 January 1731. It was sent by Evan Powell, who was the curate of Lanelweth (Llanelwedd) to London and in all probability would have gone from the **Swan Inn** and have incurred a fee of 4d. Prior to the postal reforms of 1840, when postage became pre-paid, the cost of a postal item was

A receipt from the King's Head gives an impression of prices in 1894

paid by the recipient, being determined according to the number of sheets and the distance involved. Between 1711 and 1765 the cost of a single sheet was 3d. up to 80 miles and 4d. above.

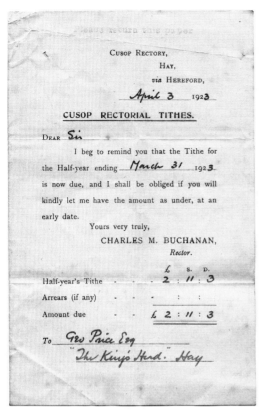

*Tithes were still payable to
the rector in 1923*

The clock tower in the centre of Hay is a natural starting point for this excursion around the present and former licensed premises of the town, as it stands to one side of the market area. Where any animals were sold, there was always a need for places of refreshment where discussions could take place and deals could be struck. There have been several inns in this area, now known as the Pavement, and along Broad Street and Newport Street.

One of the earliest pubs was the **King's Head**, adjacent to that modern landmark — the public toilets — and now called Tredegar House. The building is of 17th-century origin, and was certainly licensed in the 18th century. An engraving of the area, published in 1814, shows the inn with a sign hanging outside. However, the first directory entry, which was published in 1830, includes Thomas Jones as licensee of the **King's Head**, which was then described as being in the Coal Market. In 1835 it was in Red Lion Street. Although after 1835 the **King's Head** does not appear in a directory again until 1868, it was almost certainly the un-named beer house run by Susannah Jones which appears in directories between these dates, and which was variously described as being in Broad Street and Red Lion Street. She was probably the widow of Thomas Jones, recorded in 1835. The change to a beer-only licence is slightly unusual.

By 1861 the inn was held by James Williams and a directory of 1868 positions it in The Square. Williams was a cooper by trade and doubtless supplied many of the pubs in Hay and neighbourhood with barrels for their home-made beer. He was still at the **King's Head** in 1871, but by the time that surviving licensing records begin in 1874 the licensee was named as David James, although James Williams still owned the premises. It seems that David James may have been a rather unsatisfactory tenant, for on 1 June 1874 he was fined 6s. and costs for opening his (public) house during closing times. Two months later on 1 August 1874 he was again in front of the bench, being fined 10s. and costs for being drunk on licensed premises. On the same day, apparently because of James' misdemeanours, the licence was transferred to Frances James, presumably his wife. Matters did not improve after the transfer and on 6 September 1875 she was fined 10s. and costs for being drunk on licensed premises and the licence was endorsed. A fortnight later she was fined 10s. and costs for keeping the house open after hours and the licence was endorsed again. The result was rather inevitable — on 1 November 1875 the premises were disqualified from holding a licence for two years and notice of this was given to the owner. James Williams must have decided that tenants were not the ideal way of running a pub and he subsequently took over the business himself.

The licence was eventually renewed and on 5 June 1882 it was transferred to William Price, but by 1891 George Price held the licence. He was not the owner, for by that time the **King's Head** had been sold to the Hereford Imperial Brewery. In 1898 the inn was part of the sale of the Hereford Brewery; the particulars indicating that George Price paid a rent of £10 per annum and that the property was 'a stone and slate house situate in the centre of the town'. It apparently had a seven-day licence in 1899, but when licensing records begin again in 1919 it had only a six-day licence. The Hereford Brewery was merged to become the Hereford and Tredegar Brewery and the 1910 Land Valuation records that company as being the owner of the inn. George Price held the licence throughout the First World War and until at least 1926, but not without incident — on 5 May 1919 he was fined £13 for selling spirits at a price exceeding the maximum allowed. At that time, as a consequence of the war, there were strict controls on prices.

Price also seems to have ignored the six-day licensing regulations, as local solicitor Major Henry Rowse Armstrong apparently went there regularly for his Sunday pint — Price operating what might be described as a private client arrangement. This use by Armstrong was somewhat surprising, as the **King's Head** was considered to be rather a rough place. Armstrong was the Hay solicitor whose claim to fame — such as it was — was that he was, and still is, the only solicitor and possibly the only freemason, to receive the death penalty for murder. He was found guilty of the murder of his wife, by poisoning her with arsenic, and it was also alleged that he attempted to poison a rival solicitor, Oswald Martin, who was in practice immediately opposite Armstrong's firm in Broad Street. Armstrong was last seen in the **King's Head** on the night before his arrest.

Tony Pugh, whose reminiscences are included in *Nobody had ever heard of Hay*, recalled:

> My father lived in Hay and he told me that as a boy he used to work at the King's Head and in the mornings he had to take a broom and sweep the swill out through the door! There was a lot of drunkenness in those days.

With all this happening, it is not surprising that there was a move to close the pub and in 1938 it was referred for compensation under the Licensing (Consolidation) Act, 1910. This Act enabled owners of licensed properties to claim compensation in respect of premises that did not have their licence renewed. Compensation for the **King's Head** was agreed at £510, the owners, still the

The King's Head in retirement

Hereford and Tredegar Brewery, receiving £459 and the tenant and licensee, David James Lewis, a miserly £51 for losing both his job and his home.

The nearest licensed premises to the **King's Head** was the **Seven Stars** situated at 11 Broad Street opposite Prospect House. It was open prior to 1776 and by 1835 the landlord was John Sheen. By 1861 the tenancy had changed again, the census confirming that the landlord was Frederick Price aged 38. In 1879 the property was owned by Viscount Hereford of Tregoyd and his tenant and licensee was Jas. Maskell; by 1891 the landlord was Philip Clark.

The **Seven Stars** was included in the sale of the Hereford Brewery in 1898 and by the following year the premises had a seven-day licence. It was let at that time to Edward Williams at a rent of £28 per annum. In 1901 the tenancy had changed hands again and the landlady was Caroline Williams, possibly Edward's wife or widow. The licence had been altered by 1919 when, in accordance with the Sunday Closing Act, it had only a six-day licence. The owner then was the Hon. R.C. Devereux, of Tregoyd, the lessees being the Hereford and Tredegar Brewery Ltd. By 1910 the ownership had changed and the new owner was Penry Lloyd of Hay, the property being occupied by Robert Williams.

For many years the cattle market was held in the main streets;
the Seven Stars and the Crown Hotel are on the left-hand side

The Seven Stars is now a brasserie providing bed and breakfast

Near to the **Seven Stars**, and also on the north side of Broad Street, is the **Rose and Crown Hotel**, often simply called the **Crown**. The inn apparently opened in about 1830 and became known as the **Crown** in the second half of the 19th century. The name may have changed when the

RADNORSHIRE.

TO BE SOLD BY

Auction

By Mr. THOMAS PRICE, of Builth,

AT THE

Rose & Crown Inn,

IN THE TOWN OF HAY, IN THE COUNTY OF BRECON,

On Thursday, the 22nd of October, 1829.

Between the Hours of Two & Four o'Clock in the afternoon,

SUBJECT TO SUCH CONDITIONS AS SHALL BE THEN & THERE PRODUCED.

ALL THAT DESIRABLE

FARM;

CALLED

UPPER PENY-FOREST,

In the following or such other Lots as shall be agreed upon at the time of Sale.

Lot 1. All that Farm House and Buildings, together with several Pieces or Parcels of Land thereto belonging, with the appurtenances called **UPPER PENY-FOREST**, containing **20** Acres of Land (more or less) situate in the several Parishes of Clirow, and Llowes, in the occupation of David Herring; as Tenant from Year to Year.

Lot 2. All those Four **UPPER FIELDS** part of **PENY-FOREST FARM**, situate in the said Parishes of Clirow and Llowes, in the occupation of the said David Herring.

The Property lies in a Firtile part of the County of Radnor, and has a valuable Right of Sheep Walk upon the adjoining Hills, and is distant from the Market Town of Hay about 2 Miles, and Kington about 10 Miles, two excellent Market Towns.

The Tenant will shew the respective Lots, and further particulars may be had by applying at the Office of Mr. H. P. POWELL, Solicitor Builth Breconshire, or Mr. THOMAS PRICE Auctioneer, (if by Letter Postage Paid.)

Builth, 29th September, 1829.

In the early 19th century the Rose and Crown was host to many sales including this one for a farm in Clyro and Llowes parishes in 1829 premises were extended, but there was probably a pub on the same site prior to 1776. In 1825 Thomas James, landlord of the **Rose and Crown**, placed an advertisement in the paper as follows:

HAY, BRECONSHIRE
ROSE AND CROWN INN

Thomas James, impressed with the liveliest sentiments of gratitude for the distinguished Support he has for the last Twenty Years received from the Commercial Gentlemen and Others, who have honoured the above Inn with their Support, begs leave to return them his sincere acknowledgements and thanks for past Favours; having made considerable Additions to his House, he respectfully informs them that the same is completely finished and comfortably fitted up for their accommodation; he therefore begs to solicit a continuance of their Patronage and Support, and trusts by his uniform exertions to please, and moderate Charges, to merit a continuance of public Favours.

The **Rose and Crown** was one of the main stopping places for the mail-coach in the 19th century. In 1823 the *Telegraph* from Hereford passed through Hay three days each week at 7 p.m., and the *Cambrian* from Carmarthen to London also passed through the town on three days per week at 2 p.m., both coaches calling at the inn. The inn would probably have offered food and accommodation and was obviously quite a large establishment because auctions took place there regularly from the 19th century onwards.

Municipal street lamps were organised by a company set up for the purpose and were first lit in Hay in 1841. The *Hereford Times* reported that a celebration followed and:

HAY.

Rose and Crown Benefit Club and Amicable Society.—The members of the above club held their anniversary on Monday last. At a little after 10 o'clock they formed in procession, walking two and two with their staffs of the order in their hands through the principal streets of the town, preceded by the band and flag expressive of the society to the church, where a most beautiful and appropriate address was delivered by the worthy vicar, the Rev. W. L. Bevan, after which they returned in the same order to the Rose and Crown Inn, where a most sumptuous dinner awaited them, to which 110 members and friends sat down. Colonel Powell presided, supported on the left by the rev. vicar, Messrs. Latter, Proctor, Dowell, Higgins, &c., and on the right by the Rev. C. King, W. Acton and N. S. Wynn, Esqs., &c. The vice-chair was most ably filled by W. Pugh, Esq. Ample justice having been done to the very excellent dinner, and grace said, the cloth was removed, after which the usual loyal and patriotic toasts were given in rapid succession from the chair, also the army and navy, and the member and lord-lieutenant of the county, which were received with much applause. The bishop and clergy were next given—the Rev. C. King returned thanks. W. Higgins, Esq., next rose and in a very pleasing speech gave the health of the president which was received with rounds of cheers. Several other toasts were given from the chair, including the rev. vicar, who returned thanks in a very gratifying address. The healths of several other gentlemen present were given, and appropriately responded to. Many excellent songs were sung, and the whole company seemed to be at the height of happiness.

The Benefit Clubs were of great importance as this 1845 newspaper cutting shows

196

The contractors were met at the Rose & Crown by a large gathering of 'respectable' inhabitants, where their health's were drunk, together with that of the Rev. Humphrey Allen, who had so largely contributed to the founding of the company.

In 1843 the Rose and Crown Benefit Club and Amicable Friendly Society met at the inn, and it was reported that 'toasting went on until dawn'! The same society met at the premises for an anniversary celebration in 1846 when, following a procession through the town, 'a most sumptuous dinner was held, to which 110 members and friends sat down'.

The Rose and Crown is central in this c.*1860-70's photograph*

On Sunday 18 June 1843, James Spencer, who frequented the **Rose and Crown** regularly, was in the inn when he wrote to a solicitor in Hereford. His writing was extremely shaky — perhaps he had imbibed rather freely or he was recovering from the night before! Spencer practised as a solicitor in Hay from the late 18th century until the 1850s when he became bankrupt and eventually died in Hereford Gaol on 27 May 1851. His death certificate recorded that he 'died by the visitation of God' — a sobering thought for an ex-frequenter of the **Rose and Crown**!

On 21 July 1855 the *Hereford Times* reported in detail about a hoax played on the Kington band and the landlord of the **Rose and Crown**:

A fly and pair of gaily-caparisoned horses, drawing the Kington band, pulled up at the Rose and Crown inn, in this town, on Monday last; and the landlord, with his usual alacrity, was in immediate attendance. The leader of the band blandly inquired after his health, and that of the hostess and family, and added a hope that he would 'have a fine day, and a good attendance to the dinner'. 'What dinner,' exclaimed the surprised landlord. 'Oh!' was the reply, 'we received your secretary's letter to be here in attendance at your club-feast to-day'. 'We have heard nothing about it,' exclaimed the landlord. The letter was produced, and immediately pronounced to be a forgery, the secretary being at present in London. The length of the visitors' visages may be guessed at more easily than described. The good-natured landlord, commiserating their situation, kindly regaled then with 'cwrw da' and luncheon, and sent his guests back not quite so happy as they came.

The 1861 census confirms that the landlord was George Hope who was then only 23. He was still licensee when the **Rose & Crown** was very much involved in the celebrations that took place when the railway was officially opened in 1864. A newspaper report of the day recorded that:

> The opening of the Hereford, Hay & Brecon Railway on 19 September was marked with a monster picnic at Hay. The day had a bad start, however, when the landlady at the Swan Hotel, who had agreed that the picnic should be held in the Tump Meadow, finding that Mr. Hope of the Rose & Crown was to supply the refreshments, cancelled the use of the ground and at the last moment the Hereford Horticultural Society had to erect their tents on a nicely enclosed sward surrounded by orchards in the occupation of the respected landlord of the Nelson Inn. A train of thirteen carriages left Hereford at 9 o'clock having on board Mr. E Merrick's Rifle Corps Band of 16 performers and a large number of citizens of great respectability. At Hay a large number of visitors assembled and the Hay and Hereford Rifle Corps Band led the immense concourse of persons through the principal streets back to the Rose & Crown Hotel where Mr. Hope and his wife had caused an excellent dinner to be prepared for the band and those engaged.

By 1874, George Hope, despite the fact that he was not very old, must have died, his executors having transferred the licence to Thomas Price.

It wasn't long before the landlord of the **Rose & Crown** was in trouble with the Public Health Authority. In 1876 the minutes of the local board stated:

> 17th April 1876. Resolved that the Clerk write peremptorily to the proprietors of the Swan and the Rose & Crown hotels giving notice that in any future cases in which they may convey any deceased person or child who has died from any infectious or contagious disease or any person suffering from such disease the Board will be compelled to institute proceedings unless they immediately provide the disinfection of such conveyance.

By 1945 the Crown was being described as 'newly rebuilt'

The licence was transferred to Lucretia Williams on 3 September 1877, but she remained as licensee only until October when it was transferred to Fanny Edith Hickman. The owner at that time was Arthur Cheese Esq. from Llandrindod Wells.

The *Firefly* was one of the most important amenities in Hay in the early 1900s. It was a fire-fighting apparatus and was drawn by two black horses owned by the proprietor of the **Crown Hotel**, the horses being kept in a field on the far side of the river. The use of horses was discontinued in 1925, but the *Firefly* survived until 1942.

In 1919 the owners were the executors of Thomas Joseph Stokoe, deceased, but by August 1921 George Cranbrook Barber had bought the inn from the executors. He was clearly not a satisfactory publican because in 1923 he was fined £10 and half the costs of £2 3s. 6d. for supplying liquors during other than permitted hours. Even so, he remained there for several more years until he was declared bankrupt in 1926. The building was really in two parts — the **Crown** and the **Rose and Crown**. The **Crown** closed and has since been converted to residential flats; the **Rose & Crown**, which is brewery owned, was retained and is still a licensed premises. The original building was approximately one third larger than it is now.

The **Black Swan** was on the same side of the road as the **Rose and Crown**, on the north-western corner of Broad Street and Bridge

NOTICE.

Pursuant to the Licensing Act, 1953, intoxicating Liquors are permitted to be sold and supplied in these Premises between the hours of 10 a.m. and 11 a.m. and 3 p.m. and 5 p.m. on Mondays and Thursdays except Christmas Day, for the accommodation of persons attending the Marts and Markets

Market licences allowed pubs to open for a longer period during the day

199

The front of the Crown and its pavement display in 2005

The one time Black Swan in 2005

Street. It was in existence as early as 1808 being shown on a shield in the National Library of Wales. Indeed, a **Black Swan** is depicted on Dineley's sketch of 1689. It is probably not the present building, but clearly represents a pub of the same name in Hay. The landlord at the time of the 1861 census was William Gwilliam and he was still there in 1874 when the owner was recorded as James Holt. In 1891 the landlady was Mary Powell and in 1901 William Thomas. The pub had a seven-day licence in 1899. In 1919 the licensee was Thomas Price who, on 19 January 1920, fell foul of the law and was fined £8 3s. for permitting intoxicating liquors to be consumed during prohibited hours. The pub changed hands several times during the next few years, the final owners being the Hereford and Tredegar Brewery Ltd., who purchased the premises in 1926. On 28 August 1944 the pub was referred for compensation under the Licensing (Consolidation) Act 1910. The estimated value of

The Firefly in front of the Black Swan, about 1912

*Looking westwards along Broad Street. The Black Swan and
the Three Tuns are on the right*

the property as licensed premises was £1,969 5s. and when delicensed it
would only be worth £1,609 5s. The gross trade for 1942 and 1943 was
£2,434 10s. and the cost of conversion of the property was estimated at
£50. It was finally delicensed in 1946 due to illegal betting on the
premises. The property is now a private house, but the £50 must not have
been fully spent for it still retains the pub interior.

Bridge Street about 1897 with the Three Tuns on the right

The **Three Tuns** on the opposite corner of Bridge Street to the **Black Swan**, is one of the oldest houses in Hay. The 16th-century timber front was exposed on the Bridge Street frontage in the 1970s during reconstruction work, but is now mainly concealed. It is known that the building was an inn in the 18th century if not earlier, when it was known as the **Spread Eagle**. At that time it was associated with an extensive tan yard, which is described in a schedule to a deed of sale dated 28 October 1817. It was bought from Edmund Hallard by a consortium consisting of Nathaniel Purchas the younger (his father Nathaniel senior was a wine merchant who lived at Fownhope just outside Hereford; he died in 1817 and the business was taken over by another son, William), Robert Purchas, a timber merchant in the Monmouth area, Thomas Purchas, James Williams, a tanner in Hay, and Stephen Ball from Hay, who was described as a gentleman. The property was clearly much more substantial in 1817 than it is now, and when it changed hands for the sum of £1,068 15s. the deed of sale included:

> All those Messuages Burgages or Dwelling houses theretofore called or known by the sevl. names of the Spread Eagle and the Tanhouse but then called the Three Tons and Tanhouse together with the Tanyards and Pits covered & uncovered Gardens & Orchards thereunto adjoining.

The name change had taken place before 1761 as the Turnpike Trust met at the **Three Tuns** in March of that year. The tan house was between the **Three Tuns** and the malthouse on the Broad Street frontage.

The first landlord following the 1817 sale was James Byron who, by 1835. was also described as a dyer. By 1861 the landlord was James Morris and by 1874 the property was owned and run by William Lewis. In 1881 he was one of the many landlords in Hay who fell foul of the law when he was fined 10s. and costs for permitting drunkenness and his licence was endorsed. The census details give the tenant in 1891 as Edward Lloyd and in 1901 as James Swinburn, who was also an ostler. In 1904 the property was purchased by Messrs. Arnold, Perrett & Co. of Hereford for £1,000, and in 1919 their tenant was Edward John Jenkins who had a seven-day licence.

Timber-framing on the Three Tuns exposed in the 1970s

Jenkins was clearly not a good tenant, because on 20 October 1919 he was fined £1 for permitting intoxicating liquor to be consumed in prohibited hours — this seems to have been a rather common 'crime' in Hay in the post-war years!

Leslie Edward Powell, the father of the present landlady Lucy Powell, took over the tenancy in 1922, his son Albert being born there in the same year. Albert later became licensee of the **Wheatsheaf** (Chapter 13). Leslie Powell eventually purchased the property from Arnold, Perrett & Co. on 13 March 1925. He was a man of many parts — a carpenter by trade, but he also worked as a ghillie for the gentry. During the Second World War

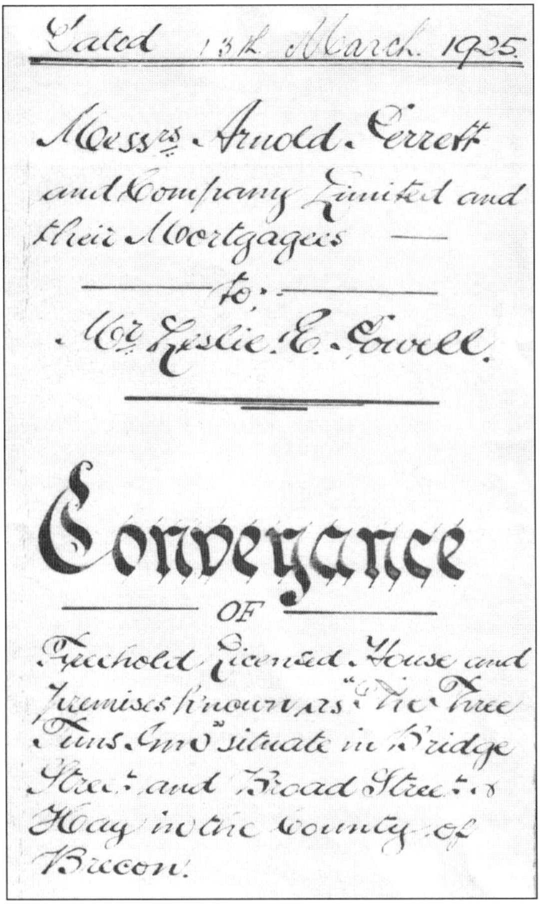
Dated 13th March 1925

Messrs. Arnold Perrett and Company Limited and their Mortgagees —

— to: —

Mr Leslie E. Powell

Conveyance

— of —

Freehold Licensed House and Premises known as "The Three Tuns Inn" situate in Bridge Street and Broad Street in Hay in the County of Brecon.

The 1925 conveyance of the Three Tuns from Arnold, Perrett and Co. Ltd. to the Powell family

he managed the **Crown**, leaving the **Three Tuns** to be run by his wife, Marion, and their daughter, Lucy. After the war he continued to run the inn until his death in 1959, after which his widow became licensee — once again running the pub with the assistance of Lucy. Marion unfortunately suffered from arthritis in her later years and Lucy became the licensee in 1973. Over the years she became well known as somewhat of a Hay character. In the late '60s the beer was kept in the back passage and brought into the bar in pint pots; if your face did not fit, the beer came out of the oldest barrel — Lucy was not to be trifled with! One American visitor, trying to discover her age, asked how long she had been in the pub. The response 'I've always been here' floored him completely! One of the regulars at the pub is Haydn Pugh, who organises the 'St. Lucy' festival on 12 December each year. The annual celebration, which is part of the Hay Festival of Light, is to show the regulars' appreciation by turning Lucy into a saint for the day.

Lucy continued to run the pub until February 2005 when a fire severely damaged the property. It was early in the morning when a resident, taking her children to school, raised the alarm after seeing smoke coming from the building. Her friend, Haydn Pugh, also noticed the smoke as he was bringing Lucy's morning newspaper. At that time, Lucy was downstairs in the pub and did not realise that there was a fire upstairs until worried neighbours banged on the door and managed to get her out.

Albert and Lucy Powell in 2005

The seven-day licence for the Three Tuns

Lucy and a young visitor in the bar of the Three Tuns in 2004

Fire engines from Hay, Eardisley and Talgarth attended the blaze and were watched by a crown of almost a hundred. The blaze ripped through the upper floors and the street was filled with smoke. After the fire had been put out the tiles had eventually to be removed from the roof for safety reasons and the whole building was then boarded up. The pub had been run by one family for most of the 20th century and the fire was effectively the end of an era.

Above: The Three Tuns plaque

The **Tanners' Arms** was a little further down Broad Street at nos. 31 and 32, on the far side of the road to the **Three Tuns** and opposite Underhill's Garage. The licence was transferred to Rice Davies, late of Newbridge, on 3 April 1876. He didn't stay long, and neither did William Cole, his replacement, who was followed by James Williams, both in

Above: The Three Tuns in 2004, before the fire.

Left: The sad sight of the Three Tuns with all its windows boarded up after the fire

1879. At that time the owner was M.S. Reynolds who became the licensee in 1881. The pub had a seven-day licence in 1899 and by 1901 the landlord was Sidney Meadows. It had a relatively short life, being delicensed soon after 1910. For some time the building was a fish shop; it has since been converted to residential flats.

The **Ship Inn** was on the south side of Newport Street at the top of Ship Pitch. It was already in existence in 1815, when land was advertised to be sold by auction there. By 1846 it was a coaching inn with the *Prince*

A party at the Tanner's Arms in the late 1940s

The Ship Inn about 1901

of Wales coach leaving there every Monday, Wednesday, Friday and Saturday mornings at 6 a.m., returning from Hereford the same afternoon at 4.45 p.m. In 1861 the landlord was John Farr, aged 49. who was also a pig dealer. In 1874 the owner was John Allen and the licensee Luke Jones. Mary Jones, possibly his widow, had taken over by 1891. By the turn of the century Mrs. Allen had become the owner, the licensee being William Williams. The

Sale of the Ship Inn in 1851

Ship was still licensed in 1910, but closed soon afterwards and the property was demolished in 1978 to allow for road widening.

The exact whereabouts of the **Old White Lion** is unknown, but it is believed to have been in the same area. The only directory mention is in 1835 when William Pitt was landlord. No other reference has yet been found and it was presumably de-licensed by the mid-19th century.

HAY, HEREFORD, GLOUCESTER AND LONDON, TO ALL PARTS OF THE KINGDOM,

IN ONE DAY.

THE PRINCE OF WALES COACH

LEAVES the Swan Inn, HAY, every Monday, Wednesday, Friday, and Saturday Mornings, at Six o'clock, in time for the following Coaches, viz.:—

MAZEPPA COACH to Gloucester in time for the following Trains :—

	Departure from Gloucester.	Arrival at Paddington.
London	12 55	5 30
Ditto express	1 20	4 30
	Departure from Gloucester.	Arrival at Bristol.
Bristol	2 5	3 40

QUEEN COACH to Worcester, arriving at Spetchley in time for the Two o'clock Train, arriving in Birmingham at 3 35.

The PRINCE OF WALES returns from the Greyhound Inn, Hereford, the same Evenings at a quarter before Five, after the arrival of the Champion and Mazeppa Coaches from Gloucester, likewise the Prince of Wales Coach from Worcester.

The Proprietor has the pleasure of announcing that he has, for the convenience of the Public, commenced running to Hereford on Fridays as well as his usual days, which has been much desired, and will, he trusts, receive the patronage of the Public.

WM. MOORE, Proprietor.

May 21, 1846. [272

Stage coaches ensured that connections
could be made from the Ship Inn,
through Hereford, to the railway at Gloucester

The **Lamb Inn** was on the north side of Newport Street at the bottom of Ship Pitch. Morgan, writing in 1932 explains 'that the East Gate of the town walls was at the bottom of Ship (Sheep) Pitch, and that there was a recess in the wall of the Lamb Inn to show its position'. There is now a plaque on the premises marking the site of the gate.

Regular auctions took place at the **Lamb**, such as one on 27 January 1802 when a 'Farm [was] to be sold by auction at the dwelling house of David Morgan, known by the sign of the Lamb Inn, in the town of Hay'. The **Lamb**, like many inns in that period, was used for the transaction of business.

A report of the Royal Commission on the state of the roads in 1840 stated that 'W. Maddy (landlord of the Lamb) gave evidence that on travelling through Hay two tolls had to be paid within 300 yards'. The toll bridge at Whitney is now the only one that affects the crossing of the Wye, all the toll gates in Hay being abolished in 1878.

The landlord in 1861 was a local man, Charles Price, aged 24. In 1879 the landlord was Alfred Pembridge. By June 1881 he had been replaced by John Davies.

Changes followed rapidly and by February 1882 the tenancy had been transferred to Lewis Evans, and by April the following year to Edwin Hathaway. In 1919, when the premises had a six-day licence, the owner and licensee was Thomas Joseph Stokoe who, on 2 November of that year, was fined £12 2s. for permitting intoxicating liquor to be consumed in prohibited hours. Licence offences were common in Hay and on 1 November 1920 the new landlord, Arthur Tucker, was fined £5 for permitting gambling on licensed premises.

It was on 8 July 1931 that the **Lamb** was referred for a claim of compensation for non-renewal of licence under the Licensing Act, 1910. The owner and licensee at that time was Jack Coles and the property had a full on-licence. The

Numb. 17056.   [1765]

The London Gazette.

Publiſhed by Authority.

TUESDAY, AUGUST 29, 1815.

THE Creditors of **John Jones**, late of Hay, in the County of Brecon, Gent. who has been lately discharged from the custody of the Marshal of the King's Bench prison, under and by virtue of an Act of Parliament made and passed in the 53d year of the reign of His present Majesty, intitled "An Act for the Relief of Insolvent Debtors in England," are requested to meet on the 14th day of September next, at Ten o'Clock in the Forenoon, at the House of Walter Maddy, commonly called or known by the name or sign of the **Lamb** Inn, at Hay aforesaid, in order to choose an Assignee or Assignees of the estate and effects of the said **John Jones**.

In August 1815, a notice was published in the London Gazette *concerning a meeting to be held at the Lamb Inn*

The Lamb Inn in 2005 is a veterinary surgery

The one-time Bridge End Inn is now a canoe centre

average retail sales for the three years ended 31 December 1930 were £1,136; the estimated rental value being £27 10s. and the cost of converting to a private house £20. The claim was for £1,416 14s. The total value of the premises licensed was £1,242 10s. and delicensed £1,096 10s. The property is now the premises of Coles Veterinary Surgery. The sign on the wall — Lamb House Veterinary Surgery — is a slight reminder of the time when the building provided a service for humans rather than animals.

The **Bridge End Inn** was on the south side of Newport Street near Dulas Bridge and was recorded in the 1874 Register of Licences as a beer house. The owner was George Mills of Talgarth and the landlady was Elizabeth Price. By 1899 it had a seven-day licence and in 1901 the landlord was Thomas Williams who was also a gardener. In the Hay Urban District Land Valuation of 1910 the occupier was E. Buckett and the owners were the Hereford and Tredegar Brewery. It closed soon afterwards as it is not referred to in the licensing records from 1919 onwards. A business called Celtic Canoes is now run from the premises.

CHAPTER THIRTEEN

Hay-on-Wye:
Lion St., Bell Bank & Bear St.

This chapter starts once again at the Clock Tower, but this time proceeds along Lion Street, turning into Oxford Street, then Bell Bank and finishing in Bear Street.

The **Mitre** was at 43 Lion Street, but in older directories it was given the number 42 (next door to the large bookshop with the tiles on the outside). The renumbering has inevitably caused a few problems in identification. The first mention of the **Mitre** is in the census of 1861, when the landlord was Thomas Probert; it is not mentioned in Slater's *Directory* of 1859. James Morris was there by 1871— he was also a butcher. It was

The one-time Mitre in 2005

still open in 1884, but must have closed soon afterwards as it is not in any later directories. The premises eventually became a dentist's surgery and were the subject of a siege in December 1993. Edward Mark Williams attempted to murder his foster mother in Llangammarch Wells then fled to Hay. He tried to sell her car and the proposed purchaser took him to a bank in Hay. The police were called and when a Hay policeman, Constable Ken Murray, approached him in the bank, Williams produced a gun and forced the constable to hand over his police radio and keys. Williams eventually ended up at the dentist's surgery and held a number of patients and staff as hostages. The siege went on throughout the night and only ended when he dozed off and was overpowered by two of the hostages and his gun, which turned out to be an imitation, was taken from him. Thankfully the siege was over, but perhaps this event caused more excitement in the building than there ever was when it was a pub!

The **Red Lion** was two doors along and on the same side as the **Mitre** at number 41. The building's core is of 17th-century, timber-framed construction, but substantially altered in the 19th century. In the minute book of the Bredwardine and Whitney Turnpike Trust there is an entry concerning a meeting at the **Red Lion** on 1 September 1760 and there is a further entry confirming that there was a further meeting at the dwelling of Stephen Prichard, inn keeper, known by the sign of the **Red Lion,** Hay, on 19 February 1762. The 1765 order book for Brecon Quarter Sessions refers to the registration of the **Red Lion** for Quaker worship. It is believed that the actual meeting place was a shed at the bottom of the garden.

On 23 February 1798 James Spencer, a Hay solicitor (see also p.197), received a letter from Thos. Parker of Northumberland Street, London, who was writing on behalf of Thomas Phillips, the brother of the late John Phillips of the **Red Lion**, claiming £8 from the estate of John Phillips. The letter was written in response to a notice in the *Hereford Journal* of 31 January 1798 to the creditors/debtors of the late John Phillips, of the **Red Lion**. The contents of the letter are as follows:-

> Sir,
> Mr. Thomas Phillips claims the sum of £8 due to him from the Estate of his late brother Mr. John Phillips of the Red Lion in your town deceased for money paid by him in London upon a bill of exchange due the 27th of May last.
> Mr. Thomas Phillips has desired me in compliance with your advertisement to send you the above amount and he relies you will put him on the same footing with the other creditors.
> I am Sir
> Your obedient Servant
> Thos. Parker
> 23rd February 1798
> Northumberland St. Strand.

The letter was posted in Charing Cross and cost 8d. to send. Subsequently, on 7 March 1798, notice was given that the lease of the **Red Lion** was to be sold by auction. Undoubtedly this sale took place because of the death of the previous occupier, John Phillips.

The **Red Lion** was a popular venue for property auctions and general meetings during the 18th and 19th centuries. There was a meeting on

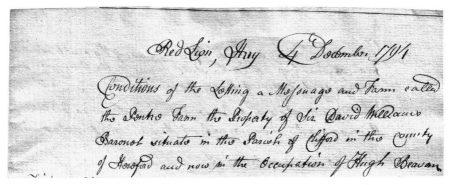

*The start of a tenancy agreement prepared at the Red Lion
and dated 4 December 1794*

2 September 1779, regarding proposals to build the bridge across the river Wye at Whitney, the notice about the meeting stating that 'any undertaker willing to engage to attend at the Red Lion, Hay'. On Thursday 4 December 1794 the terms of a tenancy agreement, relating to a property called Thom Pentro Farm at Clifford, were agreed between the owner and the proposed tenant. As was the custom at that time the agreement was drawn up at an inn, it happening to be the **Red Lion**. In 1801 the **Red Lion** was occupied by William Johnes, confirmed by a notice stating that on 23 February 1801 an estate was to be sold by auction 'at the Dwelling-house of William Johnes, known by the sign of the **Red Lion**, in the town of Hay'.

In 1830 the pub was referred to as being in the Pig Market and in 1835 the landlord was William Boore. On 20 October 1841 a notice in the *Hereford Times* stated that the **Red Lion** was to be sold by auction and commented that 'a very prosperous business had been carried on at this Inn for more than half a century'.

By 1859, when the pub was described in Slater's *Directory* as being in Red Lion Street, the landlord was William Price. He was still there, aged 29 years, in 1861. Thomas Morgan of Hay owned the pub in 1874 when the licence was held by Henry John Moro; it

Once the Red Lion Inn

215

was transferred to Llewellyn Lewis on 1 Feb 1875, then to Henry John Moro's widow, Sara, on 3 September 1877. The pub had a six-day licence from 5 September 1881, when the Welsh Sunday closing regulations came into force. The last directory entry referring to the **Red Lion** as a pub is in 1884. By 1891 the occupier was Elizabeth Davis who was described as a coffee-house keeper. This does not necessarily mean that the licence had lapsed as coffee houses were often rather up-market drinking houses. The pub was referred to by name in the 1910 Land Valuation listings for Hay, when the occupiers were a Mrs. Cook and J. Phillips and the owner was J.C. Morgan. The premises are now a shop.

4 Lion Street, probably once the White Lion

The **White Lion** is not mentioned in Slater's *Directory* for 1859, but is included in the 1861 census in Red Lion Street. The occupier was then Richard Connop, aged 38 and described as an innkeeper. This is the only mention of this inn and is different to the **Old White Lion** in Broad Street — its position in the census suggesting that it may have occupied the present number 4 Lion Street.

The **Wheatsheaf** is at 38 Lion Street on the corner with Brook Street. Although Fairs doesn't record it before 1830, a meeting of the Bredwardine and Whitney Turnpike Trust was minuted as being held 'at the house of George Watkins known by the sign of the **Wheatsheaf**' on 13 November 1775. By 1830 the landlord was Charles Parry, whose address was given as the Pig Market and an entry in Pigot's *Directory* confirms that Hannah Parry was the landlady in 1835. An advertisement in the *Hereford Times* on 12 January 1841, by James Macken, the proprietor of the **Wheatsheaf**, invited would-be tenants to apply to him for details. He must have been successful for on 14 August of that year he placed a notice in the same paper:

The Wheatsheaf in 2005

that in leaving the Inn, begs to return his best thanks to his friends and the public for the encouragement that he has met with during the last six years, and at the same time to inform them that the business will be in future conducted by Mr.Thomas Norman, whom he recommends to their notice.

George Tilley had become licensee by 1861 and was still there in 1884; in 1874 the owner was William Games of Brecon. On 4 June 1883 Tilley was fined £2 and costs for permitting drunkenness on the premises, and his licence was endorsed. Even so, he committed the same offence again some six months later and on 7 January 1884 he received another fine and a second endorsement. Perhaps that was enough, for by 1891 the landlord was William Webb who was described in the census as a farmer/inn-keeper.

It was sometime before 1898 that the **Wheatsheaf** became the property of the Hereford Brewery which was sold in that year. At the time of the sale the inn was let to Mr. George Phillips at a rent of £19 10s. per annum. Prior to taking up occupation of the **Wheatsheaf** George Phillips had been a beer retailer in Bear Street and according to the 1901 census he was also a carpenter.

The Tredegar Brewery bought the Hereford Brewery and were described as the owners in the Hay Urban Land Valuation in 1910, when the tenant was

Fred Price. It was owned by them until July 1931, during which period there were several landlords including Albert William Ree and Henry Williams. When it was sold their tenant was Frank Smith. In the sale details the inn was described as:

> A brick, stucco, and slated Corner House, in the Centre of the Stock Market, Containing Bar, Tap Room, good Smoke Room, Parlour, Lean-to Kitchen, Scullery, Workshop fronting Brook Street, Large Cellar in Basement, Four Bed Rooms, Box Room, Two Attics, Small Paved Yard, W.C., and Yard in rear extending to Parry's Lane.

The inventory of the contents shows clearly how pubs, and habits of customers, have changed since 1931. The contents for the direct benefit of the customers included 'Bagatelle table with top and marker, Quoits Board & Rings and table skittles'. Also included in the contents were 5 spittoons in the bar and 4 in the market room!

The pub was referred to the General Annual Licensing Committee on 17 February 1936 when the question of the renewal of the licence was raised because, it was alleged, there were too many pubs in the immediate vicinity. The premises were also referred under the Licensing (Consolidation) Act 1910 to ascertain the value of the property if the licence was to be removed. The Police, on behalf of the Licensing Authorities, objected to the renewal of the licence under the terms of the Act. Their case was that the **Wheatsheaf** was not required to meet the needs of the neighbourhood and the number of licensed houses in the immediate vicinity was excessive, there being eight fully-licensed houses within 230 yards of the **Wheatsheaf** namely:

Half Moon	52 yards	Rateable Value	£15
Black Lion	144 yards	-do-	£19
King's Head	104 yards	-do-	£17
Seven Sisters	164 yards	-do-	£21
Crown Hotel	180 yards	-do-	£56
Black Swan	220 yards	-do-	£12
Three Tuns	230 yards	-do-	£15
Masons Arms	210 yards	-do-	£18

The police stated that

> There are 12 fully licensed houses within the Hay Urban District with a population of 1,509, which gives an average of 126 persons including children, to each licensed house. This is the most congested area in the County. The average population of each licensed house, taking the County as a whole is 220, and the average for the whole of Wales is 526, according to the last figures available.

Mr. E.A. Capel, a solicitor from Hereford, appeared on behalf of the owners to object to the licence being referred for compensation. It took from February until October for a decision to be made, but finally, on 7 October 1936, at the County Hall, Brecon, it was unanimously resolved that the renewal of the licence of the **Wheatsheaf** be granted.

Albert Powell, the brother of Lucy Powell from the **Three Tuns** (chapter 12), was landlord of the **Wheatsheaf** from 1957 until 1970, but had to give up because of difficulties with the licensing authorities who alleged that he was running an unofficial betting business from the pub. When he left the **Wheatsheaf** he purchased the former **Castle Inn** and ran an official betting business for several years from those premises. The **Wheatsheaf** is still a popular pub in Hay with a good local clientele.

The **Castle Inn** was situated at 1 St. John's Place, next to St. John's church. The street was renamed Lion Street, whereupon the property was listed as no. 6. The first reference is in the 1858-9 directory when the landlady was Ann Byron and it was described as being in Red Lion Street; by 1861 the licensee was Thomas Williams, who was 39. In 1862 the **Castle Inn** was mortgaged to Thomas Carlton Skarratt, a draper and member of a well-known Kington family. The mortgage must have been taken up, for in 1889 the premises were conveyed by Williams, who was described in the deed as a blacksmith and innkeeper, to Skarratt. It would appear that the pub had closed some time before 1874 for there is no mention of the **Castle Inn** or Williams in the 1874 to 1884 licensing records and a deed of 1896 refers to the property as the former **Castle Inn**.

The **Harp Inn,** which was at 7 Lion Street, only appears in the 1874 Register of Licences, which stated that the owner and licensee was Elizabeth Stant and that it was a beer house. Previously, Elizabeth Stint had been at an unnamed establishment in Brecon Road in 1861, and at the same venue in a directory for 1868. By 1871 she had become a cider dealer in Gravel Lane; she was still at 7 Lion Street in 1875, but the licensing records do not show a renewal after 1874. The final reference to her in the premises was in 1881, although she is mentioned in a directory in 1884, but as it does not state her occupation it can be inferred that the **Harp Inn** had closed soon after 1874. The place has been completely rebuilt since the closure of the pub.

The **Half Moon** was at the junction of Lion Street and Chancery Lane and was in existence by 1830. Richard Williams, the landlord in 1844, was reported in the *Hereford Journal* for 28 February that year as having appeared before Hay Petty Sessions charged with having suffered persons to play cards in his house, contrary to the tenor of his licence. The court referred to an earlier offence of allowing drunkenness and disorderly conduct in the June of the previous year and fined him £2 with costs of 8s. 6d.

The Alton Court Brewery of Ross were obviously very pleased with their aquisition of the Half Moon Inn in 1891. Their faith was reasonably justified — it stayed open until 1970

The landlady in 1859 was Priscilla Dearden, a widow aged 62, but by January 1874, when the owner was recorded as Peter George, the licensee was the oddly-named Tamelane Linwall. On 3 June 1876 she was fined £1 plus costs and had her licence endorsed for permitting drunkenness on the premises. On 5 February 1877 the licence was transferred to Evan Davies who was licensee until 5 August 1878 when it was transferred to G.G. Tumbling as a temporary measure whilst the licence was transferred to Thomas Bidmead on 19 August

The Half Moon is now a rather smart looking house, but has lost much of its character

1878. In May 1889 Mrs. Martha Jones bought the **Half Moon** as sitting tenant and then conveyed the pub to the Alton Court Brewery in September 1891. By 1901 Evan M. Jones, who was also a wool merchant, had taken over.

In July 1931 the **Half Moon** was valued under the Licensing Act, 1910 in the sum of £1,242 10s. as a going concern and at £1,096 delicenced; the cost of conversion to a private house being £20. The valuation was done preparatory to the licence being refused, but this clearly did not happen because the pub remained open until 1970. It was only on 3 May 1971 that it was sold by the owners, West Country Breweries, and became a private house.

The one-time New Inn

Remains of the inn sign from the 1850s.
[N]EW INN
[JO]HN HIGGINS
[Lic]ensed to Brew
[&] Retail, Ale, Beer
[C]ider, Spirituous
[Li]quors, Tobacco &c

The **New Inn** was on the south-west corner of Lion Street and Bear Street. Bear Street appears as New Street in the 1830s and 1850s. The directories state that the **New Inn** was at no. 13 although it was originally described as being at no. 12. This beer house had a relatively short life and was only open until sometime between 1884, when it last appeared in a directory, and 1891. The named occupiers were John Smith in 1830; James Davies in 1835; John Higgins Jnr. in 1850 (who was also a butcher); and finally Silvia Higgins.

Slater's *Directory* of 1859 describes Alfred Halford of New Street as a retailer of beer and cider and, by time of the 1861 census, he was described as a spade tree maker — a master employing 17 men and two boys. Halford appeared in the Register of Licences for 1874 as the owner of the **New Inn** when the licensee was James Jenkins.

In 1879 the owners were Messrs. James & Bodenham — a firm of solicitors practising in Hereford. Bodenham was the solicitor for James Spencer (see also p.197) and was described in a letter written by Spencer in the 1840s as 'The Rogue Bodenham'. By 1881 the tenant was Andrew Preece and a year later it was James Saunders. In an 1891 directory George Philips was described as a beer retailer in Bear Street, and in the census of the same year George Phillips was a carpenter at 13 Bear Street, the number of the **New Inn**, suggesting that the licence had been given up in that year. Certainly the **New Inn** does not appear in any later directories. In the 1910 Land Valuation the occupier of the 'Old New Inn' was Mrs. Price and the owner W.M. Watkins of Lion Street. The premises, like many other former public houses in Hay, is now a private house, and during renovations in 2003 an original sign, which had been covered up from the time that John Higgins was landlord 150 years ago, was found on a wall in the house.

A busy scene at the Black Lion about the beginning of the 20th century

The **Black Lion** is at no. 26 Lion Street, opposite the end of Bear Street and close to the south gate in the Hay town wall. A black lion was part of the arms of Owain Glyndwr. The earliest known mention of the pub is a reference to a William Seward of Badsey in Worcestershire, who was killed by a stone thrown at him whilst preaching at the Black Lion Green, Hay, on 22 October 1740. The reference to Badsey is taken from *A Historical Guide To The Town And Castle Of Hay,* published in 1877. However, the author throws some doubt on the way that Seward was killed by prefixing the story with 'Tradition affirms that ...'. Whatever the case, Seward's grave can be found in Cusop churchyard.

The **Black Lion** Friendly Society had sufficient funds to erect a tomb to the memory of Rev. Richard Lloyd, who died aged 67 on 19 October 1797. The inn must have had some local standing for the Bredwardine and Whitney Turnpike Trust met there quite regularly from 1760 to 1802.

In 1843 there was a court case between the landlord of the **Black Lion** and a superintendent constable William McMahon who accused each other of being drunk and disorderly — unfortunately the result is unknown! Sales were common at the **Black Lion** — one example being when the effects of a surgeon, Mr. Groman Woodcock, were removed from his property in Oxford Terrace by the Hay auctioneer David Jones and were delivered to the large room at the **Black Lion** in readiness for a sale to take place on 21 January 1850.

The Black Lion continues to serve visitors to Hay into the 21st century

John and Hester Williams ran the **Black Lion** between 1861 and 1871 — he was recorded as the owner in 1874. In 1891 the landlord was John Probert, but by 1901 John Jones had taken over. The pub had a seven-day licence in 1899 but along with the other pubs in Hay (and Wales as a whole) it was reduced to a six-day licence by 1919. At this time the licensee was James Williams and the owners the Builth Wells Brewery. Trade must have continued reasonably well, for Williams was still at the premises in 1926.

There is a recent story contained in the book *Nobody had heard of Hay* where Vera Fairfax recalled her grandfather saying that the **Black Lion** was the worst pub for rowdiness in Hay. Apparently he lived in a cottage at the back of Hendre and the noise was so awful that even he did not dare to go down there. He said that in Hay you had either to be a drunkard or a religious fanatic, there was nothing else to do. Judging by the number of pubs in Hay in the 19th and early 20th centuries the former category was most likely! The **Old Black Lion** is still open today, but the noise is now not so great.

The **Volunteer Institute and Drill Hall** in Lion Street was opened in about 1870, when it was described as:

> A neat and substantial looking edifice. The hall is neatly decorated, and is let for concerts, entertainments and public meetings. It is capable of seating about three hundred persons.

224

George Jenkins may well have had a licence there in 1871 because he also had a licence for the **Drovers' Arms** by 1874, which was in close proximity. The premises were the focal point for entertainment in Hay, and apart from concerts the premises also operated as a working men's club with reading and coffee rooms. In 1910 the property was owned by Edmund Cheese, the Hay solicitor who was a partner of H.R. Armstrong.

On 17 January 1890 there was a complimentary luncheon and presentation to Sir R.D. Green-Price at the **Drill Hall**. He was chairman of the Golden Valley Railway and was instrumental in ensuring that the Hay extension line was built by putting up £15,000 worth of debentures. The project had difficulties throughout its life and his debentures were only worth £444 when he died in 1909.

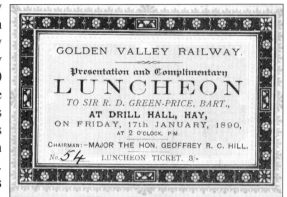

What a great railway it would be if it was still running!

The **Drovers' Arms** was at Beech House and on the same side of Lion Street as the **Drill Hall**. It was a beer house and in the Licensing Records for 1874 the owner was given as Elizabeth Ricketts and the licensee George Jenkins. It is not mentioned in the licensing records from 1879 onwards and in all probability closed to customers some time between 1874 and 1879. Although it is not shown as a pub on the 1882 Ordnance Survey map, according to Fairs it was not finally delicensed until 1902.

There is nothing known about the history of the **Traveller's Trap** which

The Traveller's Trap was probably in the predecessor of this building

225

was also in Lion Street, but it is believed to have been in the premises once occupied by Bryntiron Dairy. No documentary evidence has been traced and the information has been gathered solely from local memory.

The **Bell Inn**, which was on the east side of Bell Bank nearly half-way down the street, was already open in 1830 when the landlord was William Woodhill, but at that time it was placed in Horsefair. However, by 1835 it was described as being in Bell Bank — perhaps the street took its name from the pub? By 1859 the landlord was Daniel Minard, but by 1861, when it was known as the **Bell Bank Inn**, the landlord was Edward Bowen. By 1874 the owners were the trustees of a deceased person named Price and the tenant was George Lovett. G.H. Page, a solicitor who

Above: This fine building was once the Bell Inn or Bell Bank Inn

practised in Hay, owned one fifth of the property under a deed dated 16 December 1875, but by 4 September 1876 Page owned the whole of the premises, the licence being transferred to David Price on 2 May 1877. On 4 August 1879 the licence was transferred again, this time to one Edward Bruntnell who, on 15 December the same year, was fined 10s. and costs and had his licence endorsed for permitting drunkenness. By 1910 the **Bell Inn** was owned by Arnold, Perrett and Co. Ltd; and the occupier was Elizabeth Meadows.

The Bear Inn provides bed and breakfast accommodation in 2005

The licence changed hands rapidly in the 1920s from George Bailey to A.G. Lawrence and then Alfred Galliers. It is not therefore surprising that in February 1922 it was referred for compensation. Although the licence was provisionally renewed on 20 February, the owner of the **Bell** was compensated and so presumably the inn closed later that year, there being no application in 1923.

The **Bear**, a former pub at the west end of Bear Street, is a timber-framed, two-storey building dating from the 16th or 17th centuries. The earliest reference to the **Bear** is in the Bredwardine and Whitney Turnpike Trust minute book, which records that two meetings were held at the dwelling house of Edward Drew at the sign of the **Bear** on 25 June 1768 and 15 February 1770. In 1771 the property was owned by Edward Allen, Attorney at Law, who practised in Hay. In his will he left the **Bear** to his son William. The will stated:

> also I give to my said Son William Allen from and after my said Wife's Death and to his Heirs and assignees for ever all that Messuage or Tenement with the Outbuildings and Gardens thereto belonging and adjoining with their appurtenances called and known by the name of the Bear now in the possession or occupation of Edward Drew and Mr John Jones.

William Gane's early 1920s Bear Inn sign

Kilvert's in 2005

The licence stayed in the Watkins family for many years. In 1830 the landlord was William Watkins and by 1844 Fanny Watkins. Hannah Watkins had joined Fanny by 1859 and they were still there in 1884. In 1910 the property was owned by the Old Brewery, Brecon, and was occupied by a Mrs. Price, but by 1919 the licensee was William Thomas. Licensing records state that William Gane took over the **Bear Inn** on 6 February 1922. Gane had a sign painted which showed his name prominently, and also showed a polar bear. On his departure the sign was placed in the cellar where it has remained ever since. In 1926 William Gane was followed as licensee by William Evans.

On 18 January 1943 the premises was sold by the owner, William Lilwall, to Thomas Henry Price for £295. In the conveyance the property was described as 'formerly an Inn or Alehouse' so must have closed before that date. At that time the premises were in a dilapidated condition, hence the price, but after renovation they were used as a private residence. The former pub was owned by a trust from 1979 to 1982 — the Tyn-y-Pwll School of Outdoor Pursuits. The Trust, whose main object was to help deprived children from the north of England, ran an outward-bound centre in Wales and the premises in Hay was used as a branch. A change of use followed — the premises was then used as a retail outlet for the restoration and sale of antique clocks. There has since been a more recent change and the **Bear** is now a bed and breakfast establishment. However, the modern sign outside still shows a polar bear.

One of the newest licensed premises in Hay is **Kilvert's** in the Bull Ring. The original building is of 17th-century date but the front of the premises was rebuilt in the 19th century. The property, which was originally called Pemberton House, was a doctor's surgery for many years and Dr. L.D. Heather practised from there until his death in 1912. The practise was then taken over by Dr. R.J. Shepherd who left Hay in 1919, and then by Dr. Hugh Powell until his death in 1955. The premises have fairly recently been converted by local builder Terry Salter, and **Kilvert's** is now a flourishing business in the centre of Hay.

Pemberton House was a doctor's surgery for many years before becoming a pub called Kilvert's

BRIDGENORTH TO BRECON, BY CLEOBURY MORTIMER, TENBURY, LEOMINSTER, AND HAY.

WHITNEY. Whitney Court, *Tomkyns Dew*, Esq.

CLIFFORD. Here are the ruins of a castle, which gave name to the Lords Clifford, afterwards Earls of Cumberland.

HAY. The Castle, *Henry Wellington*, Esq.

HAY, pleasantly situated on a gentle eminence on the southern bank of the Wye, consists principally of one street running in the direction of the river, with a short cross-street near the eastern end; just beyond which it is divided from the county of Hereford by the little river Dulais, which here discharges its waters into the Wye. The houses are generally of the inferior class; but a few of a better description occasionally occur, that indicate the presence of some more opulent inhabitants. Hay is a borough by prescription, but possesses at present no privileges. The bailiff or chief magistrate, whose official duties are now restricted to receiving the tolls at the fairs and markets, is annually appointed by the lord of the manor, to whom they belong, and who holds a court-leet here annually. The parish-church, dedicated to St. Mary, is most delightfully situated on a precipitous bank of the Wye, on a bold reach of that noble river, and commanding an extensive prospect down the vale. There is some appearance of its having been once separated from the town by a deep ditch, through which the waters of the Wye may have flowed. The church is small, consisting of a nave and chancel, with a tower at the west end, and contains no object of curiosity, excepting the silver chalice used in the administration of the sacrament, which bears the following inscription, "Our Ladie Paris of the Haia," and is of ancient date. The river Wye is crossed near the eastern extremity of the town by a long bridge, constructed partly of stone and partly of wood. It appears, however, only to be a temporary erection; its predecessor, a handsome stone bridge of seven arches, having been destroyed in the year 1795, by a flood. The walls that formerly surrounded the town may yet be seen in some places, and a part only of the castle stands upon an eminence in the town. A dwelling house has been built out of the remains; but a Gothic gateway has been preserved, which frowns with venerable and baronial dignity upon the inhabitants of the town below. This place has been on the decline since the time of Owen Glendower, who committed great devastations in this neighbourhood; it appears also, from the various antiquities found here, to have been of some consequence in the time of the Romans, and to have experienced its share of martial vicissitudes in the contentious struggles between the native princes and the crown of England. The situation of Hay on the borders of the two counties, and in a rich agricultural district, seems to afford it considerable advantages as a mart for inland commerce. At present there is but one market here in the week, which is on Thursday, though formerly it had the right of holding another on Monday. It has five fairs in the course of the year, all of which are well attended, and afford opportunities for the sale of considerable numbers of cattle and horses.

From Brecon		From Bridgen.
	Cross the river Teme	
46	* *TENBURY, Worcestershire*	$21\frac{1}{4}$
	☞ *to Worcester 20 m.* / *to Bromyard 11 m.*	
$42\frac{1}{4}$	Layster's Pole, *Hereford.*	25
$39\frac{1}{2}$	Kimbolton	$27\frac{3}{4}$
$38\frac{1}{2}$	Stockton Cross	$28\frac{3}{4}$
	To Ludlow 9 m. ☞	
	Cross the river Lugg	
$36\frac{3}{4}$	* *LEOMINSTER*	$30\frac{1}{2}$
	To Ludlow $10\frac{1}{4}$ m. ☞	
	☞ *to Hereford 13 m.* / *to Bromyard $11\frac{1}{2}$ m.*	
	1 m. beyond Leominster, To Presteign 13 m. ☞	
	Near Monkland, Cross the river Arrow	
$34\frac{1}{4}$	Monkland	33
$32\frac{1}{4}$	Junction of the Roads	35
	To Kington 9 m. ☞	
	☞ *to Hereford $12\frac{1}{4}$ m.*	
$30\frac{1}{2}$	Dilwyn	$36\frac{3}{4}$
$28\frac{1}{2}$	White Hill Turnpike	$38\frac{3}{4}$
	☞ *to Weobly, $\frac{3}{4}$ m., thence to Hereford 11 m.*	
	Bridgenorth to WEOBLY $39\frac{1}{2}$ m.	
27	Sarnesfield	$40\frac{1}{4}$
	$\frac{1}{4}$ m. farther,	
	☞ *to Hereford 12 m.*	
	To Kington 7 m. ☞	
25	Kinnersley	$42\frac{1}{4}$
$22\frac{3}{4}$	Cross	$44\frac{1}{2}$
	To Kington $5\frac{1}{2}$ m. ☞	
	☞ *to Hereford $13\frac{1}{4}$ m.*	
	☞ to Willersley,	
$22\frac{1}{4}$	*Turnpike*	45
	Forward to Hereford $13\frac{1}{4}$ m.	
$21\frac{1}{4}$	*To* Winforton ☞	46
$19\frac{1}{4}$	Whitney	48
	$\frac{1}{2}$ m. farther, Cross the river Wye	
$17\frac{3}{4}$	Clifford	$49\frac{1}{2}$
$15\frac{1}{4}$	* *HAY, Brecknockshire*	52
	* *BRECON, page 147*	$67\frac{1}{4}$

LEOMINSTER, 2 m. distant, Eyeton Hall, *Edward Evans*, Esq.

MONKLAND, 2 m. beyond, Burton Court, The Misses *Evans*.

DILWYN. Henwood, *Lacon Lambe*, Esq.

WHITE HILL TURNPIKE, 1 m. distant, Garnstone Castle, *Samuel Peploe*, Esq.

SARNESFIELD. Sarnesfield House, Mrs. *Salisbury*.

KINNERSLEY, 2m. distant, Newport House, *B. Hall*, Esq.

WILLERSLEY, $1\frac{1}{3}$ m. distant, Eardisley Park, *Thomas Perry*, Esq.

CLIFFORD. Cabalva, *W. Davies*, Esq.

BRECON, near, Fried Gruch, *S. Church*, Esq.; and Ter Maur, *C. C. Clifton*, Esq.

Above: a page from Paterson's 1828 Road Book

CHAPTER FOURTEEN

Hay-on-Wye:
High Town, Castle St. & Church St.

The starting point for this chapter is once again the Clock Tower, and will deal with the pubs in part of High Town, Castle Street and Church Street. These streets, like those in most of Hay had other names previously and to make things more confusing, mistakes were made in directories and even in the census. However, the continuity of the pubs themselves enables these problems to be resolved.

Local memory (and this seems to go back a long while in Hay) places the **Three Horse Shoes** at 7 High Town, but there is no reference to an inn of that name in any directory since 1830. The only possible entry is of a beer retailer called George Lewis of 'Craneborne' Alley, in an 1850 directory. Three horse shoes feature in the arms of the Worshipful Company of Farriers, so the name may indicate that one of the early innkeepers was, or had been, a farrier by trade. 7 High Town has been a chemist's shop since at least 1852 when J.L. Davies & Son, dispensing & manufacturing chemists, was established, so the pub must have closed before that date. However, John Frederick Davies, who occupied the premises in the early 1920s, also had a wine off-licence and this may have given rise to the building's reputation as a pub.

Possibly the Three Horse Shoes

231

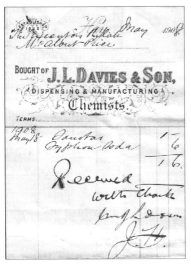

Was this chemist' shop once the Three Horse Shoes Inn?

J.F. (Fred) Davies was the chemist involved in the Henry Rowse Armstrong case (Chapter 12). Not only did he innocently supply Armstrong with arsenic, but he was also the father-in-law of Oswald Martin, who was the rival solicitor that the courts found Armstrong attempted to poison.

In 1924 Thomas Dixon Nutt took over the premises from Davies and was followed by R.M. Jones & Sons who still occupy the building. In June 1962 Ronald Middleton Jones applied to Hay Magistrates Court for a licence to sell spirits at his chemist shop, in addition to the wine off-licence. According to a report in the *Hereford Times* the application was:

> supported by a petition signed by 200 people in three days. Ladies figured prominently among those who sought to buy spirits, and they generally called in the afternoon after licensed houses were shut.

The Hay Licensed Victuallers Association objected to the application on the grounds that the state of the licensed trade in Hay was so bad that the licensees had to take extra jobs, leaving their wives to run the pub. The magistrates must have had some sympathy with the publicans in Hay for the application by Mr. Jones was refused.

The **Fountain Inn** was situated in the High Street/High Town area about where the building occupied by the HSBC Bank now stands. The name may indicate that the inn had a spring of clean water, or that it was near to a public

The Fountain stood near this building

drinking fountain. The earliest reference to the **Fountain** is in the minute book of the Bredwardine and Whitney Turnpike Trust for the period 1760/77, which recorded that there was a meeting at the dwelling house of Thomas Price, at the **Fountain** on 28 October 1762. A little later, a notice in the *Hereford Journal* dated 2 March 1780 advised that Corn Grist Mills were to be let by auction at the **Fountain Inn** in the Borough of the Parish of Hay.

Social conditions in the 18th century were different to the present day and there were many paupers and vagrants. According to Fairs, prior to the provision of workhouses the poor were looked after by the overseers of the poor, and many were housed in single rooms in houses rented for the purpose. Food was also provided, and in 1782 a contract was entered into with John Powell of the **Fountain Inn** to supply all necessary food for £130 per annum.

On 18 December 1822 an advertisement in the *Hereford Journal* stated that the 23 ton barge, *Liberty*, was for sale by auction at the **Fountain**. Curiously, another barge called the *Liberty* was built in Hay in 1824 by James Prout. Navigation took place up the Wye as far as Hay, in suitable conditions, during the 18th and the early part of the 19th centuries.

The only directory entry is in 1830, when the **Fountain** is shown as being in High Street, now called High Town. William Spillman was the licensee at that time, but by 1835 he had moved to the **Swan**, and as the **Fountain** is not mentioned in that or later directories, in all probability he was the last licensee of the inn.

The occupiers of the building in 1844 were Charles and Benjamin Hadley, chemists and druggists. Between 1868 and 1871 Thomas Stokoe took over from Charles Hadley and the building was probably demolished about that time. In the 1874 Register of Licences Hadley owned a shop in Castle Street (presumably built on the site) and he and Stokoe had an additional spirits licence. From 1879 Stokoe had an off-licence and was also agent for W. & A. Gilbeys wine and spirit merchants. By 1879 Stokoe was the sole occupier and the premises were used solely as a bottling plant for soft drinks. As part of the business, Stokoe continued to act as the the local chemist and veterinary. In 1880 their address was given as 12 High Town — the same address as the current occupiers, the H.S.B.C.

The **Market Tavern/George** stood at the south-west end of Market Street, but the building was demolished in about 1958 to make room for a car park. The 1929 Ordnance Survey map, and a photograph taken in 1920 at the War Memorial before it was moved, both indicate that this was quite a substantial property. The documentary evidence regarding occupation of the building supports the view that the **Market Tavern** was originally called the **George**, but that the name changed by common usage because of its location.

The earliest reference to the **George** is in 1691 when, on 26 August the Almoners of Christ's Hospital travelled to Hay from Wobley [Weobley] to inspect Mr. Pennoyre's School and stayed at the **George**. One wonders which George was celebrated by the pub's name for, this is too early for King George I. According to Fairs (1972), Friendly Societies met at the **George**

*The Market Tavern/George at the inauguration of
the war memorial in 1920*

Inn in the 18th and 19th centuries. In addition, the 1765 order book for Brecon Quarter Sessions refers to the registration of three premises for Quaker worship in the Hay area, one of which was the **George Inn Barn**.

On 17 March 1769 there was a meeting of the Bredwardine and Whitney Turnpike Trust at the 'Dwelling House of Matthew Kinsey Innholder, known by the sign of the George Inn' and there was a further meeting at the house of Mary Kinsey (his widow) at the inn on 23 January 1777. She was still there in December 1778 when there was another meeting of the Hay Turnpike.

Thomas James was named as landlord of the **George** in Castle Street in 1830 and 1835, but from 1844 he was listed as being at the **George** in Market Place. The corner site must always have led to some confusion — there is no known evidence that he moved premises. Joseph Prosser moved to the **George** from the **Black Swan** in the 1850s presumably after the departure or death of Thomas James, because in Slater's *Directory* for 1859 he was named as the landlord and by 1874 as the owner. Prosser had at least one break in tenure because in the 1871 census Ann Wilce was named as the licensee of 1 Market Street — it could only be the **George**, but the pub name was not mentioned. Prosser was in constant trouble with the law — on 5 October 1875 he was fined £1 and costs for permitting drunkenness on his licensed premises and his licence was endorsed, on 6 March 1877 he was fined £2 and costs for the same offence and his licence was endorsed again. His final recorded misdemeanour was on the 20 May 1878 when he was fined £5 and costs for permitting drunkenness and on the same date the premises were

234

disqualified for two years. There is no evidence of the licence subsequently being renewed and in the 1881 census Joseph Prosser was listed as a retired innkeeper aged 67 residing at Market House. The confusion of names and addresses continued — the **George Inn** is listed as 1 Market Place in the 1871 census and as 2 Market Street in an 1880 directory. Little is known about the later history of the building, but in *Nobody had heard of Hay* there is reference to the occupier of the premises that used to be the **George/ Market Tavern** selling faggots and peas that were clearly enjoyed by the locals.

Documentary sources seem to be somewhat confused between George House and the **George Inn**. However, the present George House (for a period the vicarage) has been called by that name since the 18th century as an inspection of the deeds covering the period 1760 to 1843 has shown. They indicate that in 1762 the premises were purchased by John Watkins and settled on his daughter on her marriage to Edmund Cheese. In 1806 the property was purchased by Thomas Howells, a Quaker and successful businessman — he was a woollen manufacturer, who lived at George House until his death in 1824. Part of the property passed to his daughter Susannah Swetman, who was also a Quaker, and the remainder to his son. In 1829 one part was sold to William Enoch who, like his predecessor Thomas Howells, was clearly a man of means. In 1833 he financed the rebuilding of the Butter Market in Hay and there is now a plaque on the wall commemorating his generosity. The only William Enoch in Pigot's *Directory* 1835 is described as a Linen and Woollen Draper residing in High Town. George House was the main house of an estate in Hay, the house next door being in the same ownership. The deeds do not mention any use as licensed premises and indeed, the building seems to be rather up-market for that. In 1851 George House was occupied by Mary Jones, a 70-year-old widow, described as an Annuitant, and definitely not a publican.

As previously mentioned, in the 1835 directory and in the 1851 census Thomas James is named as the licensee of the **George Inn**, so at this period George House and the **George Inn** were two different places. George House was advertised for sale in 1907 and in the particulars it was stated that the house stood well back from the street — another indication that it was a private residence and not a pub.

The **Talbot**, which was originally known as the **Dog**, was at 8 Castle Street. According to Fairs it was a pub prior to 1776. A talbot according to the *Oxford Dictionary* was:

A kind of large whitish hound now extinct with long hanging ears and heavy jaws, formerly used for tracking and hunting and supposed to be an ancestral stock of bloodhound; representation of this is in heraldry, as an inn-sign.

The Talbot in the early 20th century

This may well explain why the **Dog** was eventually re-named the **Talbot**. In 1830 James Price was listed as landlord of the **Dog** but by 1835 he was listed as landlord of the **Talbot** — undoubtedly it was the same pub. In Slater's *Directory* for 1859 James Maskall is listed as landlord of the **Talbot**, but by 1861 Thomas Hayson, who was a widower aged 56, had taken over. He was also a labourer and had been born in Ewyas Harold. By 1871 John Probert was the licensee and he was followed by 1891 by Llewellyn Lewis.

The licensing records confirm that the owner in 1874 was Lord Viscount Hereford from Tregoyd. However, in 1898 the **Talbot** was listed as one of the leasehold inns in the sale of the Hereford Brewery. The lease at £25 per annum, was for a term of 10 years from 2 February 1892. The Brewery had let the property to David Jarman at a rent of £19 10s. — he was still there in 1901 when he was aged 37. In the 1910 Land Valuation for Hay, the owner and occupier was the Hereford and Tredegar Brewery. In 1919 the landlord was Joseph Phillip who, on 19 May, was fined for selling two pints at a price exceeding the maximum controlled price. In addition, for not exhibiting a list of

The one-time Talbot in 2005

HEREFORDSHIRE AND BRECONSHIRE.

TIMBER AND COPPICE.

MR. THOS. PRICE

WILL SELL BY AUCTION,

At the TALBOT INN, in the Town of Hay,

On Friday, 25th March, 1881,

At TWO o'clock in the Afternoon; subject to Conditions;

THE UNDERMENTIONED

TIMBER

VIZ:

Lot 1.   800 LARCH, numbered 1 to 800, and 100 SPRUCE, felled and lying in the LOWER WOOD, and marked with Red Paint.

Lot 2.   60 OAK TREES, numbered 1 to 60, standing in CWMGWILLIM PLANTATION.
The above Lots are situate on TREGOYD ESTATE, within about Two Miles from Glasbury, and Four from Hay Railway Stations.   Edward Lane, Woodward, Tregoyd, will shew the above Lots.

Lot 3.   500 LARCH TREES, numbered 1 to 500, lying in WERN-Y-VIRIG PLANTATION.

Lot 4.   50 LARCH TREES, in the ALLT PLANTATION.

Lot 5.   30 ASH and 9 WYTCH, standing in PENHENALLT MEADOW.

Lot 6.   118 OAK TREES and POLES, standing in the OPEN WOOD.

Lot 7.   160 OAK TREES and POLES, standing in the LONG WOOD.
Lots 3 to 7 are standing on PENYWORLODD ESTATE, in the Parish of Llanigon, near the Town of Hay. William Lewis, Woodward, Llanigon, will shew the same.

Lot 8.   About 13 Acres of good COPPICE WOOD, standing in ASPER WOOD, near the Bage, within One Mile of Dorstone Railway Station, and Five of Hay, close to a good Road. Mr. Jones, the Bage Farm, will appoint a person to shew the Coppice.

Further Particulars to be obtained on application to

Mr. CHARLES GRIFFITHS, Estate Agent, Hay.

LUNCHEON at Half-past One prompt.

GEORGE HORDEN, PRINTER AND BOOKSELLER

*Sales of timber often took place in pubs as with this one
at the Talbot Inn in 1881*

prices in the bar, contrary to the regulations, he was fined £10. Possibly as a result, Mary Howells took over the licence on 20 October 1919, but by 1923 she had been succeeded by Charles Walters.

The pub was referred for compensation twice, there was a provisional renewal in 1922 then, in 1927, there was another provisional renewal on

21 February. This was the last act for the **Talbot** — the owner was finally compensated and the inn closed its doors on 30 December 1927.

The **Mason's Arms** was on the south side of Castle Street at number 26. It is known to have had a licence granted prior to 1776 but the first known documented evidence relating to the pub is a notice by Richard Phillips, dated 15 June 1784, which reads as follows:

> Whereas Richard Phillips, late of the Mason's Arms in this town, has separated from his wife: this is, therefore, to all persons from giving her credit on my account, and will not pay any debt she may contract. Richard Phillips.

Those were the days when a husband was responsible for his wife's debts!

The pub appears to have changed landlord on a regular basis, for in 1830 it was William Jones, then in 1835 Mary Jones, possibly his widow. In 1844 the landlord was George Thomas and by 1850 it had changed hands again and Richard James was in charge. Pigot's *Directory* for 1859 lists the landlord as Edward Williams, but he did not last long because, by the time of the 1861 census, it was James Davies aged 61 from Titley near Kington, and later the same year it was Eliza Davies who was in charge. Between 1861 and 1871 the pub changed hands again because by 1871 the licensee was Naomi Winton, a widow at the early age of 35. She was there until the licence was transferred to James Morgan on 21 June 1874. The **Mason's Arms** was then another of the Hay pubs listed as being owned by the Hereford solicitor, Francis Bodenham. William Powell from Usk took up brief occupation from 1879 until 4 April 1881 when James Watkins became licensee. Watkins had

The Mason's Arms is on the right beyond the café in this old photograph

only been at the pub for three months when he fell foul of the law, because on 4 July 1881 he was fined 10s. and costs and his licence was endorsed, and on 2 October he was fined £2 10s. with 7s. 6d. costs for permitting drunkenness, his licence being endorsed for the second time.

There was then a period of some stability James Holbrow being listed as landlord in 1891 and 1901, although the address of the **Mason's Arms** varied between 24 and 26 Castle Street. The 1910 Land Valuation indicates that the owners were the Alton Court Brewery of Ross and the occupier was John Wiseman. By 1919 the licensee was Frank Warren Webb who was still there in 1926.

The Mason's Arms is now a Spar supermarket

One of the most well-known customers of the pub, according to *The Book of Hay* was Richard Booth of bookshop fame. The landlords at the time were Ken and Violet Jenkins who endured many late night drinking sessions when he was present. The licence was not renewed in 1971 — the year that Hay lost two pubs, the other being the **Half Moon**. Lucy Powell from the **Three Tuns** (Chapter 12) said that when the **Mason's** closed it became a guest house, but by 1987 it was a branch of Fine Fare and is now a Spar supermarket.

The **Golden Lion** was on the south side of Castle Street at number 21. The golden lion is an emblem from the Royal Arms so it must be assumed that the owners wished to proclaim their allegiance to the crown. The earliest reference so far found, is on 8 October 1760, when there was a meeting of the Bredwardine and Whitney Turnpike Trust at the **Golden Lyon**, followed by another meeting on 10 August 1761 'at the Dwelling House of Dugal McGibbon known by the sign of the **Golden Lyon**'. McGibbon had a second job being postmaster at that time. On 11 December 1794 a notice advertising a change of landlords stated that Joshua James has taken the **Golden Lion Inn**, lately occupied by John Savagar:

> which he has fitted up in a neat and commodious manner for the reception of those Ladies and Gentlemen who may please to honour him with their company, assuring them that they may depend on the greatest attention and civility.

By 1835 the spelling had changed again from **Lyon** to **Lion**, the landlord being William Jones. In 1859 the licensee was Charles Gibson and by 1861 Ann Wilce, who was then aged 40. In 1874 the owner was recorded as James Bevan Lloyd and the following year the licence was transferred from Ann Wilce to Mary Ann Price. She presumably celebrated her new job by marrying a Mr. Biddle because on 6 September 1875 the licence was transferred to Mary Ann Biddle!

All things come to an end, and by 1891, according to Kelly's *Directory*, the premises had become a shop occupied by Charles Gorst. The **Golden Lion** must have closed its doors to customers some time between 1875 and 1891. For almost 45 years from 1920 the building was Madigan's cycle shop — proudly described as a 'Motor and Cycle Works' as there was a petrol pump on the edge of the pavement.

The **Wine Vaults/Bunch of Grapes** was in Castle Street. It was clearly much more than a beer house and sold wines and spirits as well. While in the past distinctions have been made between the **Grapes, Bunch of Grapes**, and **Wine Vaults** in Castle Street, documentary sources show that these were all names for the same up-market establishment, although directories in particular have errors in location which have been corrected from other sources. Charles Minton was at the pub in 1830 and in 1835.

It was on 29 August 1846 that Elizabeth Morris, described as being of the **Wine Vaults**, placed an advertisement in the *Hereford Times* announcing that she was retiring from business and introducing Mr. John Yate Wheeler as her successor. It turns out that Elizabeth Morris was the widow of the partner of Charles Minton because in the same notice Wheeler wrote:

> In taking on the old Established Business, for many years conducted by Mr. Charles Minton and Mr. Morris, begs to assure the inhabitants of Hay and neighbourhood that it will ever be his study and desire to keep nothing but Wines Spirits etc of the best quality, at the lowest possible price, for ready money, and he trusts that by personal attention and regularity in the despatch of all orders for which he may be favoured to merit and retain them. Ale, prime bottled cider, and beer of the very best quality.

By 1859 the property was described as the **Bunch of Grapes/Wine Vaults**, the landlord being John Humphris. At that time the address was given as Church Street, the building being close to the junction of Castle Street and Church Street and different directories placed it in one or the other. The 1861 census gives the occupier of the **Bunch of Grapes Inn** as Mary E Harris; it must be assumed that her husband was away as she is described as the innkeeper's wife. Her husband was presumably the John Harris recorded

The entry to the re-opened Wine Vaults

in the 1874 licensing records as the owner and licensee of the inn. The licence was transferred to James Evans on 17 April 1876; by 1879 the records show that the owner was Jno. Jarvis from 'Bronith' (Bronllys) and the licensee was Lewis Evans, perhaps a relative of James. In the latter part of the 19th century the property was generally known as the **Wine Vaults** and at the beginning of the 20th century Thomas Stokoe was the licensee, apparently employing a manager.

The establishment had ceased to be an inn by the time of the 1910 Land Valuation, having become the Wye Hotel. Later it came down the social scale a little, becoming the Wye Café. However, the wheel has now turned a full circle and the property is once again the **Wine Vaults**.

The **Cock Inn**, also known as the **Cock & Hen,** was at 12 Castle Street and according to Fairs was there prior to 1776. The name suggests that cock fighting took place there regularly, there having been a cock painted on a door panel of one of the upstairs rooms which regrettably has now disappeared. By 1815 the inn had closed and the premises had became the offices for the Hay Tramroad Company who operated the horse-drawn tramway from Brecon to

Above: The West or Carles Gate plaque
Left: the one-time Cock Inn

241

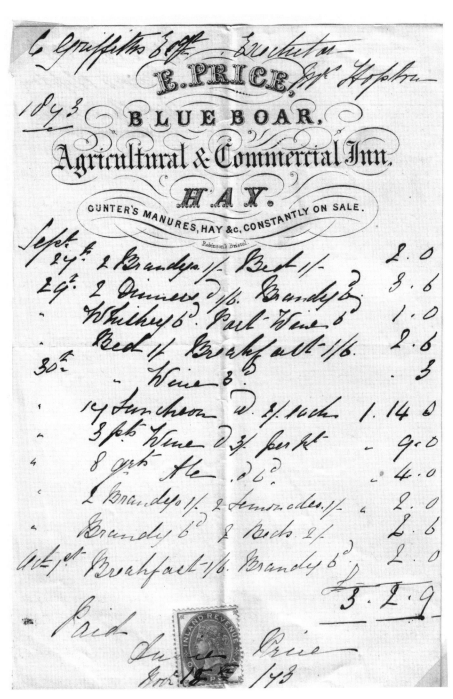

*An 1873 receipt from the Blue Boar indicating the landlord's
other services in the title*

Eardisley. In 1817 the building, then known as the Cock with Hen, was leased from Viscount Hereford for a period of 21 years at a rental of £64 per annum. The premises are now a general store, and there is a plaque on the wall recording that it is built on the original site of the 'Carles Gate'.

The **Blue Boar Inn** is on the corner of Castle Street and Oxford Road and, like many of the older pubs in Hay had a mounting block outside for the benefit of customers. A blue boar was the badge of the Earls of Oxford who supported the Lancastrian cause in the Wars of the Roses. The **Blue Boar** was one of the few pubs where the Turnpike Trustees did not meet, but it is mentioned in the minute book dated 16 August 1775:

> It is ordered ... to repair, out of hand, the roads leading from the Widow Prosser's House near the Hay Pound to the Blue Boar in the town of Hay.

John Nixon was landlord from before 1830 until at least 1850. Elizabeth Price had become landlady at the **Blue Boar** according to the 1851 census which shows that John Nixon was in the licensed trade round the corner in Horse Fair. Perhaps he made use of part of the premises, for an advertisement in the *Hereford Times* in March 1861 records:

> John Nixon, Blue Boar Inn, Hay — still the owner of the celebrated thorough-bred horse 'Hereford' and he intends the following season to travel his usual rounds.

Many sports took place at inns in the 19th century and it is not surprising to see advertised in the *Hereford Journal* that a pigeon match was to to take place on 1 January 1847 at the **Blue Boar**. By 1871 Elizabeth Price had been joined by her son Thomas and was still at the inn, whatever her relationship with John Nixon.

Kilvert's diary contains an entry dated 8 March 1870 detailing the unfortunate death of a barmaid from the **Blue Boar**:

> Yesterday there was an inquest at the Blue Boar, Hay, on the body of the barmaid of the Blue Boar who but a day or two ago went out at night on an hour's leave, but went up the Wye to Glasbury and threw herself into the river. She was taken out at Llan Hennw. She was enceinte.

Elizabeth Price was the sole licensee of the **Blue Boar** in November 1873, according to a bill she delivered to Mr C. Griffiths, the local solicitor, on behalf of the late Mrs. Hopton. Included in the bill, which was for September and October of that year, was bed 1s., breakfast 1s. 6d., 17 luncheons £1 14s. and several brandies at 1s. each. The bill head advertised the pub as an Agricultural and Commercial Inn which, in addition to bed and breakfast advertised 'Gunter's Manure, Hay etc, constantly on sale'.

The Blue Boar in 1910

A reminder of the winter of 1947

A Blue Boar receipt from 1910

By 1874 the owner was William Aston, but Elizabeth Price was still at the helm. She died in 1877 and on 4 June the licence was transferred from the executors of her will to Thomas and William Price. By 1879 the owner was Mrs. Aston, the licensee being the afore mentioned Thomas Price. Thomas had departed by 1891 when the landlord was James Webb, who was also a carpenter and builder. The licensee in 1901 was Thomas Turner who, in 1906, was an agent for Anglo-Bavarian Ales and Stout. In the 1910 Land Valuation the owner/occupier was given as Robert Thomas. The sign on the side of the premises offered 'accommodation for tourist cyclists'. In 1910 Thomas apparently had at least one satisfied client as she sent a postcard from Hay on 23 August saying 'this is a lovely place' — she could of course have been referring to Hay and not the **Blue Boar**!

By 1919 Arnold, Perrett & Co had purchased the pub, the licensee being William Gane who was there until 1923. He may have been the person of the same name who took over the **Bear Inn** in 1922, and if so must have run both establishments for a while. William Thomas took over the inn on 6 February 1922, when ownership was transferred to him from Arnold, Perrett & Co. The ownership was then transferred to Sarah Ann Thomas on 19 June of the same year, although she did not take over the licence until the following year. She must have been a little careless for on 5 November in the following year she was convicted for supplying intoxicating liquor during other than permitted hours and was fined £1. Perhaps she was over-tired, for according to Kelly's *Directory* she led a double life, being a midwife as well as running a public house! The **Blue Boar** is one of the pubs in Hay that has weathered the storm, especially

245

The Blue Boar in 2005

the snow of 1947, and is still open, being one of the town's more popular pubs.

The **Swan Inn** in Church Street was originally called the **White Swan** and is one of the oldest pubs in Hay. The swan may well have been derived from the badge of the Bohuns (Earls of Hereford). The **Swan** was rebuilt as a coaching inn about 1812, but it had been popular since the 18th century, not just as an inn, but as a venue for auctions and a post and coach house. The earliest known reference is in 1771, where it is mentioned in the will of Edward Allen — a solicitor practising in Hay as well as the owner of more than one licensed premises. He bequeathed property to his second son Edward Allen including, as recited in his will:

> all that my Messuage or Tenement known by the name of the White Swan with the Outbuildings Garden and Orchard thereto belonging, and one meadow thereto, also belonging with their appurtenances situate and being in the Town and Parish of Hay in the said County of Brecon and now rented by the said Widow Minors.

It would seem that 'The Widow Minors' wanted to leave the **White Swan** in 1773 as there was an advertisement on 11 March:

> to be lett and entered upon immediately, the Swann Inn, in this town, held by Elizabeth Minors, widow. The stock in hand and household goods to be disposed of, apply to the said Elizabeth Minors, or Mr. Allen in the Hay.

A further notice dated 10 June 1773 stated that the **White Swan Inn**, had been taken by William Powell, but he lasted less than two years, Samuel Hill taking it over on 9 March 1775. The importance of the **Swan** is endorsed by an advertisement dated 26 October 1775:

> Concert in the church at Hay on Tuesday 31 October, and in the evening, at the Swan Large room, will be a Concert of Vocal and Instrumental Music, and a Ball, to which no person will be admitted without a ticket. Tickets at 2s. 6d. each, to be had at the principal inn, at which places Ordinaries will be provided. To begin at six o'clock.

An early sketch of the Swan Inn

Prior to the arrival of the railway in 1864, horse transport was usually available at the larger inns in every town throughout the country. Post chaises were a favoured means of transport for those able to afford them and an advertisement in the *Hereford Journal* of 1775 offered 'Good Post Chaises and able horses with careful drivers to all parts of England from the Swan Hotel at the Hay'.

For those travelling by stagecoach, the *Hereford Journal* of 9 April 1778 contained the following notice:

> The Hay Diligence sets out from the Swan Inn in the Hay every Wednesday at six o'clock in the morning to the Red-Streak in Hereford, and returns to the Swan Inn in the Hay the same day.

There were numerous auctions of property and meetings at the inn during the latter part of the 18th century and the early part of the 19th. Thus on 2 December 1801 it was advertised that the household furniture and the stock of the late Howell Powell was to be sold by auction at the Swan Inn, Hay — including two post chaises, seven post horses and two milking cows. On 21 June 1820 it was advertised that Tithes of Hay were to be sold by auction at the Swan Inn, Hay, and also a messuage or Inn, called the Swan Inn, situate in the village of Llanigon.

SWAN HOTEL.

❈ FAMILY AND COMMERCIAL HOTEL. ❈

HAY, *May 25* 190*8*

M Executors of the late Mr A Price

Dr. to E. T. POWELL.

POSTING IN ALL ITS BRANCHES. ❈ ORDINARY ON MARKET AND FAIR DAYS.

1908

Date		£	s	d
March	1 Load of Manure & Hauling		7	0
April	1 Load of Manure		5	0
May 9.	1 lb of Beef for Tea			6
12.	Ditto			6
	1 Bottle of Martells 3 Star Brandy		6	6
	Eggs.			6
from May 9	Milk 4 quarts at 3 d		1	9
to 16	7 quarts Milk		1	9
15	Packet Matches			3
	Eggs.			6
16	2 oz of Tobacco.			9
	1 lb of Composites			4½
	1 Bottle of Enos Fruit Salts		2	3
17.18.19.	2 quarts Milk			6
22	7 Pints Beer *Received*		1	9
	with thanks.	£ 1	9	10½
	June 12 1908 E Powell			

The Swan sold a wide variety of goods ranging from manure to milk!

Throughout this period the **Swan** was one of the most popular and one of the largest establishments in the whole of the Hay area. Thomas Morgan became licensee on 6 April 1796, to be followed, on 7 April 1802, by Joseph Ward from London. By July 1814 George Walton had taken over and advertised his services in the usual rather flowery language:

> Most respectfully returns his grateful acknowledgments to the Nobility, Gentry, Commercial Gentlemen, and the Public, for the liberal encouragement hitherto shown him, and begs leave to Inform them, that

the whole of the above Inn, is now fitted up in a very modern and commodious manner. He also assures them that no effort will be wanting to render every thing as comfortable as possible, and hopes by strict attention to the accommodation of his Friends, to merit a continuance of their Patronage and Support. Well-aired Beds, and a Good Larder. — Neat Post Chaises, Good Stables, and Lock-up Coach Houses.

The Swan Inn in 2003

In 1811 Paterson recorded that the mail coaches arrived at the Swan at Hay where fresh horses were supplied, at 11 in the evening, and returned at four in the morning. In Pigot's *Directory* of 1835 the premises were described as the **White Swan** (and Posting and Excise Office) and the occupier was Wm. Spillman. Spillman was still there in 1861, when he was aged 71, and described as both a hotel keeper and a farmer. By 1868 Spillman had gone and the landlord was John Howells, who was also a farmer. The owner in 1874 was Lord Tredegar, John Howell being his tenant.

In the 1910 Land Valuation the owner was still Lord Tredegar, but by then the licensee was Evan Powell. Surviving records from 1919 show that Cecilia Powell, his widow, had taken over the licence by that time and that she also owned the premises. On 1 February 1926 she was succeeded by William Samuel Jones, after which she retired to Talgarth.

W.J. Humfrys, a Hereford solicitor who practised from 1871 until his death in 1924, recalled in his book *Memories of Old Hereford* a memorable auction at the **Swan Hotel**, which he attended with his father whilst he was still in articles:

But one of the customs which, from the point of view of sobriety was as mischievous as any, was the holding of auctions of landed property at public houses where the sellers provided wines or spirits for all comers. There were occasions when the practice led to very evil results even in Hereford, but in some of the towns in Radnorshire and Brecknockshire the consequences were positively disgraceful. I recollect, soon after I entered on my articles, my father taking me to a sale held at the Swan Hotel, Hay. The sale had been fixed at 'three for four' o'clock, the idea being that the company should assemble between those hours and the sale commence punctually at four. When we entered the room about a quarter before four several persons interested were already seated round a long table, and several more arrived very shortly. The first question was 'what will you drink?' and the order given by the auctioneer for a bowl of Punch met with general approval. By the time it arrived the clock was striking four, and the auctioneer proceeded to read the Conditions of Sale, a lengthy document, some forty folios or more (about 3,000 words) in length. Few of those present paid much attention, and fewer still understood the conditions, but the punch disappeared rapidly. Ultimately, however, the biddings began and proceeded in usual leisurely fashion, until after our reserve price had been reached. The auctioneer however thought he saw his way to a little further competition, and pressed one of his earlier bidders to advance on the last bid. 'Well, Mr. Auctioneer', was the answer, 'I did think to give you a bid or two more, but the way you are conducting this sale is such that I won't bid any more'. 'Why, what is the matter, Mr. —?' said the Auctioneer. 'Can't you see that bowl?' pointing to the empty punch bowl. 'I never bids dry'. So the punch bowl had to be replenished, while we talked about the weather and the crops and such matters; and when it returned refilled, the old gentleman who never 'dry bid' made, I should think, from a dozen to twenty fresh bids, all of them being advances of not more than £5 on the preceding one. And he took care to consume a glass of punch after a great many of them. I remember that the sale began at four and was not over till past six, though there was but a single lot. But the proceedings on this occasion were quiet and rational compared with some I have seen.

I recollect a sale in the early seventies (also at Hay) where there was much more enthusiasm. There was but one lot to sell, a small farm, to which was appurtenant a right of common pasture for sheep on the adjoining hill. The room was well filled, chiefly with farmers, some in a very small way of business, and very few intending to bid. I had instructions to sell the farm for almost anything it would fetch, although I had been advised it ought not to be sold for anything below £1,700. I suggested that the liquor for consumption should be port and sherry, as I did not want to give them the fiery brandy which in those days was a favourite beverage. As soon as the conditions had been read the bidding, to my surprise, began at once, and before I could make a note of the offers, £1,900 had been bid; and then by smaller advances we reached, I think, £2,150. Meanwhile the fun was beginning. A well-known character who rented his farm from a neighbouring squire had come to the sale very far gone in liquor, and was amusing himself by baiting his landlord's agent, who happened to be present. ''Tis a fine farm', he declared, 'and I'd buy it myself if Mr. — (his landlord) would but pay me what he owes me'. After this kind of abuse had gone on for some time, the agent turned on him, remarking 'you know, you scoundrel, you are years behind in your rent, and but for Mr. —'s good nature you would have been turned out from your farm long ago'. 'Behind with my rent? I should think so; I've paid no rent for years. But where is the compensation promised for the rabbits? The Squire do owe me hundreds of pounds beyond the rent, for the mischief they beasts do do'. Such sallies were received with cheer and laughter, and it was not without a good deal of trouble and after a threat to have the interrupter forcibly removed, that the auctioneer, who was a very able and determined man, succeeded in establishing something like order.

Meanwhile the bidding was proceeding and bottle after bottle of port and sherry disappeared. By the time the bidding had reached something approaching £2,500, nearly everyone in the room was more or less drunk, and the competition was confined to two farmers seated on opposite sides of a long table at the top of which was the Auctioneer. Each bidder had beside and behind him a group of friends who cheered in turn as the bids were made. Shortly after the biddings rose to £2,600, and the excitement was at its height. £2,605 was bid from one side of the table, followed by cheers from the supporters of the bidder. 'You've done him, Jack'. 'Well done'. 'You've got him', and the like; while from the other side of the table came shouts 'Have another, Tom'. 'Don't let him beat you', 'Stand up to him', and the like. The Auctioneer, who knew his business and understood his audience, waited a minute or two, and then you heard: 'Now gentlemen any advance on £2,605, once at £2,605; twice at £2,605, for the third and last time, £2,605' raising his hammer. 'Any advance?' 'I'll have another £5' comes from the other bidder; then the same cheers from his supporters, and the same appeals to his opponent by his friends, the same process by the Auctioneer, and the last moment a nod or a bid. This was repeated until the biddings reached £2,650, at which price the farm was knocked down. The purchaser was a man I knew as a good and most respectable farmer, who was probably in a position to pay the whole of the purchase money. But he staggered up to the table, and producing his cheque book, with a cheque in blank already signed, asked me to fill in the amount of the deposit. 'Missus told me', he said, 'if I bought the farm I should not be able to sign my name by the time I had bought it,' and I recollect that his signature to the contract was such that I doubt whether his Bankers would have paid a cheque so signed. The quantity of wine said to have been drunk was quite preposterous. I know I was made to pay for something between six and twelve dozens, the exact quantity I forget. But as I had made nearly a £1,000 more than I expected for the farm, I asked no questions.

The Swan sign in 2003

In May 1947 the *Brecon & Radnor Express* advertised that the **Swan** was for sale for £16,500, with an annual turnover of £8,000. The asking price must have been too high, for the property was eventually sold for £12,000 allowing the old owner, F.C. Martin, to emigrate to New Zealand.

The **Swan** was again on the market in the year 2000, when Colin and Rosemary Vaughan, having been there for nearly 11 years, decided to move. The asking price had gone up since 1947 — it was on the market at £695,000. The **Swan** is now a modern establishment with its own web page and offering 18 luxury rooms all with *en suite* facilities and televisions in all rooms.

Although the **Sun Inn** is described as being a cider house prior to 1776, no evidence for this has been found, the earliest certain record being in 1871 when it was described as a beer house run by Edward Evans who was also a quarryman and, by 1881, a general labourer and innkeeper. Although it is claimed that it was at no. 3 Brecon Road, both directory and census evidence place it at no. 4 and it is so marked on the 1889 1:2,500 Ordnance Survey map. Moreover, the licensing records from the 1870s show that the licensee and owner of no. 4 was Lewis Havard of Ystradgynlais, whereas the deeds of 2 and 3 Brecon Road show that at that time the owners of those properties were members of the Price family. By 1891 the **Sun Inn** was being run by John Powell, a local man, and he was succeeded by his widow, Jane. The 1901 census is a little unclear but seems to indicate that she may have moved to the house next door (no. 3), which is consistent with Fairs statement that the **New Sun Inn** was adjacent to the **Sun Inn**, although not in the exact position that he indicated! Whatever the case, the inn closed soon afterwards and when the chapel adjoining the former Sun Inn was reconstructed the two properties were made into one.

On the opposite side of Brecon Road, at no. 18, is a house known as the **Royal Oak**. This name is indicative of a public house, but as no documentary evidence has so far been found it is suggested that any such use was a very long time ago. The Royal Oak symbol celebrated the restoration of Charles the Second and refers to the avoidance of capture by hiding in an oak tree at Boscobel in Staffordshire. In 1851 the **Royal Oak** was occupied by Mary Morris, a dressmaker aged 23, while in 1861 Sarah Jones, an invalid widow, then aged 85, lived there. Clearly, at this period it was not a licensed premises.

THE HOLLY BUSH INN
Small Country Inn - Bed and Breakfast
Coarse Fishing Available

HAY-ON-WYE   Tel. : Glasbury 371

A typical plain 1960s advertisment for the Holly Bush Inn

The **Holly Bush** at Pont-yr-Angel is outside the town of Hay, but is within the parish and is covered by the Hay licensing records. According to the 1859 Slater's *Directory* the landlord was John Powell. In the 1874 register of licenses the owner was Mrs. Stephens and the licensee Henry Jones; the licence was transferred to Jno. Hardern Watkins on 2 April 1877. In 1879 the owner was John Stephens. It stayed in the same family, for in 1910 the owner was Maria Stephens and the licensee W.F. Ammonds. He was followed about 1919 by John Lewis. Mrs. Maria Stephens was recorded as the owner in the licensing records from 1919 to 1926.

Interesting to see that on this letter to Mrs. Lewis at the Holly Bush Inn, Hay is described as being 'near Glasbury'.

George Lewis, known as 'Dovey', who kept the **Holly Bush Inn** for 47 years, was deprived of his favourite drink when he was captured by the Germans during the Second World War. He escaped and was on the run for 18 months. After his experiences he swore that he 'would never go thirsty again' — and, after taking over the **Holly Bush Inn** in 1954, he kept to his promise with his usual drink 'half a Welsh'. He died, aged 87, some 18 months after leaving the Holly Bush, one of the last of the old-fashioned landlords who knew how to run an orderly house and keep good relations with his locals.

MEASURED from TYBURN TURNPIKE.	LONDON TO BRECON.			THROUGH HEREFORD and HAY.
	From Brecon		*From London*	
occasional visitor at Hom-Lacy, wrote his 'Man of Ross,' and the apartments then occupied by the poet may still be seen in their former state. Among the venerable ornaments of the interior should also be noticed the elaborate carvings by Gibbons, which are little inferior to those at Petworth and Chatsworth; and indeed so completely is this mansion preserved from the incongruities of modern alteration, that it deserves to rank among our national curiosities. The limner will here be gratified by surveying, besides numerous family portraits, a choice and valuable selection of paintings by the most eminent artists, among which he will find a capital one of Solomon and the Queen of Sheba, that has been exactly copied in stained glass for a window in Arundel castle. The grounds are extremely pleasant, and the old garden, on the south front, which has a very spacious terrace, was formed on the model of that of Hampton Court, in Middlesex.		*To Kington, by Weobley,* 18¾ *m.* *To Presteign, by Pembridge,* 22 *m.*		BREDWARDINE. After crossing the Wye, leave Burbridge Hill to the south, and a fine valley to the north, watered by the river Wye, on the north bank of which are the villages of Letton, Willersley, Winforton, and Whitney. ——— 1 m. from Willersley is Eardisley Park, *Thos. Perry*, Esq.; and at Whitney, the most westerly of these villages, is the seat of *Tomkyns Dew*, Esq. ——— Beyond Bredwardine, you pass over a high hill, called Penna Park, in the parish of Clifford: from this hill, see, on right, the ruins of Clifford Castle.
	32¼	*to* King's Acre, *Green Man*	138¾	
		To Kington, by Yazor, 17½ *m.*		
	30¾	Sugwas Pool	140¼	
	29¾	New Ware	141¼	
	28½	Bridge Sollers	142¼	
	26	Portway	145	
	24¼	Hanmer's Cross	146¾	
		To Kington 10 *m.* *To Hay, by Whitney,* 10¾ *m., thus,*		
HEREFORD, 1 m. distant, Hinton House, *R. Jones Powell*, Esq.; and Pool House, *J. G. Cooke*, Esq.		*To Letton* 1¼ *m., thence to Willersley* 2 *m., to Winforton* 1 *m., to Whitney* 2 *m., to Clifford* 2¼ *m, and to Hay* 2¼ *m.*		GLASBURY. Within 1 m. of the north bank of the Wye, Maeslough, *Walter Wilkins*, Esq.; near Glasbury, Tregoyd, Lord Viscount *Hereford*; and 4 m. distant from Glasbury, on left of the road to Built, Llangoed Castle, *A. Macnamara*, Esq. This delightful seat derives its chief beauty from the magnitude and position of its woods, which extend two miles and a half on a hill that slopes towards the Wye, whose banks are overhung with forest trees. The scenery of this place is perhaps inferior to none in the kingdom, and to enable the traveller the better to enjoy the windings of the river, which here pursues a rapid course, walks have been cut upon its margin, which add greatly to the facility of following the Wye, that here assumes a most romantic appearance, being broken into many falls, formed by the detached masses of the rock by which it is on every side surrounded.
		Or,		
		Over Tin Hill, and across the river Wye, to		
SUGWAS POOL. Sugwas Court, *Philip Jones*, Esq.	22¼	Bredwardine	148¾	
	19¼	Clockmill	151¼	
BRIDGE SOLLERS, 3 m. distant, Tibberton Court, *Henry Lee Warner*, Esq.	17¼	Hardwick Green	153¾	
	15¼	* HAY, Brecon.	155¾	
		To Kington 12 *m.*		
BREDWARDINE, 1 m. distant, Moccas Court, Sir *G. Cornewall*, Esq.	11¾	Glasbury, *Cock Inn*	159¼	
		Beyond Glasbury, *To Built* 15 *m.*		
HARDWICK GREEN, Hardwick Court, Col. *Powell*; and ¼ m. distant, The Moor, *T. Stallard Penoyre*, Esq.		*to Crickhowel* 16½ *m.*		
	7¼	Brunllys	163¾	
BRUNLLYS. Tregunter House, *W. A. Madocks*, Esq.	4¼	Vellinvach	166¾	BRUNLLYS. Pontywall, Mrs. *Clarke.*
		* BRECON	171	

Above: a page from Paterson's 1828 Road Book

Sources & References

Most Approved and Long experienced Water-Workes, Rowland Vaughan, 1610 (1897 reprint).

The Antiquities of England and Wales, Francis Grose, 1784 (new edition).

The River Wye, Rev. W. Gilpin, 5th edition, 1800.

Malcolm's Excursions, J.P. Malcolm, second edition, 1814.

Topographical Description of the County of Hereford, C. Cooke, *c.* 1830.

Mansions and Manors of Herefordshire, Rev. C.J. Robinson, 1872.

The Golden Valley, Herefordshire, Thomas Powell, n.d. *c.*1882.

An Historical Account of the Town and Castle of Hay by an Old Inhabitant, Anon., 1877 (1890 edition).

St. James' Church, Llangua and its surroundings, Anon., n.d. (*c.*1890?).

Nooks and Corners of Herefordshire, H.T. Timmins, 1892.

The History of Ewias Harold, its Castle, Priory, and Church, Rev. A.T. Bannister, 1902.

History of Monmouthsire. Volume I Part I, Hundred of Skenfrith, Part II, Hundred of Abergavenny, Joseph Bradney, 1904 & 1906.

Outlines of Old and New Hereford, W. Collins, 1911.

Royal Commission on Historical Monuments, Herefordshire, Vol. I South-West, 1931.

The History of Saint Clodock: British King and Martyr, Rev. F.G. Llewellin, 1919.

Memories of Old Hereford, W.J. Humfrys, (1925).

Hay and Neighbourhood, Rev. W.E.T. Morgan, 1932.

The Jubilee of County Councils 1889 to 1939, Anon, 1939.

Eaton Bishop. Its History 1855 – 1955, Eaton Bishop W.I., 1955.

The Inns of Herefordshire, H.P. Bulmer, *c.*1955.

Kilvert's Diary, Ed. W. Plomer ,Vol. 1, Vol. 2 , Vol. 3, 1960.

The Buildings of England. Herefordshire, N. Pevsner, 1963.

The Golden Valley Railway, W.H. Smith, n.d.

A History of the Hay, G.L. Fairs, 1972.

Monmouth. The Making of a County Town, Keith Kissack, 1975.

Herefordshire, J.W. Tonkin, 1977.

The Drovers' Roads of Wales, Fay Godwin and Shirley Toulson, 1977.

Farm and Furrow. A local farm study by Ewyas Harold and District WEA Research Group, n.d. *c.*1978.

Yesterday in Ewyas Harold, Ewyas Harold and District W.E.A. Research Group, n.d. *c.*1980.

Craftsmen at Monnowside 1867-1980, Sheila E.M. Parry, 1980.

Domesday Book, Herefordshire, F. & C. Thorn (eds), 1983.

Early Railways between Abergavenny and Hereford, R.A. Cook and C.R. Clinker, 1984.

Real Ale and Cider in Herefordshire (CAMRA), Ian Wraight and Mark Dyer, 1985.

Golden Valley Days, R. Graves, 1986.

Hando's Gwent, ed. Chris Barber, 1987.
The Herefordshire Village Book, HFWI, 1989.
Bloody Jeffreys. The Hanging Judge, Robert Milne-Tyte, 1989.
Dorstone 1890-1990. A centenary celebration, comp. Jones, Morgan and Morgan, 1990.
Monmouthshire Houses, Sir Cyril Fox and Lord Raglan, second edition, 1994.
Memories of Newton, 1995.
The Hay and Kington Railway, Gordon Tattenbury and Ray Cook, 1996.
Kingstone. The story of a Herefordshire Village from Domesday to the present time,
	Delphine Coleman, 1996.
A Definitive History of Dore Abbey, eds. R. Shoesmith and R. Richardson, 1997.
Herefordshire Constabulary 1857-1967, comp. V. Hadley, 1999.
The Buildings of Wales. Gwent/Monmouthsire, John Newman, 2000.
Longtown Millenium Domesday Book, 2000.
The Book of Hay, Kate Clarke, 2000.
The Pubs of Ross and South Herefordshire, Heather Hurley, 2001.
Welsh Cattle Drovers, Richard Moore-Colyer, Second edition 2002.
Nobody had Heard of Hay, 2002.
A History of Theatres & Performances in Herefordshire, Robin Haig, 2002.
Herefordshire's Postcard Past, Tim Ward, 2003.
Exploring Kilvert Country, Chris Barber, 2003.
Herefordshire Maps 1577 to 1800, Brian Smith, 2005.
Oxford Dictionary of National Biography, 2005.

JOURNALS AND NEWSPAPERS ETC.
Transactions of the Woolhope Naturalists' Field Club, 1851 to date.
Directories as quoted.
Hereford Journal.
Hereford Times.

INNS AND TAVERNS
Pub Names of Britain, L. Dunkling and G. Wright, 1994.
Beer and Britannia. An inebriated history of Britain, Peter Haydon, 2001.

MSS MATERIAL
Minutes of Bredwardine and Brobury Turnpike Trust 1760 - 1776.
Estate maps of the Moccas Estate, 1772.
W.H. Fussell's diary.
Dore Division Licensing records 1872-1901.
Hay Division Licensing records 1874 – 1884, 1919 – 1928.
Bredwardine Division Licensing records 1923-1927.
Deeds as quoted.

OTHER
Printed list of licensed establishments in Herefordshire, 1903.
Sale particulars as quoted.

Index of Pub Names

In the following index the latest name of the establishment is used, although with some cross-referencing. All main entries are in bold; illustrations are in italics.

Abbey Hotel (Traveller's Rest, Llanthony Abbey Hotel)
    (Llanthony)   **66-71**, *67, 69,70*
Anchor (Longtown)   **91-2**, *92*
Ancient Camp (Camp Inn) (Ruckhall Common,
    Eaton Bishop)   **159-61**, *160*
Apple Tree (Oak) (Bacton)   **128-9**, *128, 129*
Apple Tree (Pine Apple) (Ruckhall Common, Eaton Bishop) **159**

Bear Inn (Hay-on-Wye)   **227-9**, *227, 228*
Bell Inn (Bell Bank) (Hay-on-Wye)   **226-7**, *226*
Bell (Longtown)   **107**
Black Lion (Cwmyoy)   **63-4**
Black Lion (Hay-on-Wye)   **223-4**, *223, 224*
Black Lion (Longtown)   **92-3**, *92*
Black Swan (Hay-on-Wye)   **199-201**, *200, 201*
Blue Boar (Hay-on-Wye)   **243-6**, *244, 245, 246*
Board (Old Thatched House) (Preston on Wye) **165-6**
Boat (Sugwas Boat) (Eaton Bishop/Stretton Sugwas) **157-9**, *157, 158*
Boughton Arms (Peterchurch)   **137-40**,*137, 138, 139*
Bridge End (Newton)   **110**, *110*
Bridge End (Bach, Dorstone)   **152-3**, *152, 153*
Bridge End (Hay-on-Wye)   **212**, *212*
Bridge Inn (Michaelchurch Escley)   **118-121**, *121*
British Oak (Oak) (Kenderchurch)   **48**
Brydges Arms (Mason's Arms) (Tyberton)   **167**, *167*
Bull Ring (Kingstone)   **44-6**, *44*
Bull's Head (Forest House) (Craswall)   **103-5**, *104, 105*
Bull's Tail (Cusop)   **122**
Bunch of Grapes (Hay-on-Wye) see Wine Vaults

Carpenter's Arms (Wormbridge)   **48**, *48*
Carpenters' Arms (Michaelchurch Escley)   **121-2**, *121*
Carpenters' Arms (Walterstone)   **87-9**, *88*
Castle (Clifford)   **179-80**, *178, 179*
Castle (Fwddog, Cwmyoy)   **63**
Castle (Hay-on-Wye)   **219**
Castlebury (Madley)   **165**
Castlefield Inn (Clifford)   **176-7**, *176*
Chapel House (Capel-y-ffin)   **72**
Cherry Tree (Allensmore)   **40-1**, *40*
Coach and Horses (Turnastone)   **132-3**, 132
Cock (Michaelchurch Escley)   **115**

Cock (Fwddog, Cwmyoy) — **62**
Cock/Cock with Hen (Hay-on-Wye) — **241-2**, *241*
Comet Inn (Madley) — **161-2**, *162*
Cornewall Arms (Clodock) — **89-91**, *90*
Court House (New Inn) (Longtown) — **96-8**, *96*
Crossway (?Cross Keys) (St. Margaret's) — **114**, *114*
Crown (Longtown) — **93-5**, *94*
Crown (Peterchurch) — **136**, *136*
Cwm (Crown) (Llanveynoe) — **99**, *99*

Daw (Moccas) — **168**, *168*
Dog (Bell, Dog, Castle) (Ewyas Harold) — **78-82**, *79, 81*
Drill Hall (Hay-on-Wye) — **224-5**, *225*
Drovers' Arms (Hay-on-Wye) — **225**

Ely Dawn (Lower Maes-coed, Longtown) — **108**

Fidler's (Craswall) — **103**
Fountain (Hay-on-Wye) — **232-3**, *232*

George (Hay-on-Wye) see Market Tavern
Golden Lion (Craswall) — **101**, *100, 101*
Golden Lion (Hay-on-Wye) — **239-40**
Goytre Inn (Llanfihangel Crucorney) — **55**
Greyhound (Longtown) — **95-6**, *95*
Griffin (Ewyas Harold) — **124**

Half Moon (Hay-on-Wye) — **219-21**, *220, 221*
Half Moon (Llanthony) — **71-2**, *71*
Harp (Hay-on-Wye) — **219**
Holly Bush (Hay-on-Wye) — **253-4**, *253*

Kilvert's (Hay-on-Wye) — **229-30**, *228, 229*
King's Arms (Michaelchurch Escley) — **115-7**, *115, 116, 117*
King's Head (Hay-on-Wye) — **191-3**, *191, 193*

Lamb (Hay-on-Wye) — **210-2**, *211*
Lancaster Arms (Llanfihangel Crucorney) — **55-6**, *57*
Little Green Farm (Newton) — **109-10**, *109*

Marbach (Clifford) — **175-6**
Market Tavern (George) (Hay-on-Wye) — **233-5**, *234*
Mason's Arms (Hay-on-Wye) — **238-9**, *238, 239*
Mason's Arms (Kingstone) — **46-7**, *46, 47*
Mitre (Hay-on-Wye) — **213-4**, *213*
Monmouth Cap (Llangua) — **51-54**, *53*

Nag's Head (Peterchurch) — **141-3**, *142, 143*
Nelson (Cusop) — **181-3**, *181, 182*
Neville Arms (Ewyas Harold) — **124-5**, *125*
New House (Cusop) — **122**, *122*
New House Inn (Ewyas Harold) — **82-4**, *83*
New Inn (?Drum and Monkey) (Peterchurch) — **145**
New Inn (?Portway) (Peterchurch) — **141**
New Inn (Bacton) — **127-8**, *128*
New Inn (Fwddog, Cwmyoy) — **62**

New Inn (Gate) (Michaelchurch Escley)   **117-8**, *117*
New Inn (Hay-on-Wye)   **222**, *221, 222*
New Inn (Lower Maes-coed, Longtown)   **107-8**, *107*
New Inn (Vowchurch)   **130**
New Sun (Hay-on-Wye)   **252**

Old Pandy (Pandy) (Llanfihangel Crucorney)   **55-6**, *58, 56*
Old White Lion (Hay-on-Wye)   **209**

Pandy Inn (Dorstone)   **147-51**, *146,148, 149, 150*
Pear Tree (Dorstone)   **151-2**, *151*
Pelican Inn (Allensmore)   **39-40**, *40*
Plough (?Raven) (Blakemere)   **167**, *167*
Plough (Plough and Harrow) (Peterchurch)   **144-5**, *144*
Portway (Peterchurch)   **141**, *141*
Prill (beer house) (Ewyas Harold)   **84**
Prince of Wales (Ewyas Harold)   **76-7**, *76*

Queen's Head (Cwmyoy)   **61-62**, *61*

Red Cross Inn (Turnastone)   **132**, *132*
Red Lion (Abbey Dore)   **126-7**, *126*
Red Lion (Bredwardine)   **170-5**, *170, 171, 173, 174, 175*
Red Lion (Ewyas Harold)   **75-76**, *74*
Red Lion (Hay-on-Wye)   **214-6**, *215*
Red Lion (Madley)   **163-4**, *163, 164*
Rising Sun (Sun) (Llanfihangel Crucorney)   **58**, *57, 58*
Rose and Crown/Crown (Hay-on-Wye)   **194-9**, *194, 195, 196, 197, 199, 200*
Royal Oak (Hardwick)   **153**, *154*
Royal Oak (Hay-on-Wye)   **253**
Royal Oak (Newton)   **109**

Scudamore Arms (Pontrilas)   **49-50**, *49*
Scudamore Arms Hotel (Pontrilas)   **49-50**
Seven Stars (Clehonger)   **155-6**, *155*
Seven Stars (Hay-on-Wye)   **193**, *194*
Ship (Hay-on-Wye)   **207-9**, *208, 209, 210*
Skirrid Mountain (Llanfihangel Crucorney)   **58-61**, *59*
Spiteful Inn (Fwddog, Cwmyoy)   **63**, *63*
Sun (?Crown and Anchor) (St. Margaret's)   **110-2**, *111, 112, 113*
Sun (?White Hart) (Michaelchurch Escley)   **118**, *119*
Sun (Cusop)   **154**
Sun (Hay-on-Wye)   **252**
Sun (Longtown)   **98-9**, *98*
Sun (Lower Maes-coed, Newton)   **108-9**, *109*
Sun (Peterchurch)   **136-7**
Swan (White Swan) (Hay-on-Wye)   **246-52**, *247, 248, 249, 252*

Tafarn Twlch (Craswall)   **101**
Talbot (Dog) (Hay-on-Wye)   **235-8**, *236, 237*
Tanners' Arms (Hay-on-Wye)   **206-7**, *208*
Temple Bar (Ewyas Harold)   **77-8**, *77, 78, 79*
Temple Bar (Peterchurch)   **145**
Three Horse Shoes (Allensmore)   **41-4**, *41*

Three Horse Shoes (Craswall) **101-2**, *101*
Three Horse Shoes (Hay-on-Wye) **231-2**, *231, 232*
Three Tuns (Spread Eagle) (Hay-on-Wye) **202-4**, *202, 203, 204, 205, 206, 207*
Trap (Brobury) **169-70**
Traveller's Trap **225-6**, *225*
Trout Found Out (New Inn) (Dulas) **84-86**, *85*

Unicorn (Hardwick) **177-8**, *177*

Victoria Inn (Michaelchurch Escley) **114-5**, *114*
Vine Cottage (Peterchurch) **145**

Walk Mill (Ewyas Harold) **84**
Well (Clifford) **180-1**, *180*
Wheatsheaf (Hay-on-Wye) **216-9**, *217*
White Lion (Craswall) **102**, *102*
White Lion (Hay-on-Wye) **216**, *216*
Wine Vaults (Grapes/Bunch of Grapes) (Hay-on-Wye) **240-1**, *241*

Yew Tree (Preston on Wye) **166**, *165*

Index by Place

Abbey Dore
    Red Lion — **126-7**, *126*

Allensmore
    Cherry Tree — **40-1**, *40*
    Pelican — **39-40**, *40*
    Three Horse Shoes — **41-4**, *41*

Bacton
    Apple Tree (Oak) — **128-9**, *128, 129*
    New Inn — **127-8**, *128*

Blakemere
    Plough (?Raven) — **167**, *167*

Bredwardine
    Red Lion — **170-5**, *170, 171, 173, 174, 175*

Brobury
    Trap — **169-70**

Capel-y-ffin
    Chapel House — **72**

Clehonger
    Seven Stars — **155-6**, *155*

Clifford
    Castle Inn — **179-80**, *178, 179*
    Castlefield — **176-7**, *176*
    Marbach — **175-6**
    Well — **180-1**, *180*

Clodock
    Cornewall Arms — **89-91**, *90*

Craswall
    Bull's Head (Forest House) — **103-5**, *104, 105*
    Fidler's — **103**
    Golden Lion — **101**, *100, 101*
    Tafarn Twlch — **101**
    Three Horse Shoes — **101-2**, *101*
    White Lion — **102**, *102*

Cusop
    Bull's Tail — **122**
    Nelson Inn — **181-3**, *181, 182*
    New House — **122**, *122*
    Sun Inn — **154**

Cwmyoy
    Black Lion — **63-4**
    Queen's Head — **61-62**, *61*

Cwmyoy, Fwddog
    Castle — **63**
    Cock — **62**

New Inn	**62**
Spiteful	**63**, *63*
Dorstone	
Pandy	**147-51**, *146,148, 149, 150*
Pear Tree	**151-2**, *151*
Dorstone, Bach	
Bridge End	**152-3**, *152, 153*
Dulas	
Trout Found Out (New Inn)	**84-86**, *85*
Eaton Bishop, Ruckhall Common	
Ancient Camp (Camp)	**159-61**, *160*
Apple Tree (Pine Apple)	**159**
Eaton Bishop/Stretton Sugwas	
Boat (Sugwas Boat)	**157-9**, *157, 158*
Ewyas Harold	
Dog Inn (Bell, Dog, Castle)	**78-82**, *79, 81*
Griffin	**124**
Neville Arms	**124-5**, *125*
New House	**82-4**, *83*
Prill (beer house)	**84**
Prince of Wales	**76-7**, *76*
Red Lion	**75-76**, *74*
Temple Bar	**77-8**, *77, 78, 79*
Walk Mill	**84**
Hardwick	
Royal Oak	**153**, *154*
Unicorn	**177-8**, *177*
Hay-on-Wye	
Bear	**227-9**, *227, 228*
Bell (Bell Bank)	**226-7**, *226*
Black Lion	**223-4**, *223, 224*
Black Swan	**199-201**, *200, 201*
Blue Boar	**243-6**, *244, 245, 246*
Bridge End	**212**, *212*
Bunch of Grapes see Wine Vaults	
Castle Inn	**219**
Cock/Cock with Hen	**241-2**, *241*
Drill Hall	**224-5**, *225*
Drovers' Arms	**225**
Fountain Inn	**232-3**, *232*
George Inn see Market Tavern	
Golden Lion	**239-40**
Half Moon	**219-21**, *220, 221*
Harp Inn	**219**
Holly Bush	**253-4**, *253*
Kilvert's	**229-30**, *228, 229*
King's Head	**191-3**, *191, 193*
Lamb	**210-2**, *211*
Market Tavern (George)	**233-5**, *234*
Mason's Arms	**238-9**, *238, 239*
Mitre	**213-4**, *213*
New Inn	**222**, *221, 222*
New Sun	**252**

Old White Lion	**209**
Red Lion	**214-6**, *215*
Rose and Crown/Crown	**194-9**, *194, 195, 196, 197, 199, 200*
Royal Oak	**253**
Seven Stars	**193**, *194*
Ship	**207-9**, *208, 209, 210*
Sun	**252**
Swan (White Swan)	**246-52**, *247, 248249, 252*
Talbot (Dog)	**235-8**, *236, 237*
Tanners' Arms	**206-7**, *208*
Three Horse Shoes	**231-2**, *231, 232*
Three Tuns (Spread Eagle)	**202-4**, *202, 203, 204, 205, 206, 207*
Traveller's Trap	**225-6**, *225*
Wheatsheaf	**216-9**, *217*
White Lion	**216**, *216*
Wine Vaults (Grapes/Bunch of Grapes)	**240-1**, *241*

Kenderchurch
British Oak (Oak)	**48**

Kingstone
Bull Ring	**44-6**, *44*
Mason's Arms	**46-7**, *46, 47*

Llanfihangel Crucorney
Goytre	**55**
Lancaster Arms	**55-6**, *57*
Old Pandy (Pandy)	**55-6**, *58, 56*
Rising Sun (Sun)	**58**, *57, 58*
Skirrid Mountain	**58-61**, *59*

Llangua
Monmouth Cap	**51-54**, *53*

Llanthony
Abbey Hotel (Traveller's Rest, Llanthony Abbey Hotel)	**66-71**, *67, 69,70*
Half Moon	**71-2**, *71*

Llanveynoe
Cwm (Crown)	**99**, *99*

Longtown
Anchor	**91-2**, *92*
Bell	**107**
Black Lion	**92-3**, *92*
Court House (New Inn)	**96-8**, *96*
Crown	**93-5**, *94*
Greyhound	**95-6**, *95*
Sun	**98-9**, *98*

Longtown, Lower Maes-coed
Ely Dawn	**108**
New Inn	**107-8**, *107*

Madley
Castlebury	**165**
Comet	**161-2**, *162*
Red Lion	**163-4**, *163, 164*

Michaelchurch Escley
Bridge	**118-121**, *121*
Carpenters' Arms	**121-2**, *121*

Cock	**115**	
King's Arms	**115-7**, *115, 116, 117*	
New Inn (Gate)	**117-8**, *117*	
Sun Inn (?White Hart)	**118**, *119*	
Victoria	**114-5**, *114*	

Moccas
Daw	**168**, *168*

Newton
Bridge End	**110**, *110*
Little Green Farm	**109-10**, *109*
Royal Oak	**109**

Newton, Lower Maes-coed
Sun	**108-9**, *109*

Peterchurch
Boughton Arms	**137-40**, *137, 138, 139*
Crown	**136**, *136*
Nag's Head	**141-3**, *142, 143*
New Inn (?Drum and Monkey)	**145**
New Inn (?Portway))	**141**
Plough (Plough and Harrow)	**144-5**, *144*
Portway	**141**, *141*
Sun	**136-7**
Temple Bar	**145**
Vine Cottage	**145**

Pontrilas
Scudamore Arms (Pontrilas)	**49-50**, *49*
Scudamore Arms Hotel	**49-50**

Preston on Wye, Ploughfields
Board (Old Thatched House)	**165-6**
Yew Tree	**166**, *165*

St. Margaret's
Crossway (?Cross Keys)	**114**, *114*
Sun (?Crown and Anchor)	**110-2**, *111, 112, 113*

Turnastone
Coach and Horses	**132-3**, *132*
Red Cross	**132**, *132*

Tyberton
Brydges Arms (Mason's Arms)	**167**, *167*

Vowchurch
New Inn	**130**

Walterstone
Carpenters' Arms	**87-9**, *88*

Wormbridge
Carpenter's Arms	**48**, *48*